Freedom Press

The Following are Military Manuals without Copyright released to the General Public.

They are provided for informational purposes only.

ISBN-13: 978-1508515029
ISBN-10: 1508515026

FAIR USE ASSERTION

ARMY TM 9-1005-249-23&P
AIR FORCE TO 11W3-5-5-24
COAST GUARD COMDTINST M8370.9

Supersedes Copy Dated November 1983

TECHNICAL MANUAL

UNIT AND DIRECT SUPPORT MAINTENANCE MANUAL
(INCLUDING REPAIR PARTS AND SPECIAL TOOLS LIST)
RIFLE, 5.56MM, M16 (1005-00-856-6885) (EIC:4F7)
RIFLE, 5.56 MM, M16A1 (1005-00-073-9421) (EIC:4FC)

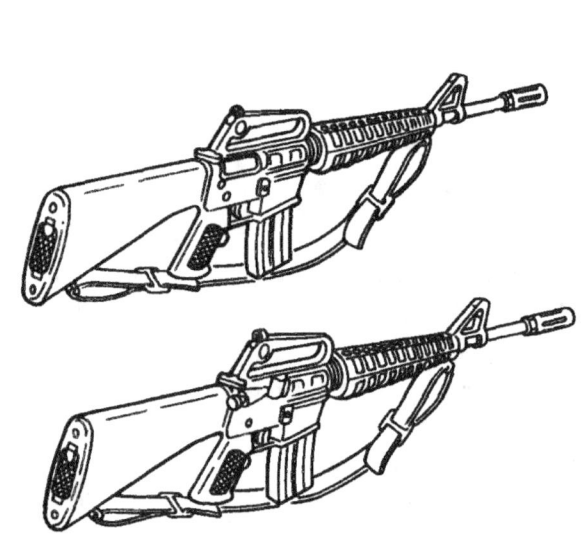

INTRODUCTION	1-1
UNIT MAINTENANCE INSTRUCTIONS	2-1
DIRECT SUPPORT MAINTENANCE INSTRUCTIONS	3-1
MAINTENANCE AUXILIARY EQUIPMENT	4-1
REFERENCES	A-1
MAINTENANCE ALLOCATION CHART	B-1
REPAIR PARTS AND SPECIAL TOOLS LIST	C-1
EXPENDABLE/DURABLE SUPPLIES AND MATERIALS LIST	D-1
ILLUSTRATED LIST OF MANUFACTURED ITEMS	E-1
TORQUE LIMITS	F-1
ALPHABETICAL INDEX	INDEX-1

**HEADQUARTERS, DEPARTMENTS OF THE ARMY AND)
AIR FORCE, COMMANDANT, COAST GUARD**

JUNE 1991

METRIC CHART
THE METRIC SYSTEM AND EQUIVALENTS

LINEAR MEASURE

1 Centimeter = 10 Millimeters = 0.01 Meters = 0.3937 Inches
1 Meter = 100 Centimeters = 1000 Millimeters = 39.37 Inches
1 Kilometer = 1000 Meters = 0.621 Miles

WEIGHTS

1 Gram = 0.001 Kilograms = 1000 Milligrams = 0.035 Ounces
1 Kilogram = 1000 Grams = 2.2 Lb
1 Metric Ton = 1000 Kilograms = 1 Megagram = 1.1 Short Tons

LIQUID MEASURE

1 Milliliter = 0.001 Liters = 0.0338 Fluid Ounces
1 Liter = 1000 Milliliters = 33.82 Fluid Ounces

SQUARE MEASURE

1 Sq Centimeter = 100 Sq Millimeters = 0.155 Sq Inches
1 Sq Meter = 10,000 Sq Centimeters = 10.76 Sq Feet
1 Sq Kilometer = 1,000,000 Sq Meters = 0.386 Sq Miles

CUBIC MEASURE

1 Cu Centimeter = 1000 Cu Millimeters = 0.06 Cu Inches
1 Cu Meter = 1,000,000 Cu Centimeters = 35.31 Cu Feet

TEMPERATURE

5/9 (°F -32) = °C
212° Fahrenheit is equivalent to 100° Celsius
90° Fahrenheit is equivalent to 32.2° Celsius
32° Fahrenheit is equivalent to 0° Celsius
9/5 C° + 32 = F°

APPROXIMATE CONVERSION FACTORS

TO CHANGE	TO	MULTIPLY BY
Inches	Centimeters	2.540
Feet	Meters	0.305
Yards	Meters	0.914
Miles	Kilometers	1.609
Square Inches	Square Centimeters	6.451
Square Feet	Square Meters	0.093
Square Yards	Square Meters	0.836
Square Miles	Square Kilometers	2.590
Acres	Square Hectometers	0.405
Cubic Feet	Cubic Meters	0.028
Cubic Yards	Cubic Meters	0.765
Fluid Ounces	Milliliters	29.573
Pints	Liters	0.473
Quarts	Liters	0.946
Gallons	Liters	3.785
Ounces	Grams	28.349
Pounds	Kilograms	0.454
Short Tons	Metric Tons	0.907
Pound-Feet	Newton-Meters	1.356
Pounds per Square Inch	Kilopascals	6.895
Miles per Gallon	Kilometers per Liter	0.425
Miles per Hour	Kilometers per Hour	.609

TO CHANGE	TO	MULTIPLY BY
Centimeters	Inches	0.394
Meters	Feet	3.280
Meters	Yards	1.094
Kilometers	Miles	0.621
Square Centimeters	Square Inches	0.155
Square Meters	Square Feet	10.764
Square Meters	Square Yards	1.196
Square Kilometers	Square Miles	0.386
Square Hectometers	Acres	2.471
Cubic Meters	Cubic Feet	35.315
Cubic Meters	Cubic Yards	1.308
Milliliters	Fluid Ounces	0.034
Liters	Pints	2.113
Liters	Quarts	1.057
Liters	Gallons	0.264
Grams	Ounces	0.035
Kilograms	Pounds	2.205
Metric Tons	Short Tons	1.102
Newton-Meters	Pound-Feet	0.738
Kilopascals	Pounds per Square Inch	0.145
Kilometers per Liter	Miles per Gallon	2.354
Kilometers per Hour	Miles per Hour	0.621

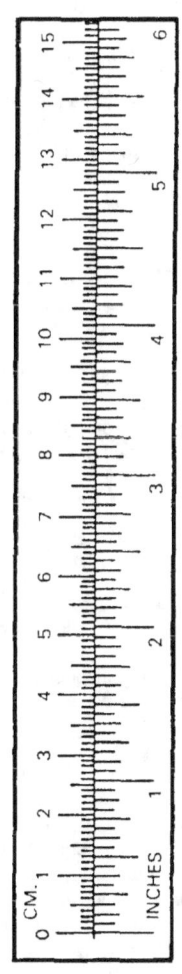

WARNING

RADIATION HAZARD

TRITIUM (H3)

A. **RULES AND REGULATIONS:** Copies of the following rules and regulations are maintained at HQ, AMCCOM, Rock Island, IL 61299-6000. Copies may be requested, or information pertinent to these rules and regulations obtained, by contacting the AMCCOM Radiological Protection Officer (RPO), AUTOVON 793-2964/2965/2966 Commercial (309) 782-2964/2965/2966.

(1) 10CFR Part 19 - Notices, Instructions, and Reports to Workers; Inspections.

(2) 10CFR Part 20 - Standards for Protection Against Radiation.

(3) NRC license, license conditions, and license application.

B. **SAFETY PRECAUTIONS.** The radioactive material used in this rifle is tritium gas (H3) sealed in a glass tube. It poses no significant hazard to the repairman when intact. The source illuminates the front sight for night operations. Tampering with or removal of the source in the field is prohibited by Federal law. In the event there is no illumination, notify the local Radiological Protection Officer. Do not attempt to repair or replace the sight in the field! If skin contact is made with any area contaminated with tritium, immediately wash with nonabrasive soap and water.

C. **IDENTIFICATION:** The radioactive self-luminous source is identified by means of a radioactive warning label (as above). This label should not be defaced or removed, and should be replaced immediately when necessary. Refer to the local RPO or the AMCCOM RPO for instructions on handling, storage, or disposal.

D. **STORAGE AND SHIPPING:** All radioactively illuminated instruments or modules which are defective will be evacuated to a depot maintenance activity. These items must be placed in a plastic bag and packaged in the shipping container from which the replacement was taken, before evacuation to a higher echelon is made. Spare equipment must be stored in the shipping container, as received, until installed on the weapon. Storage of these items is recommended to be in an outdoor shed type storage or unoccupied building.

WARNING

Read this manual carefully before performing required maintenance. This manual will be referred to for Inspection/ Maintenance and Repair procedures.

Before starting an inspection, be sure to clear the rifle. Do not actuate the trigger until the rifle has been cleared. Inspect the chamber to ensure that it is empty and no ammunition is in position to be chambered. Do not keep live ammunition near work area.

To avoid injury to your eye, use care when removing and installing spring-loaded parts.

All Active Army M161/M16A1 rifles must be inspected and gaged at least once annually for safety. All Army Reserve and Army National Guard M16/M16A1 rifles must be inspected and gaged at least once every two years, after the initial inspection/gaging procedures have been accomplished. This two year interval may be maintained unless preventive maintenance checks and services (PMCS), or other physical evidence indicates that an individual unit's M16/ M16A1 rifles require inspection at a more frequent interval. If it is determined that a yearly inspection is necessary for an individual unit, only that unit will be affected. This will not affect other units in regard to the interval of inspection.

Air Force users refer to inspection requirements in AFR 50-36, Volume 1.

WARNING (cont)

Below Direct Support Maintenance, DO NOT interchange bolt assemblies from one weapon to another. Doing so may result in injury to, or death of, personnel.

Bolt cam pin must be installed or weapon will blow up while firing the first round. If the bolt cam pin is not installed, injury to, or death of, personnel may result.

Dry cleaning solvent is flammable and toxic and should be used in a well-ventilated area. The use of rubber gloves is necessary to protect the skin when washing rifle parts.

When using solid film lubricant or dichloromethane, be sure the area is well ventilated

When using P-C-111, avoid skin contact. If it comes in contact with the skin, wash off thoroughly with running water. Using a good lanolin base cream after exposure to compound is helpful. Gloves and protective equipment are recommended.

For further information on safety, care, and handling of ammunition: Army and Air Force users refer to M16/M16A1 Operator's Manual TM 9-1005-249-10/TO 11A13-10-7; Coast Guard users refer to OP4 or OP5.

For additional first aid data, see FM 21-11

TECHNICAL MANUAL
ARMY NO. 9-1005-249-23&P
AIR FORCE TO 11W3-5-5-24
COAST GUARD COMDTINST M8370.9

*ARMY TM 9-1005-249-23&P
*AIR FORCE TO 11W3-5-5-24
COAST GUARD COMDTINST M8370.9

HEADQUARTERS, DEPARTMENTS OF THE ARMY
AND AIR FORCE
COMMANDANT, COAST GUARD
Washington, DC   19 June 1991

Unit and Direct Support Maintenance Manual
(Including Repair Parts and Special Tools List)
RIFLE, 5.56MM, M16
(1005-00-856-6885)
RIFLE, 5.56MM, M16AI
(1005-00-073-9421)

Current as of 7 January 1991

REPORTING ERRORS AND RECOMMENDING IMPROVEMENTS

You can help improve this manual. If you find any mistakes or if you know of a way to improve the procedures, please let us know.

Army users mail your letter, DA Form 2028 (Recommended Changes to Publications and Blank Forms),   located in the back of this manual direct to: Commander, US Army Armament, Munitions and Chemical Command, ATTN: AMSMC-MAS, Rock Island, IL 61299-6000.

Air Force users submit AFTO Form 22, Technical Order System Publications Improvement Report and Reply to: WR-ALC/MMDET, Robins AFB, GA 31098-5609.

Coast Guard users submit Publications Correction/Change Report form CG 4394 to: Commandant, U.S. Coast Guard (G-ODO-2), Washington, DC 20593-0001.

A reply will be furnished to you.

		Page
HOW TO USE THIS MANUAL		iii
CHAPTER	1 INTRODUCTION	1-1
	Chapter Overview	1-1
Section	I General information	1-1
Section	II Equipment Description and Data	1-2
Section	III Principles of Operation	1-4
CHAPTER	2 UNIT MAINTENANCE INSTRUCTIONS	2-1
	Chapter Overview	2-1
Section	I Repair Parts, Special Tools, TMDE, and Support Equipment	2-1
Section	II Service Upon Receipt	2-1
Section	III Preventive Maintenance Checks and Services (PMCS)	2-3
Section	IV Troubleshooting	2-12
Section	V Decontamination of Rifles and Arms Rooms	2-21
Section	VI Maintenance Procedures	2-21

---

*This manual supersedes TM 9-1005-249-24&P, dated 25 November 1983, including all changes and TO 11W3-5-5-24 dated 10 February 1972.

			Page	Illus Figure
CHAPTER	3	DIRECT SUPPORT MAINTENANCE INSTRUCTIONS	3 - 1	
		Chapter Overview	3 - 1	
Section	I	Repair Parts, Special Tools, TMDE, and Support Equipment	3 - 1	
Section	II	Service Upon Receipt	3 - 1	
Section	III	Troubleshooting	3 - 2	
Section	IV	Decontamination of Rifles Shop Area	3 - 9	
Section	V	Maintenance Procedures for the M16 and M16A1 Rifle	3 - 10	
Section	VI	Preembarkation Inspection of Materiel in Units Alerted for Overseas Movement	3 - 73	
CHAPTER	4	MAINTENANCE OF AUXILIARY EQUIPMENT	4-1	
		Chapter Overview	4-1	
Section	I	Unit Auxiliary Equipment	4-1	
Section	II	Preparation for Storage or Shipment	4-13	
APPENDIX	A	REFERENCES	A-1	
APPENDIX	B	MAINTENANCE ALLOCATION CHART	B-1	
APPENDIX	C	REPAIR PARTS AND SPECIAL TOOLS LIST	C-1	
Section	I	Introduction	C-1	
Section	II	Repair Parts List	C-1-1	
Group	0 0	5.56MMRifle M16,8448600 and M16A1, 8448500	C-1-1	C - 2
Group	01	Bolt carrier assembly 8448501	C-2-1	C - 2
		0101 Bolt Assembly 8448509	C-3-1	C - 3
		0102 Key and bolt carrier assembly 8448505	C-4-1	C - 4
Group	02	Charging handle assembly 844851 7	C-5-1	C - 5
Group	03	Upper receiver and barrel assembly 8448601 (M16) and 8448522 (M16A1)	C-6-1	C - 6
		0301 Rifle barrel assembly 8448663	C-7-1	C - 7
		0302 Upper receiver assembly 8448602 (M16) and 8448523 (M16A1)	C-8-1	C - 8
		030201 Forward assist assembly 9349 086(M16AI)	C-9-1	C - 9
Group	0 4	Lower receiver and extension assembly 8448604 (M16) and 8448578 (M16A1)	C-10-1	C - 10
		0401 Buttstock assembly 9349119	C-11-1	C - 11
		0402 Hammer assembly 8448610	C-12-1	C - 12
		0403 Trigger assembly 8448591	C-13-1	C - 13
		0404 Lower receiver and extension subassembly 84488605 (M16) and 8448579 (M16A1)	C-14-1	C - 14
Section	III	Special Tools List	C-15-1	C - 15
Section	IV	National Stock Number and Part Number Index	I-1	
APPENDIX	D	EXPENDABLE/DURABLE SUPPLIES AND MATERIALS LIST	D-1	
APPENDIX	E	ILLUSTRATED LIST OF MANUFACTURED ITEMS	E-1	
APPENDIX	F	TORQUE LIMITS	F-1	
		ALPHABETICAL INDEX	I ndex-1	

HOW TO USE THIS MANUAL

Read this manual carefully before performing required maintenance. This manual will be referred to for Inspection/Maintenance and Repair procedures.

GENERAL

There arc several things you need to know to use this manual efficiently.

1. All references in the manual are to pages only. Referencc to maintenance procedures is to the page whcre the respective initial setup appears.

2. Illustrations for the maintenance procedures show only those parts affected by the opeation being performed.

3. Whenever the male gender is mentioned in the manual (i.e., crewman, repairman), it also pertains to females.

4. When the term "evacuate to support maintenance" is used, the entire rifle must be evacuated.

INDEXES

This manual is organized to help you find the information you need quickly. There are several useful indexes.

1. Front Cove-r Index. Lists the most important areas of the manual. It is keyed to areas with bleed-to-edge indicators.

2. Table of Contents. Lists in order all chapters, sections, and appendixes. Gives page references.

3. Nomenclature Cross-References List.

4. Chapter Overviews. Summarise material covered in the chapter. Are located at the beginning of each chapter.

5. Symptom Index. Located just before the troubleshooting table in each maintenance chapter. Lists, in alphabetical order, parts of&e rifle with possible malfunctions. References pages of the troubleshooting table.

6. Alphabetical Index. Located at the end of the manual. An extensive subject index for everything in the manual Gives page references.

MAINTENANCE PROCEDURES

There are two maintenance chapters:

Army personnel use chapter two for unit maintenance procedures and chapter three for direct support maintenance procedures.

Air Force personnel: Only Air Force Specialty Code 753XX Combat Arms Training and Maintenance (CATM) specialists, technicians, and gunsmiths are authorized to perform maintenance procedures contained in this manual.

Each maintenance task has an initial setup containing a list of the following things you will need in order to do your maintenance task:

1. Tools and Special Tools. For standard and special tools, see appendixes B and C. Army uses the Tool Set, Gage Set and/or Shop Set listed in the initial setup.

2. Materials/Parts. Lists expendable materials and 100 percent replaceable parts. Each material or part is followed by a part number or appendix reference.

3. References. Lists other publications containing necessary information,

4. Equipment Condition. Lists conditions to be met before Starting the procedure. The reference on the left of the condition is a page reference to instructions for setting up the condition.

5. General Safety Instructions. Lists safety instructions to follow before performing maintenance procedures.

EXTERNAL VIEW OF 5.56MM RIFLE M16

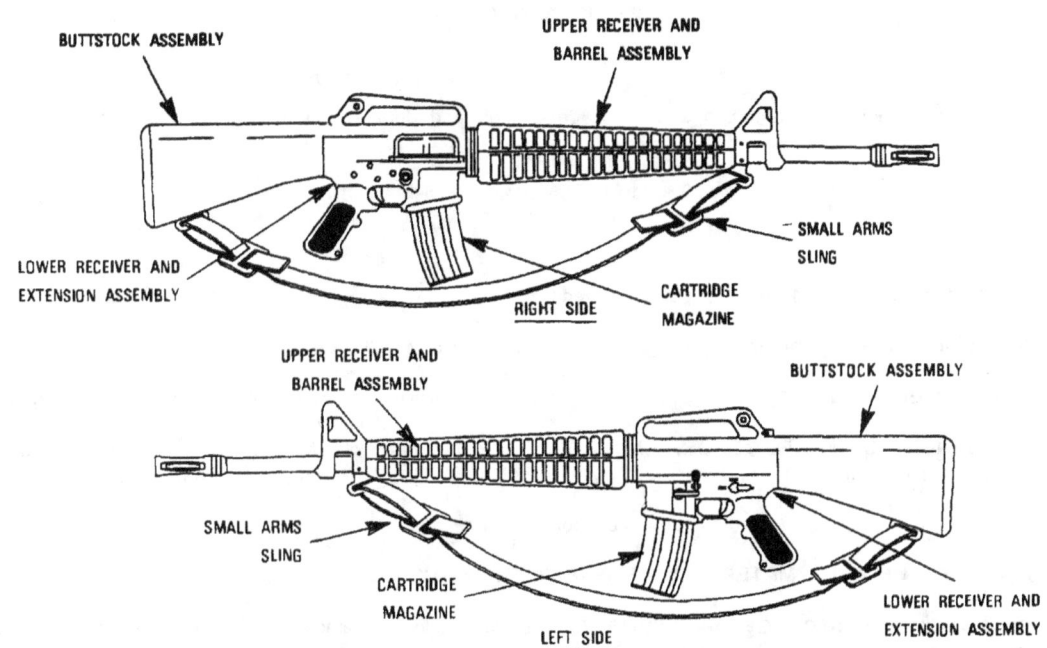

EXTERNAL VIEW OF 5.56MM RIFLE M16A1

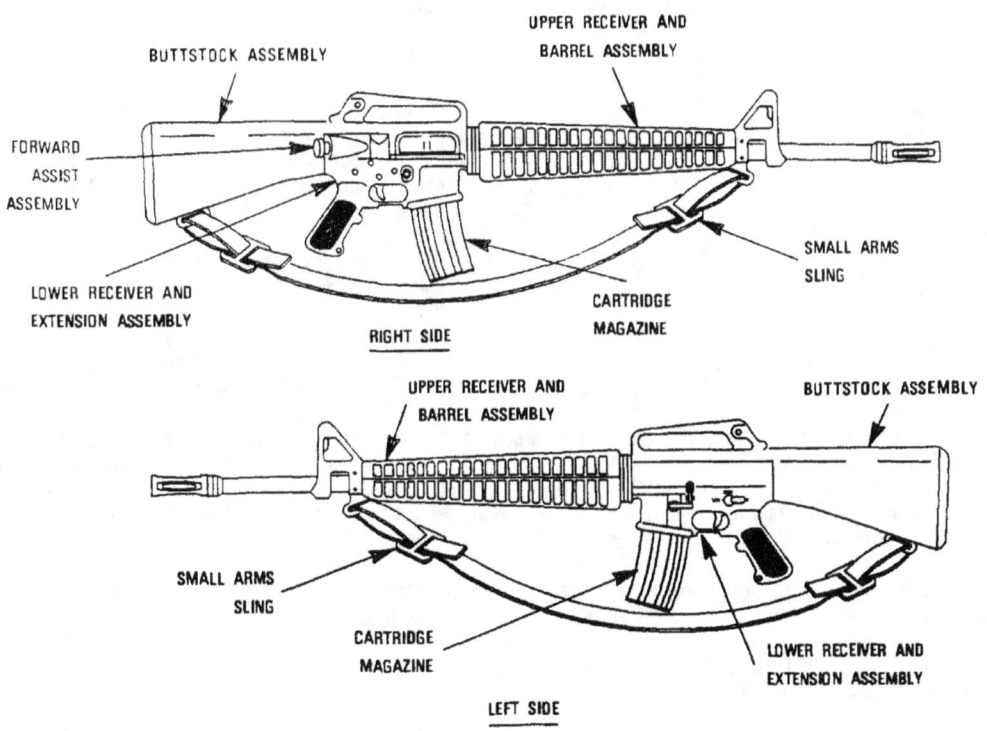

CHAPTER 1

INTRODUCTION

CHAPTER OVERVIEW

This chapter contains general information equipment description and data and principles of operation for your weapon.

Section I. GENERAL INFORMATION

1-1. SCOPE.

   a. Type of Manual: Unit and Direct Support Maintenance.

   b. Model Number and Equipment Name: 5.56mm Rifle M 16 and M16A1.

   c. Purpose of Equipment. Provides personnel an offensive/defensive capability to engage targets for field use.

1-2. MAINTENANCE FORMS, RECORDS, AND REPORTS. Department of the Army forms and procedures used for equipment maintenance will be those prescribed by DA PAM 738-750, The Army Maintenance Management System.

Air Force users refer to TO 11 W 1-10 for applicable forms and records.

1-3. DESTRUCTION OF ARMY MATERIEL TO PREVENT ENEMY USE. See TM 750-244-7.

1-4. PREPARATION FOR STORAGE OR SHIPMENT. Refer to chapter 4, paragraph 4-7. Air Force users refer to Special Packaging Instructions (SPI) 00-856-6885.

1-5. OFFICIAL NOMENCLATURE, NAMES AND DESIGNATIONS.

NOMENCLATURE CROSS-REFERENCE LIST

Common Name	Official Nomenclature
Action Spring	Helical Compression Spring (8448629)
Bolt Catch Spring	Helical Compression Spring (8448633)
Carrier	Key and Bolt Carrier Assembly (8448505)
Disconnector Spring	Helical Compression Spring (8448594)
Ejector Spring	Helical Spring (8448516)
Extractor Spring Assembly	Spring Assembly (8448755)
Hammer Spring	Helical Torsion Spring (8448611)
Magazine Catch Spring	Helical Compression Spring (8448637)
Pistol Grip	Rifle Grip (9349127)
Pivot Pin Detent	Takedown Detent (8448585)
Trigger Spring	Helical Torsion Spring (8448593)
Weapon	5.56mm Rifle M 16 (8448600) or M 16A1 (8448500)

1-6. REPORTING EQUIPMENT IMPROVEMENT RECOMMENDATIONS (EIR). If your rifle needs improvement, let us know. Send us an EIR. You, the user, are the only one who can tell us what you don't like about your equipment. Let us know why you don't like the design. Put it on SF 368 (Product Quality Deficiency Report). Mail it to us at Commander, US Army Armament, Munitions and Chemical Command, ATTN: AMSMC-QAD-I, Rock Island, IL 61299-6000. We'll send you a reply.

Air Force users submit Materiel Deficiency Report (MDR) to: DIR MAT MGT ROBINS AFB GA//MMIBTC// and Product Quality Deficiency Report to: DIR MAT MGT ROBINS AFB GA//MMQA// IAW Technical Order 00-35D-54.

Coast Guard users submit PQDRs (SF 368) in accordance with COMDTINST M4855.1 to: Commandant, U.S. Coast Guard (G-ODO-2), Washington, DC 20593-0001.

Section II. EQUIPMENT DESCRIPTION AND DATA

1-7. EQUIPMENT CHARACTERISTICS, CAPABILITIES, AND FEATURES.

a. Characteristics.

(1) Lightweight
(2) Air-cooled
(3) Gas-operated

(4) Magazine-fed
(5) Semi or automatic fire

b. Capabilities. Provides personnel an offensive/defensive capability to engage targets while in the field role.

c. Features.

(1) Receivers are made of light-weight aluminum alloys; however, the safety, durability, and function of the rifles are in no way reduced. The portability and logistical values are greatly increased, particularly when air transport is used.

(2) The bolt locking action is one of the mechanical features of the weapon. The bolt and barrel extension contains locking lugs which engage and lock the bolt firmly in the barrel extension. The initial force of the explosion of the cartridge propellant is absorbed by the barrel, barrel extension, and bolt.

(3) The trigger guard is easily adaptable to winter operations. A spring-loaded retaining pin is depressed to allow ready access to the trigger when wearing arctic mittens.

(4) The ejection port cover prevents dirt or sand from getting into the ejection port, The cover must be closed during periods when firing is not anticipated. It opens automatically by the forward or rearward movement of the bolt carrier.

1-8. LOCATION AND DESCRIPTION OF MAJOR COMPONENTS.

(A) CHARGING HANDLE ASSEMBLY. Provides a means of charging the weapon.

(B) BOLT CARRIER ASSEMBLY. Carries bolt to chamber and fires the weapon. Contains the firing pin, extractor, bolt, ejector, and cam pin.

(C) UPPER RECEIVER AND BARREL ASSEMBLY. Rifle barrel assembly is air-cooled, contains flash suppressor and front sight assembly, and holds the two hand guards and the sling swivel. Upper receiver contains rear sight, ejection port and cover, and a housing for the bolt carrier and bolt assembly. A forward assist assembly is used on the M16A1 weapon.

(D) LOWER RECEIVER AND EXTENSION ASSEMBLY. Lower receiver contains the trigger assembly, sear hammer assembly, selector lever, rifle grip, bolt catch, and buttstock assembly. The buttstock assembly houses the action spring, buffer assembly, and extension assembly.

(E) CARTRIDGE MAGAZINE. 30 round cartridge capacity.

(F) SMALL ARMS SLING. The small arms sling is adjustable and provides a means to carry the weapon.

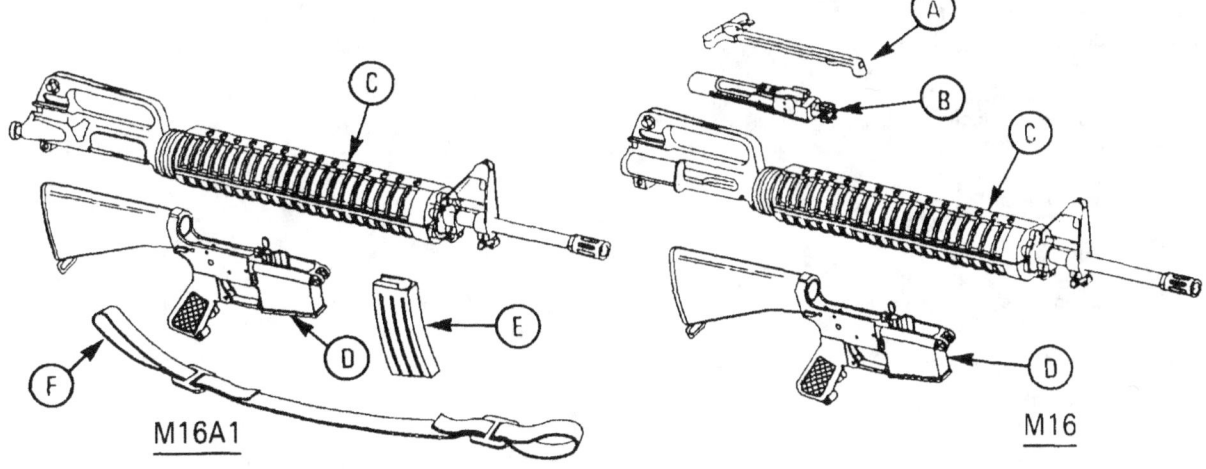

1-9. DIFFERENCES BETWEEN MODELS. The 5.56mm Rifle M16 does not contain the forward assist assembly contained on 5.56mm Rifle M16A1.

1-10. EQUIPMENT DATA.

a. Rifles and M16 and M16A1.

Weight:

Rifle M16, without magazine and Sling	6.35lb
Rifle M16A1, without magazine and sling	6.55 lb
Sling M1	0.4lb
Empty magazine	0.25lb
Loaded magazine	1.01 lb
Rifle M16, w/sling and loaded magazine	7.76 lb
Rifle M16A1 w/sling and loaded magazine	7.96 lb
Bayonet-Knife M7	0.6lb
Scabbard M10	0.3lb

Length:

Rifle w/flash suppressor	39.625 in.
Rifle w/bayonet-knife	44.875 in.
Barrel	20in.
Barrel with flash suppressor	21 in.

Mechanical features:

Rifling - RH twist, 6 grooves, 1 turn in 12 inches	
Method of operation	gas
Typeof breech mechanism	rotatingbolt
Method of feeding	magazine
Cooling	air
Trigger pull	5.5 to 8.5 lb

Ammunition:

Caliber	5.56 mm
Type	ball, blank, dummy and tracer

Firing characteristics:

Muzzle velocity (approximate)	3,250 fps
Muzzle energy	1,300. ft-lb
Chamber pressure	52,000 psi
Cyclic rate of fire (approximate)	800 rds/m

Maximum rate of fire:

Semiautomatic	45/65 rds/m
Automatic	150/200 rds/m
Sustained rate of fire	12/15 rds/m
Maximum range	2,653 meters
Maximum effective range	460 meters

b. Rifle Bipod M3.

Weight:

Bipod	0.6lb
Bipod case	0.2lb

Section III. PRINCIPLES OF OPERATION

1-11. GENERAL. The 5.56mm M16/M16A1 rifle:

a. Is gas-operated. It fires in either the automatic or semiautomatic mode.

b. Has positive locking of the bolt. Firing pin is part of the bolt and carrier assembly and cannot strike the primer until the bolt is fully locked.

1-12. PRINCIPLES OF OPERATION.

(A) **BOLT AND CARRIER ASSEMBLY.** Provides stripping, cambering, locking, firing, extraction, and ejection of cartridges using the drive springs and projectile propelling gases for power.

(B) **CHARGING HANDLE ASSEMBLY.** Provides initial charging of the weapon. The charging handle latch locks the handle in the forward position during sustained fire to prevent injury to the operator.

(C) **UPPER RECEIVER AND BARREL ASSEMBLY.** Provides support for the bolt carrier assembly. The barrel chambers the cartridge for firing and directs the projectile.

(D) **LOWER RECEIVER AND EXTENSION ASSEMBLY.** Provides firing control for the weapon and provides storage for basic cleaning materials.

(E) **CARTRIDGE MAGAZINE.** Holds cartridges ready for feeding and provides a guide for positioning cartridges for stripping. Provides quick reload capabilities for sustained firing.

(F) **SMALL ARMS SLING.** Provides the means for carrying the weapon.

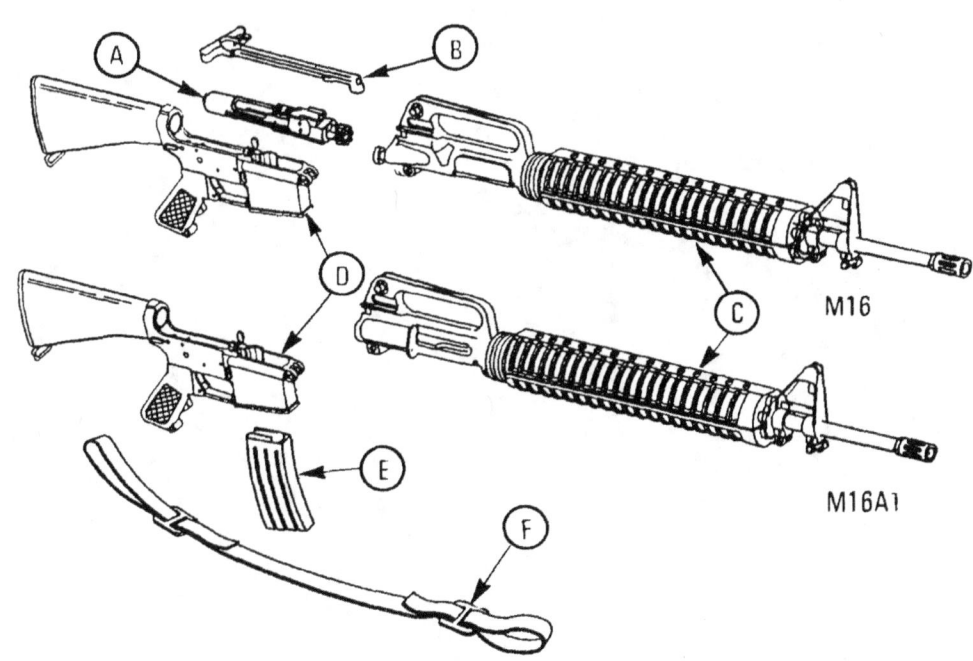

1-13. CORROSION PREVENTION AND CONTROL (CPC). CPC of Army materiel is a continuing concern. It is important that any corrosion problems with this item be reported so that the problem can be corrected and improvements can be made to prevent the problem in the future items.

While corrosion is typically associated with rusting of metals, it can also include deterioration of other materials such as rubber and plastic. Unusual cracking, softening, swelling, or breaking, of these materials may be a corrosion problem.

If a corrosion problem is identified, it can be reported using Standard Form 368, Product Quality Deficiency Report. Use of key words such as "corrosion", "rust", "deterioration" or "cracking" will assure that the information is identified as a CPC problem.

The form should be submitted to:

Commander
U.S. Army Armament, Munitions and Chemical Command
ATTN: AMSCM-QAD/Customer Feedback Center
Flock Island, Illinois 61299-6000

Air force users submit Material Deficiency Report (MDR) to:

DIR MAT MGT
ATTN: MMIBTC
Robins AFB, GA

and Product Quality Deficiency Report to:

DIR MAT MGT
ATTN: MMQA
Robins AFB, GA

CHAPTER 2

UNIT MAINTENANCE INSTRUCTIONS

CHAPTER OVERVIEW

This chapter contains information and instructions to help keep the weapon **in good repair. The chapter contains:**

a. Repair Parts, Special Tools, TMDE, and Support Equipment
b. Service Upon Receipt
c. Preventive Maintenance Checks and Services (PMCS)
d. Troubleshooting
e. Decontamination of Rifles and Arms Rooms
f. Maintenance Procedures

Section 1. REPAIR PARTS, SPECIAL TOOLS, TMDE, AND SUPPORT EQUIPMENT

2-1. COMMON TOOLS AND EQUIPMENT. For authorized common tools **and equipment refer to the Modified Table of** Organization and Equipment (MTOE) applicable to your unit. Air Force **and Coast Guard users must maintain the** following common tools:

Three-ounce soft-brass hammer	Tweezers/round nose pliers
Vise	Hammer
Flat tip screwdriver	Needle nose pliers
Punch	

2-2. SPECIAL TOOLS, TMDE, AND SUPPORT EQUIPMENT. Special tools. required for unit support are listed in appendix C. Fabricated tools are listed and illustrated in appendix E.

2-3. REPAIR PARTS. Repair parts are listed and illustrated in appendix C of this manual.

Section II. SERVICE UPON RECEIPT

2-4, GENERAL.

a. Inspect the weapon for damage incurred during shipment. If the equipment has been damaged, report the damage on SF Form 364, Report of Discrepancy (ROD).

b. Check the weapon against the packing slip to see if the shipment is complete. Report all discrepancies in accordance with the instructions in DA PAM 738-750.

Army users submit an SF 368 (Product Quality Deficiency Report) to: Commander, U.S. Army Armament, Munitions and Chemical Command, ATTN: AMSMC-QAD-I, Rock Island, IL 61299-6000.

Air Force users submit Materiel Deficiency Report (MDR) to: DIR MAT MGT ROBINS AFB GA//MMIBTC// and Quality Deficiency Report to: DIR MAT MGT ROBINS AFB GA//MMQA// IAW Technical Order 00-35D-54.

Coast Guard users submit PQDRs (SF 368) in accordance with COMDTINST M4855.1 to: Commandant, U.S. Coast Guard (G-000-2), Washington, DC 20593-0001.

c. Check to see whether the equipment has been modified.

d. Check to see if all MWOs have been applied.

2-5. SERVICE UPON RECEIPT OF MATERIEL. Refer to the following table.

<u>WARNING</u>

Before starting an inspection, be sure to clear the weapon. Do not actuate the trigger before clearing the weapon. Inspect the chamber to make sure it is empty and free of obstructions. Check to see there are no obstructions in the barrel, and no ammunition is in position to be chambered.

SERVICE UPON RECEIPT - M16/M16A1 RIFLE

LOCATION	ITEM	ACTION	REMARKS
1. Container	M16/M16A1 Rifle	a. Remove rifle from containers.	
		b. Inspect the equipment for damage incurred during shipment.	If the equipment has been damaged, report the damage on SF Form 364, Report of Discrepancy (ROD),
		c. Check the equipment against the packing list to see if the shipment is complete.	Report all discrepancies in accordance with the instructions of DA PAM 738-750.
	b. Basic issue items	Check for missing items.	TM 9-1005-249-10 (Operators Manual)
2. Rifle	a. Barrel assembly	If volatile corrosion inhibitor (VCI) is in barrel, remove and discard.	
	b. All parts	a. Field-strip rifle and inspect for missing, damaged, and rusted or corroded parts.	Refer to Operator's Manual
		b. Clean and lubricate.	Refer to Operator's Manual
		c. Reassemble.	Refer to Operator's Manual
		d. Function check	Refer to paragraph 2-22b
		e. Check to see whether the equipment has been modified.	DA PAM 25-30

Section III. PREVENTIVE MAINTENANCE CHECKS AND SERVICES (PMCS)

2-6. GENERAL This section contains the procedures and instructions necessary to perform unit preventive maintenance checks and services. These services are to be performed by unit maintenance personnel with the assistance of the operator where practical.

2-7. PREVENTIVE MAINTENANCE CHECKS AND SERVICES.

WARNING

Before starting an inspection, be sure to clear the weapon. Do not keep live ammunition near the work area.

a. General. The PMCS procedures are contained in the table following. They are arranged in logical sequence requiring a minimum amount of time and motion on the part of the persons performing them and are arranged so that there will be a minimum interference between persons performing checks simultaneously on the same end item.

b. Item No. Column. Checks and services are numbered in disassembly sequence. This column shall be used as a source of item numbers for the "TM Number" column on DA form 2404, Equipment Inspection and Maintenance Worksheet, in recording results of PMCS.

c. Interval Column. This column gives the designated interval when each check is to be performed.

d. Item To Be Checked Or Serviced Column. This column lists the items to be checked or serviced.

e. Procedure Column. This column contains a brief description of the procedure by which the check is to be performed. It contains all the information required to accomplish the checks and services.

f. Not Fully Mission Capable If: Column. This column contains a brief statement of the condition (e.g., malfunction, shortcoming (SH), deficiency (D)) that would cause the covered equipment to be less than fully ready to perform its assigned mission.

PREVENTIVE MAINTENANCE CHECKS AND SERVICES FOR M16/M16A1 RIFLE

Item No.	Interval	Item To Be Checked Or Serviced	Procedure	Not Fully Mission Capable If:

WARNING

Before starting an inspection, be sure to clear the rifle. Do not actuate the trigger until the rifle has been cleared. Inspect the chamber to ensure that it is empty and no ammunition is in position to be chambered. Do not keep live ammunition near work area.

NOTE

During periods of inactivity, perform preventive maintenance quarterly unless inspection reveals more frequent servicing is necessary.

An inactive weapon is a weapon which has been stored in an arms room for a period of 90 days without use. The weapon may or may not have been assigned to an individual.

Normal cleaning (PMCS) of an inactive weapon will be performed every 90 days. Should the unit armorer detect corrosion on a weapon prior to the end of the 90-day period, the PMCS should be performed immediately.

Solid Film Lubricant (SFL) is the authorized touch up for the M16/M16A1 Rifle and may be used on up to one third of the exterior finish of the weapon.
FOR CONUS USE ONLY: Solid Film Lubricant may be used as a touch up without limitation on the upper receiver and barrel assembly. This is to say that units which DO NOT fall under the category of Divisional Combat Units or rapid deployment type units may have up to 100% of the exterior surface of the Upper Receiver and Barrel Assembly protected with SFL. Prior to application of SFL the surface must be thoroughly clean and inspected for corrosion and/or damage. If corroded or damaged the part must be repaired or replaced prior to application of SFL. Continued use under combat conditions would result in an unprotected surface when the SFL wears off. This would result in a large light reflecting surface and accelerated deterioration of the unprotected surface. Therefore, Divisional Combat Units and units which fall under the definition of Rapid Deployment type must adhere to the limitation of NOT over 1/3 of their exterior surface covered by SFL.

| | Quarterly | Cartridge magazine (serviceability check) | a. Disassemble as in operators manual Inspect tube (1) for bulges, dents, or damaged feeder lips (2). Inspect spring (3) and follower (4) for kinks or damage. | SH - Replace the magazine if any of these conditions exist. |
| | | | b. Reassemble magazine and check for binding during operation of follower (4). | SH - Replace the magazine if the follower binds |

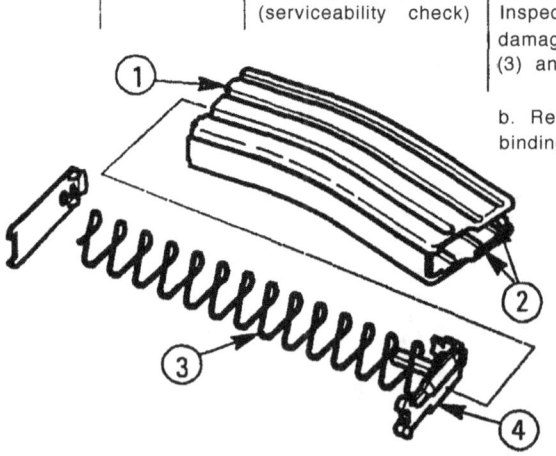

PREVENTIVE MAINTENANCE CHECKS AND SERVICES FOR M16/M16A1 RIFLE (Cont)

Item No.	Interval	Item To Be Checked Or serviced	Procedure	Not Fully Mission Capable If:
2	Quarterly	Charging handle assembly and selector lever.	**WARNING** **If the weapon fails any of the following selector lever teats, evacuate it to Direct Support Maintenance. Continued use of the weapon could result in injury to, or death of, personnel.** Pull charging handle (1) to rear. Check that chamber is clear. Let bolt and bolt carrier (2) close. Leave hammer in cocked position. Do not pull trigger.	D - Charging handle must lock in place when in the forward position.
			Place selector lever (3) in SAFE position. Pull trigger. Hammer should not fall.	D - Hammer falls.
			NOTE **For the purpose of the following test "SLOW" is defined as 1/4 to 1/2 the normal rate of trigger release.**	
			Place selector lever (3) in SEMI position. Pull trigger. Hammer should fall.	D - Hammer does not fall.
			Hold trigger to the rear, charge weapon, and release the trigger with a slow, smooth motion, without hesitations or stops, until the trigger is fully forward. (An audible click should be heard.) Hammer should not fall.	D - Hammer falls.
			Repeat the above SEMI position test five times.	D - The weapon malfunctions during any of these five tests.
			Place in AUTO position. Charge weapon and pull trigger. Hammer should fall.	D - Hammer does not fall.
			Hold trigger to the rear, charge weapon, and release trigger. Pull trigger. Hammer should not fall.	D - Hammer falls.
			NOTE **Automatic sear should have released hammer while holding trigger in the pulled position before releasing and pulling the trigger.**	
			With hammer in forward position, attempt to place the selector lever (3) in SAFE position using finger/thumb pressure only..	D - Finger/thumb pressure moves fire control selector to SAFE position.

PREVENTIVE MAINTENANCE CHECKS AND SERVICES FOR M16/M16A1 RIFLE (Cont)

Item No.	Interval	Item To Be Checked Or Serviced	Procedure	Not Fully Mission Capable If:
3	Quarterly	Upper receiver and barrel assembly (handguards)	**CAUTION** **Do not use screwdriver or any other tool when removing the handguards, doing so may damage the handguard and/or slip ring.** **NOTE** **Refer to operator's manual for "buddy system" procedure on removing handguards.** Remove and inspect handguards (1) internally and externally for cracks and/or damage. Cracks up to one inch in length are acceptable providing they do not extend into the handguard retaining flange or adversely affect weapon operation, operator safety, or proper retention of handguard.	SH - Discard and replace the handguard assembly (1) if the heat-shield is loose enough to rattle when installed on the rifle or it fails the inspection.
4	Quarterly	Upper receiver and barrel assembly (serviceability check)	**WARNING** **Dry cleaning solvent is flammable and toxic and should be used in a well-ventilated area. The use of rubber gloves is necessary to protect the skin when washing rifle parts.** Release takedown pins and open and separate receivers Hand check flash suppressor (1) for looseness on barrel (2), then hand check barrel for looseness on upper receiver (3). Check gas tube (4), forward assist (5), and rear sight (6) for damage. Using finger pressure, check the rear sight for firmness. The rear sight spring shall retain the rear sight in either position with Firmness. Check front sight post, plunger, and spring (7) for damage and corrosion. Clean and lubricate them (p 2-22). Check charging handle (8) and ejection port cover (9) for defects and proper function. Check sling swivel (10) and pin/rivet(11) for damage and proper function.	D - If flash support or barrel are loose, evacuate to direct support maintenance. **D - If barrel is loose on upper receiver, evacuate to support maintenance.** SH - If damaged, evacuate to direct support maintenance. **D - Charging handle (8) is defective.** **SH - Replace defective components as necessary.**

PREVENTIVE MAINTENANCE CHECKS AND SERVICES FOR M16/M16A1 RIFLE (Cent)

Item No.	Interval	Item To Be Checked Or Serviced	Procedure	Not Fully Mission capable If:

CAUTION
Do not use a wire brush to roughen surfaces. Use a well-ventilated area during cleaning and application of solid film lubricant. If solid film lubricant comes in contact with moving parts or functioning surfaces of the rifle, remove lubricant immediately by washing with dry cleaning solvent.

NOTE
Shiny metal exterior surfaces of the rifle should be recoated with solid film lubricant (item 19, app D). Clean surface with dry cleaning solvent (Item 15, app D), dry, roughen with abrasive cloth (item 12, app D) and apply solid film lubricant

Item No.	Interval	Item To Be Checked Or Serviced	Procedure	Not Fully Mission capable If:
4	Quarterly	Upper receiver and barrel assembly (serviceability check) (cent)	Inspect upper receiver (3) finish for scratches or worn shiny spots.	SH - If scratched or worn, to allow a shiny, light reflecting surface, apply solid film lubricant.

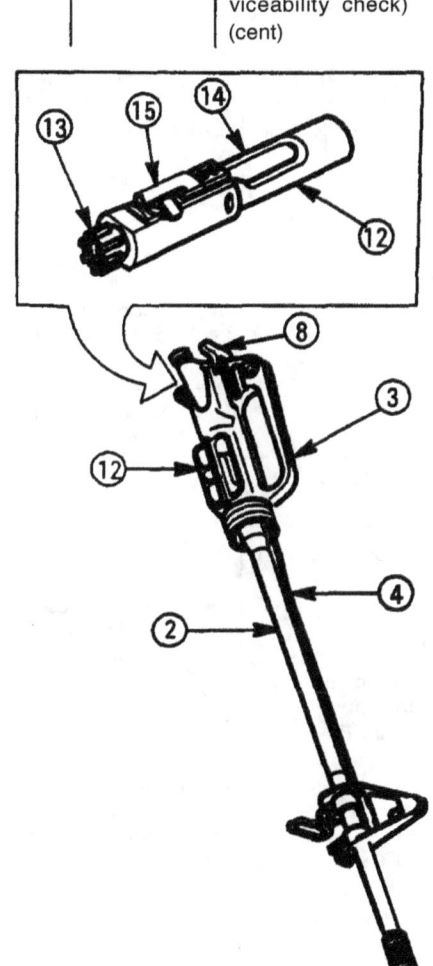

If scratched or worn shiny in spots, disassemble and remove all lubricant from surface with dry cleaning solvent (item 15, app D). Wear rubber gloves (item 16, app D) and use a wash pan (item 22, app D) to apply solvent. Let parts dry thoroughly. Roughen the surface using abrasive cloth (item 12, app D) and apply solid film lubricant (item 19, app D). Allow 16 to 24 hours to dry before handling.

Hold barrel (2) at 40-degree angle (muzzle down). Pull charging handle (8) to rear. Hold bolt carrier assembly (12) to rear and push charging handle forward. Release bolt carrier assembly (1 2). The bolt carrier assembly should close and lock under its own weight. If it does not, remove the bolt (13) from the carrier(14) and slide the carrier (14) (without bolt) back and forth in the upper receiver and barrel assembly. If the gas tube (4) hits the carrier key (15) or if the gas tube binds on the carrier key, try to correct the malfunction by adjusting (slightly bending) the gas tube in the area of the handguards.

D - If this does not correct the malfunction, evacuate to direct support maintenance.

PREVENTIVE MAINTENANCE CHECKS AND SERVICES FOR M16/M16A1 RIFLE (Cont)

Item No.	Interval	Item To Be Checked Or Serviced	Procedure	Not Fully Mission Capable If:
			WARNING	
			Below direct support maintenance, do not interchange bolt assemblies from one weapon to another. Doing so may result in injury to, or death of, personnel.	
5	Quarterly	Bolt carrier assembly (serviceability check)	Remove and disassemble. Visually inspect bolt assembly (1) for cracks, especially in the area of the cam pin hole (2). Check for cracks on locking lugs (3), for a cluster of pits or chipped bolt face (4), and for an elongated firing pin hole (5).	ID - If defects are found, evacuate to direct support maintenance for repair.
			Check for missing or broken retaining pin (6)/bolt cam pin (7), or cracks on bolt cam pin.	ID - Replace retaining pin/bolt cam pin.
			Check for worn bolt rings (8). Insert the bolt assembly (1) into the bolt carrier (9). Turn bolt carrier assembly (9) so the bolt assembly (1) points down. The bolt must not drop out.	ID - If the bolt assembly drops out of the bolt carrier due to its own weight, evacuate to direct support maintenance for repair (usually bolt ring replacement).
			Check extractor and spring (10) and ejector and spring (11) for dirt and serviceability.	SH - Clean, lubricate (p 2-22) and assemble.
			NOTE Do not remove extractor spring assembly from extractor except for replacement.	D - Replace extractor and spring, and ejector and spring as necessary.
			Check bolt carrier (9) and carrier key (12) for damage and looseness.	D - If bolt carrier or carrier key is damaged or carrier key is loose, evacuate to direct support maintenance.
			NOTE Dented carrier keys may be repaired (p 2-25) using the fabricated key tool (fig E-3, app E).	
			Check firing pin (13) for chips or breaks.	D - If firing pin is damaged, evacuate to direct support maintenance.
			Pits or wear in area illustrated is permissible (14).	

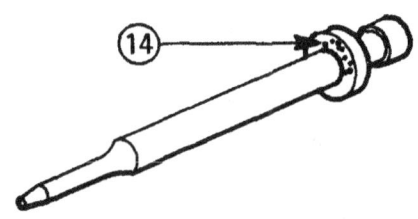

PREVENTIVE MAINTENANCE CHECKS AND SERVICES FOR M16/M16A1 RIFLE (Cont)

Item No.	Interval	Item To Be Checked Or Serviced	Procedure	Not Fully Mission Capable If:
6	Quarterly	Lower receiver and extension assembly (serviceability check)	Remove buffer (1) and action spring (2). Check buffer for cracks.	SH - Replace buffer if racked.

Check action spring (12) for kinks and free length. Free length should be 11 3/4 minimum to 13 1/2 maximum inches.

SH - If kinked or incorrect length replace. Do not attempt to adjust spring length.

Remove rifle grip (3), spring (4), safety detent (5), pivot pin (6), detent (7), and spring (8). Clean and lubricate metal components (p 2-22). Also clean and lubricate pivot pin holes and spring/detent holes.

D - Replace defective/damaged components as necessary.

Compress helical compression spring and takedown pin detent (9) using a jeweler's screwdriver or fabricated tool depicted in appendix E (fig E-2).

D - If helical compression spring will not compress, or takedown pin detent will not return to its original position, refer to page 2-41 for repair procedure.

Lubricate (p 2-22) helical compression spring and takedown pin detent (9) by placing one drop of lubricant on detent and lowering the buttstock assembly (10) to vertical position. Allow the lubricant to work its way around the helical compression spring and takedown pin detent (9).

Check buttstock assembly (10) components for damage.

Under the following conditions, hairline cracks (no chipped away material allowed) originating from the buttplate end of the buttstock are acceptable without repair.

D - Replace damaged components as necessary.

 a. One hairline crack, not to exceed one inch in length, per side of buttstock.

 b. Two additional hairline cracks up to 1/4 inch in length, per side of buttstock.

 c. A total of three cracks per side of the buttstock, originating from the buttplate end, are allowable.

Cracks in the critical area (11) at the front end of the buttstock are not acceptable.

PREVENTIVE MAINTENANCE CHECKS AND SERVICES FOR M16/M16A1 RIFLE (Cont)

Item No.	Interval	Item To Be Checked Or Serviced	Procedure	Not Fully Mission Capable If:
6	Quarterly	Lower receiver and extension assembly (serviceability check) (cent)	Check buttstock assembly (10) for forward to rear movement and/or a 1 /32" gap between the buttstock assembly (10) and the lower receiver (11). If forward to rear movement and/or a 1/32" gap appears, tighten butt cap screw. If still not tight, replace buttplate.	

If movement and/or gap remains, a loose lower receiver extension may be the cause.

NOTE
Small amounts of side-to-side, up-and-down or rotational movement of the buttstock assembly is acceptable without repair.

Replace the butt plate (12) if any of the following conditions exist:

(1) Cracks around the mounting holes are visible when installed on the weapon.

(2) Cracks or separations around the door assembly are visible when the door assembly is closed.

(3) If any crack is in excess of 1/4 inch in length and extends through the butt plate (12).

(4) The butt plate (12) should not be removed other than for repair or replacement of parts at which time a new, self-locking screw must be used.

Function check the magazine catch (13) and bolt catch (14).

Check lower receiver (11) finish for scratches and worn shiny spots.

NOTE
If a M16/M16A1 Rifle LOWER RECEIVER is missing one third or more of its exterior protective finish, resulting in an unprotected/light reflecting surface, it is candidate for overhaul. This missing finish will be considered a shortcoming. This shortcoming requires action to obtain a replacement weapon. Once a replacement has been received, evacuate the original weapon to depot for overhaul.

D If a loose lower receiver extension is suspected, remove buttstock (p 2-45) and check for tightness. If loose, evacuate to direct support maintenance for repair, Clean and lubricate all components before reassembly.

SH - If defective, replace necessary parts.

D - If defective, evacuate to direct support maintenance.

PREVENTIVE MAINTENANCE CHECKS AND SERVICES FOR M16/M16A1 RIFLE (Cont)

Item No.	Interval	Item To Be Checked Or Serviced	Procedure	Not Fully Mission Capable If:
6	Quarterly	Lower receiver and extension assembly (serviceability check) (cont)	If scratched or worn shiny in spots, recoat with solid film lubricant (item 19, app D) as stated in item 4 (p 2-7).	
7	Quarterly	M16/M16A1 Rifle	Assemble as in operators manual.	
			Check for broken, missing, or damaged parts and check over all general appearance.	D - Replace parts as required and authorized, or evacuate to direct support maintenance for repair.
			Check small arms sling for damage.	SH - Replace if damaged.
8	Quarterly	Bipod assembly M3 (serviceability check)	Check spring tension for retention to rifle barrel. Check legs (1) for damage.	SH - If defective, replace M3 bipod.

Item No.	Interval	Item To Be Checked Or Serviced	Procedure	Not Fully Mission Capable If:
9	Quarterly	Annual DS safety and serviceability inspection and gaging	Check the DD Form 314 to insure annual DS safety and serviceability inspection and gaging has been done and that the next gaging and inspection is scheduled.	D - If annual gaging has not been performed within the last year, notify direct support maintenance.

Section IV. TROUBLESHOOTING

2-8. GENERAL.

a. This section contains troubleshooting information for locating and correcting most of the operating troubles which may develop in the 5.56mm Rifle M16 and M16A1, Each malfunction for the individual part or assembly is followed by a list of tests or inspections which will help you to determine the corrective actions to take. You should perform the tests, inspections and corrective actions in the order listed.

b. This manual cannot list all malfunctions that may occur, nor all tests or inspections and corrective actions. If a malfunction is not listed or is not corrected by listed corrective actions, see individual repair sections for maintenance instructions on each major assembly.

2-9. TROUBLESHOOTING PROCEDURES. Refer to troubleshooting table for malfunctions, tests, and corrective actions. The symptom index is provided for a quick reference of symptoms covered in the table.

SYMPTOM INDEX

	Troubleshooting Procedures Page
Failure of magazine to lock in weapon	2-13
Failure to feed	2-13
Failure to chamber	2-14
Failure to lock	2-14
Failure to fire	2-15
Failure to unlock	2-15
Failure to extract	2-16
Failure to eject	2-16
Failure to cock	2-16
Short recoil	2-17
Weapon cannot be zeroed	2-18
Failure to cycle with selector lever set on AUTO	2-19
Fires two rounds with one pull of trigger with selector lever set on SEMI (double firing)	2-19
Fires with selector lever on SAFE or when trigger is released with selector lever on SEMI	2-19
Bolt fails to lock to rear after firing last round	2-20

TROUBLESHOOTING

MALFUNCTION
 TEST OR INSPECTION
  CORRECTIVE ACTION

1. FAILURE OF MAGAZINE TO LOCK IN WEAPON.

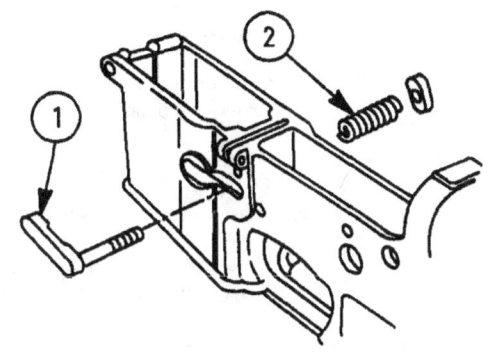

 Step 1. Dirty or corroded magazine catch (1).

  Disassemble and clean.

 Step 2. Defective magazine catch spring (2).

  Replace spring (2).

 Step 3. Worn or broken magazine catch (1).

  Replace magazine catch (1).

2. FAILURE TO FEED.

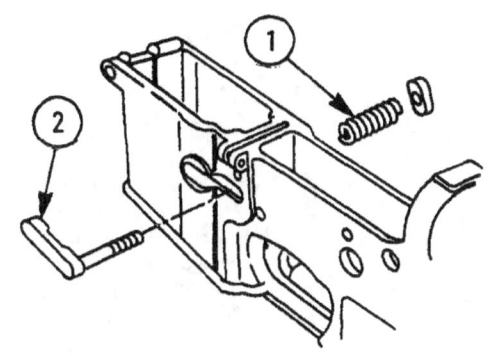

 Step 1. Magazine catch spring (1) weak or broken.

  Evacuate to direct support maintenance.

 Step 2. Magazine catch (2) defective.

  Evacuate to direct support maintenance.

 Step 3. Magazine catch (2) out of adjustment (will not retain magazine).

  Refer to operator's manual

 Step 4. Magazine catch notch (3) defective.

  Replace magazine assembly.

 Step 5. Magazine lips (4) burred or broken.

  Replace magazine.

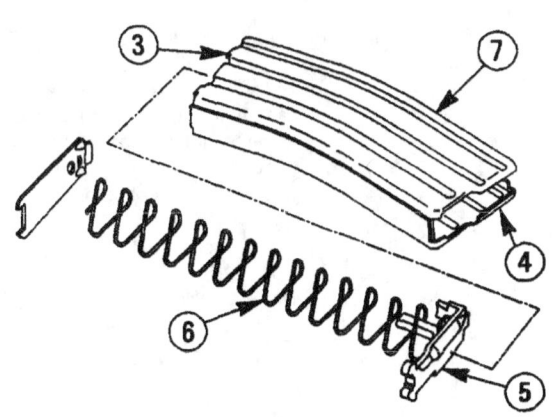

 Step 6. Magazine follower (5) defective, or binds during operation.

  Replace magazine.

 Step 7. Magazine spring (6) weak or broken.

  Replace magazine.

 Step 8. Magazine tube (7) dented.

  Replace magazine.

 Step 9. Short recoil.

  Refer to page 2-17.

TROUBLESHOOTING (CONT)

MALFUNCTION
   TEST OR INSPECTION
      CORRECTIVE ACTION

3. FAILURE TO CHAMBER.

Step 1. Weak or broken action spring (1) (free length 11 3/4 inches minimum to 13 1/2 inches maximum).

   Replace action spring (1) (p 2-45).

Step 2. Obstruction in bore/chamber.

   Remove obstruction; if unable to remove obstruction, evacuate to direct support maintenance.

4. FAILURE TO LOCK.

Step 1. Dirty or damaged ammunition (1).

   Replace ammunition.

Step 2. Bolt cam pin (2) broken or missing.

   Replace bolt cam pin (p 2-24).

Step 3. Loose or damaged bolt carrier key (3).

   Evacuate to direct support maintenance. Dented carrier keys (3) may be repaired (p 2-22) using the fabricated key tool (fig E-3, app E).

Step 4. Improperly assembled extractor spring assembly (4) to extractor (5).

   Assemble correctly (p 2-29).

Step 5. Bent gas tube (6).

   Adjust/bend gas tube in area of the handguard to its original configuration. If the gas tube cannot be repaired to its original configuration, evacuate weapon to direct support maintenance.

Step 6. Weak or broken action spring (7).

   Replace action spring (7) (p 2-45).

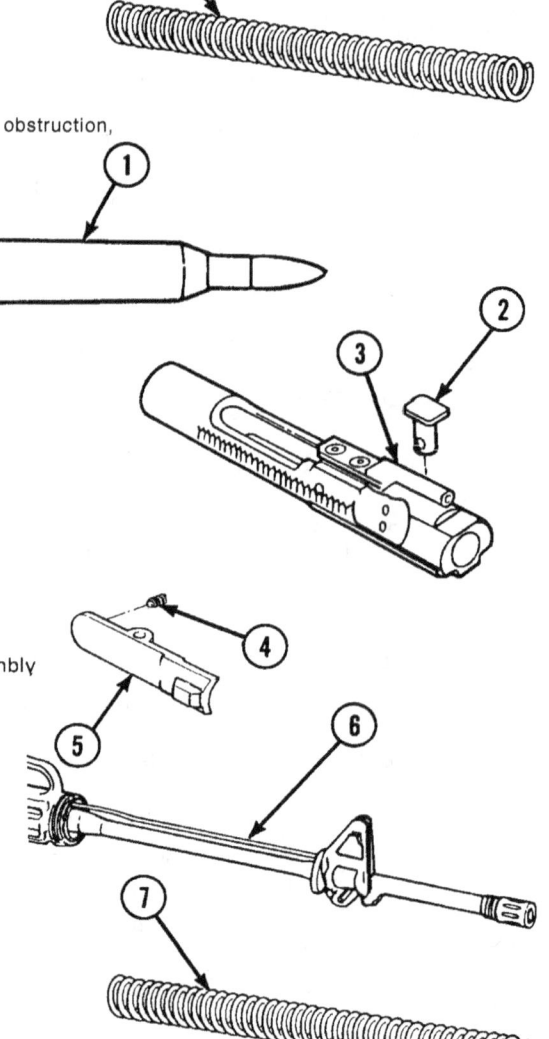

TROUBLESHOOTING (CONT)

MALFUNCTION
    TEST OR INSPECTION
        CORRECTIVE ACTION

5. FAILURE TO FIRE.

    Step 1. Broken, chipped, or deformed firing pin (1).

        Evacuate to direct support maintenance.

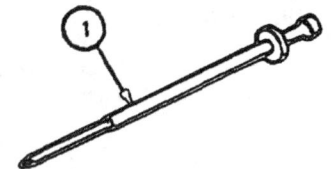

    Step 2. Firing mechanism (2) and/or lower receiver assembly (3) improperly assembled or has worn, broken, or missing parts.

        Evacuate to direct support maintenance

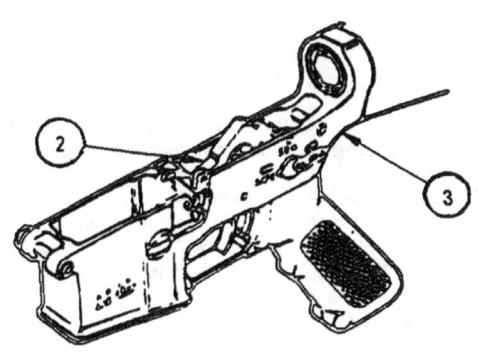

    Step 3. Broken, missing, or defective retaining pin (4).

        Replace retaining pin (p 2-24).

6. FAILURE TO UNLOCK.

    Step 1. Burred locking lugs (1) on bolt assembly (2).

        Evacuate to direct support maintenance.

    Step 2. Burred locking lugs (3) on barrel extension.

        Evacuate to direct support maintenance.

    Step 3. See short recoil (p 2-17).

    Step 4. Broken bolt assembly (2).

        Evacuate to direct support maintenance.

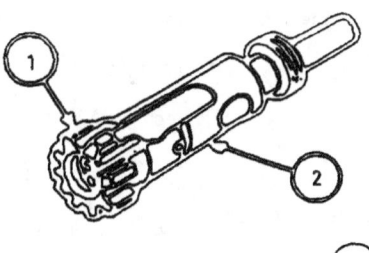

TROUBLESHOOTING (CONT)

MALFUNCTION
    TEST OR INSPECTION
        CORRECTIVE ACTION

---

7. FAILURE TO EXTRACT.

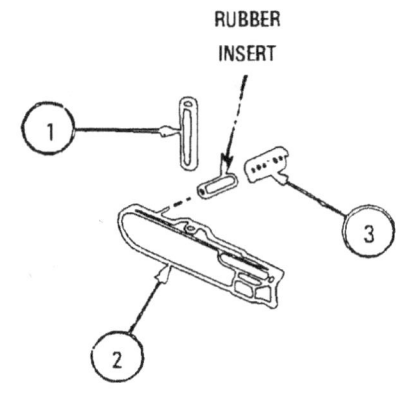

RUBBER INSERT

> **Step 1.** Defective extractor pin (1), extractor (2), and/or extractor spring assembly (3).
>
> > Replace extractor pin (1), extractor (2), and/or extractor spring assembly (3) (p 2-24).
>
> **Step 2.** Short recoil.
>
> > Refer to page 2-17.

NOTE

Rubber insert and spring are an assembly. Illustration shows insert out of assembly for clarification only. Do not remove rubber insert from spring.

> **Step 3.** Badly pitted chamber.
>
> > Evacuate to direct support maintenance.

8. FAILURE TO EJECT.

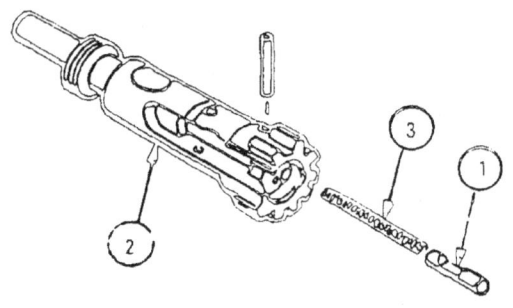

> **Step 1.** Broken or missing cartridge ejector (1).
>
> > Replace (p 2-29).
>
> **Step 2.** Ejector (1) stuck in bolt body (2).
>
> > Disassemble and clean (p 2-29).
>
> **Step 3.** Weak, broken or missing ejector spring (3).
>
> > Replace (p 2-29).
>
> **Step 4.** Short recoil.
>
> > Refer to page 2-17.

9. FAILURE TO COCK.

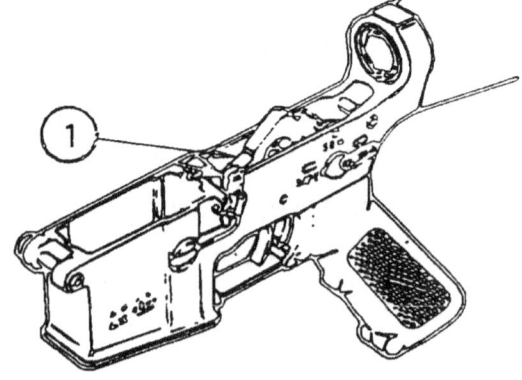

> **Step 1.** Worn, broken, or missing parts of firing mechanism (1).
>
> > Evacuate to direct support maintenance.
>
> **Step 2.** Short recoil.
>
> > Refer to page 2-17.

TROUBLESHOOTING (CONT)

MALFUNCTION
    TEST OR INSPECTION
        CORRECTIVE ACTION

10. SHORT RECOIL.

    Step 1. Improper gap space or worn, missing or broken bolt rings (1).

        Evacuate to direct support maintenance if rings are worn, broken or missing (p 2-30).

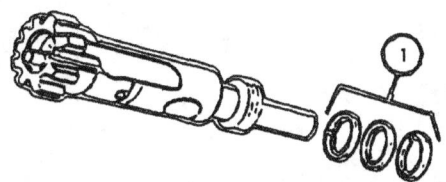

    Step 2. Partially plugged gas system because of carbon build up in gas tube.

        Evacuate to direct support maintenance.

    Step 3. Carbon buildup in the narrow passage of the bolt carrier key.

        Clean with CLP (item 9, app D) or RBC (item 11, app D). See operator's manual.

    Step 4. Gas leakage caused by broken or loose gas tube (2) around front sight base (3).

        Evacuate to direct support maintenance.

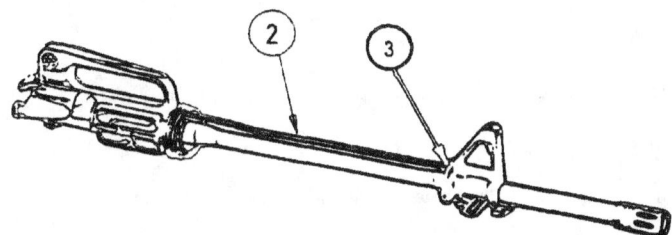

    Step 5. Improper alignment of gas tube (2) and carrier key (4).

        Refer to page 2-24.

    Step 6. Loose carrier key (4).

        Evacuate to direct support maintenance.

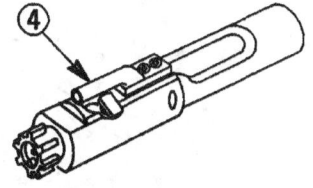

TROUBLESHOOTING (CONT)

MALFUNCTION
        TEST OR INSPECTION
                CORRECTIVE ACTION

11. WEAPON CANNOT BE ZEROED.

    Step 1. Bent or bulged rifle barrel assembly (1).

        Evacuate to direct support maintenance.

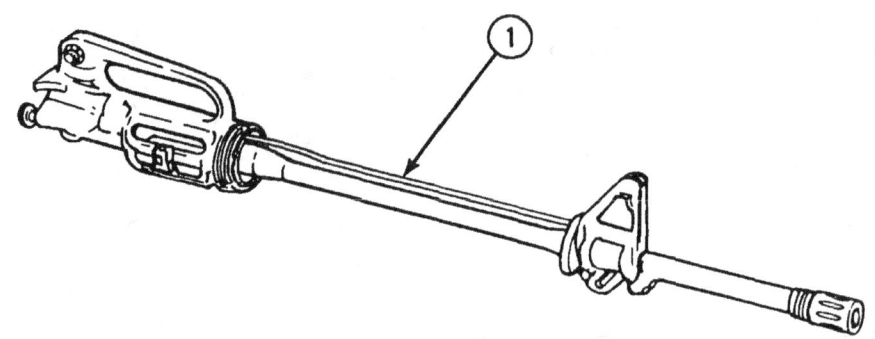

    Step 2. Barrel assembly out of alignment with rear sight on upper receiver.

        Evacuate to direct support maintenance.

    Step 3. Corroded front sight post (2).

        Disassemble, clean and lubricate (p 2-37).

    Step 4. Corroded rear sight (3).

        Clean and lubricate. Evacuate to direct support maintenance.

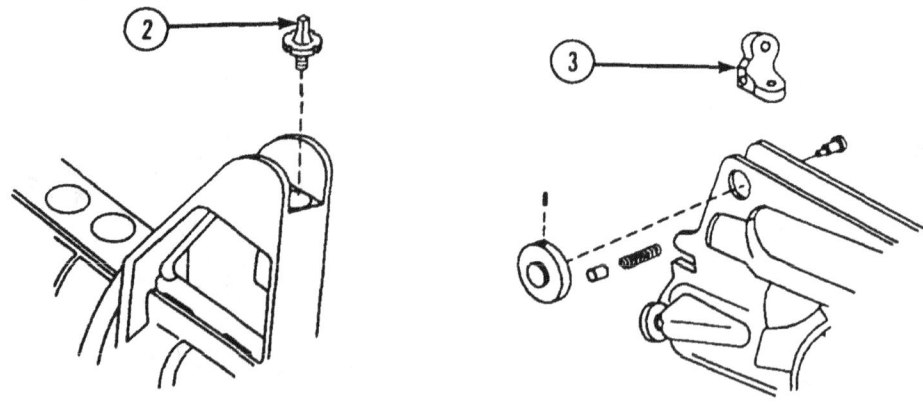

TROUBLESHOOTING (CONT)

MALFUNCTION
    TEST OR INSPECTION
        CORRECTIVE ACTION

12. FAILURE TO CYCLE WITH SELECTOR LEVER SET ON AUTO.

    Faulty selector lever (1).

        Evacuate to direct support maintenance.

13. FIRES TWO ROUNDS WITH ONE PULL OF TRIGGER WITH SELECTOR LEVER (1) SET ON SEMI (DOUBLE FIRING).

    Perform function test.

        If any part of function test (p 2-53) fails, evacuate to direct support maintenance.

14. FIRES WITH SELECTOR LEVER (1) ON SAFE OR WHEN TRIGGER IS RELEASED WITH SELECTOR LEVER ON SEMI.

    Worn, broken, or missing parts of firing mechanism.

        Evacuate to direct support maintenance

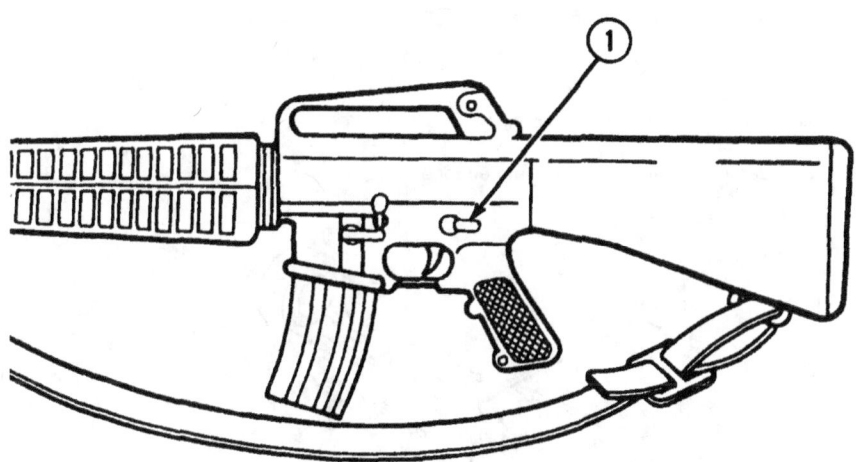

TROUBLESHOOTING (CONT)

MALFUNCTION
> **TEST OR INSPECTION**
>> **CORRECTIVE ACTION**

15. BOLT FAILS TO LOCK TO REAR AFTER FIRING LAST ROUND

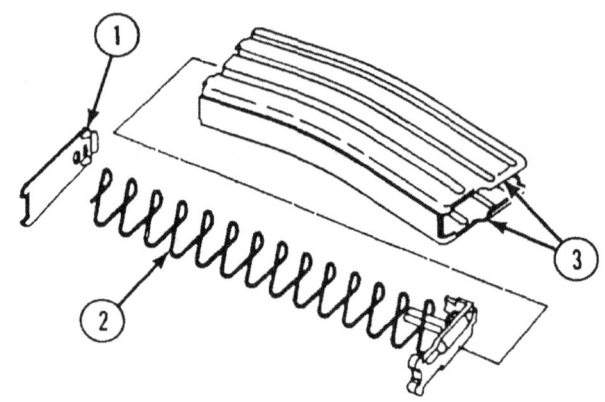

Step 1. Magazine follower (1) worn or broken.

Replace magazine.

Step 2. Magazine spring (2) weak or broken.

Replace magazine.

Step 3. Magazine feeder lips (3) bent or broken,

Replace magazine.

Step 4. Magazine follower (1) binds during operation.

Replace magazine.

Step 5. Broken bolt catch (4) and/or spring,

Evacuate to direct support maintenance.

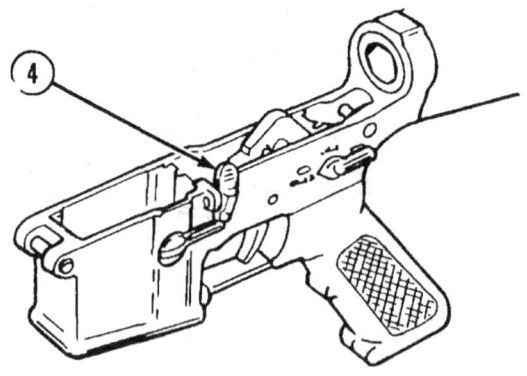

Section V. DECONTAMINATION OF RIFLES AND ARMS ROOMS

2-10. DECONTAMINATION OF SIGHTS ACTIVATED WITH TRITIUM (H3).

  a. Identification. Tritium sights will be marked with the assembly data and the radiation symbol and stamped H3, 9 mc .

  b. Damage Determination. Evidence of a break in the glass container for the H3 will be a lack of illumination (assuring the expiration data for the sight has not been exceeded). Radiation from the sight is extremely low and CANNOT be detected with standard issue radiation detectors, i.e., AN/PDR-27.

  c. Contamination. The tritium isotope used in the low light level sight is in a gaseous state and will rapidly diffuse into the atmosphere in the event of breakage. Very little residual contamination should be left on the rifle. All illumination will cease upon loss of H3 gas.

WARNING

Dry cleaning solvent is flammable and toxic and should be used in a well-ventilated area.
The use of rubber gloves is necessary to protect the skin when washing rifle parts.

  d. Decontamination. When a broken sight is found, the sight MUST be removed and turned in for disposal in accordance with AR 385-11. After removing the sight, the rifle should be cleaned with dry cleaning solvent (item 15, app D). Wear rubber gloves (item 16, app D) and use a wash pan (item 22, app D) to apply solvent. Let dry, then lubricate (p 2-22).

  e. Requirements. Because its small volume of gas and its low energy of emitted radiation. H3 does not pose a health hazard to the user. Current Army regulations NRC license conditions and Title 10, Code of Federal Regulations, Part 20 require that the above actions be carried out.

2-11. DECONTAMINATION OF SIGHTS ACTIVATED WITH PROMETHIUM (PM 147).

NOTE

PM 147 is no longer available for issue and must be replaced. It is being replaced with tritium (H3).

  a. General. When a sight activated with promethium (PM 147) is found, the sight MUST be removed and turned in for disposal in accordance with AR 385-11. Contact the local RPO.

  b. Identification. Promethium sights are marked with the assembly date, radiation symbol, and PM 147, 1 mc.

  c. Decontamination. If a sight activated with promethium (PM 147) is found, conduct a survey under the direction of the local RPO. Decontaminate as required in accordance with local procedures.

Section VI. MAINTENANCE PROCEDURES

2-12. INITIAL SETUP. The following will reduce the space required for the initial setup portion of the maintenance procedures.

  a. Materials Parts required are not listed unless they apply to the procedure.

  b. Personnel Required is listed only if the task requires more than one person. If Personnel Required is not listed, it means one person can do the job.

c. Do not scratch, etch or stamp numbers, letters or any other information on bolt, bolt carrier, buttstock or other piece parts.

d. The normal standard equipment condition is that the item is removed from end item or next higher assembly and is in the assembled condition. Equipment Condition is not listed unless some other condition is required.

e. The approximate time required is listed on the applicable Maintenance Allocation Chart (MAC).

f. When the term evacuate to direct support maintenance is used, the entire weapon must be evacuated.

NOTE

Solid Film Lubricant (SFL) is the authorized touch up for the M16/M16A1 Rifle and may be used on up to one third of the exterior finish of the weapon.
FOR CONUS USE ONLY: Solid Film Lubricant may be used as a touch up without limitation on the upper receiver and barrel assembly. This is to say that units which DO NOT fall under the category of Divisional Combat Units or rapid deployment type units may have up to 100% of the exterior surface of the Upper Receiver and Barrel Assembly protected with SFL. Prior to application of SFL the surface must be thoroughly clean and inspected for corrosion and/or damage. If corroded or damaged, the part must be repaired or replaced prior to application of SFL. Continued use under combat conditions would result in an unprotected surface when the SFL wears off. This would result in a large light reflecting surface and accelerated deterioration of the unprotected surface. Therefore, Divisional Combat Units and units which fall under the definition of Rapid Deployment type must adhere to the limitation of NOT over 1/3 of their exterior surface covered by SFL.

2-13. LUBRICATION GENERAL.

a. Whenever the term or instruction "'lubricate" is cited in this TM, it is to be Interpreted to mean CLP, (item 9, app D), LSA (item 21, app D), or LAW (item 20, app D) can be utilized as applicable The following constraints must be adhered to:

b. Under all but the coldest arctic conditions. LSA or CLP are the lubricants to use on the weapon Either may be used at -10°F and above. However, do not use both on the same weapon at the same time.

c. LAW is the lubricant to use during cold arctic conditions, +10° F and below.

d. Any of the lubricants may be used from -10°F to +10°F.

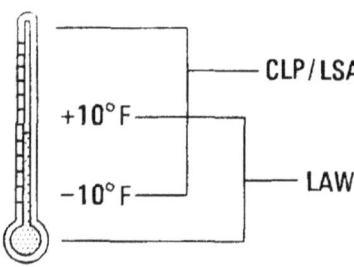

e. Do not mix lubricants on the same weapon. The weapon must be thoroughly cleaned during change from one lubricant to another. Dry Cleaning Solvent (SD) (item 15, app D) is recommended for cleaning during change from one lubricant to another.

f. Rifle Bore Cleaner (RBC) (item 11, app D), may be used to remove carbon buildup in the bore and other portions of the weapon.

2-14. MAJOR COMPONENTS OF M16/16A1 RIFLE.

This task covers disassembly.

INITIAL SETUP

Applicable Configuration
   M16/M16A1 Rifle

References
   TM 9-1005-249-10 (operator's manual)

Equipment Condition
   Weapon assembled.

General Safety Instructions
   Before starting an inspection, be sure to clear the weapon. Do not keep live ammunition near the work area.

To avoid injury to your eyes, use care when removing and installing spring-loaded parts.

Before starting an inspection on a weapon equipped with a low light level sight, check for damage to the sight and decontaminate if required. See procedures on page 2-21.

Below direct support maintenance, do not interchange bolt assemblies from one weapon to another. Doing so may result in injury to, or death of, personnel.

DISASSEMBLY

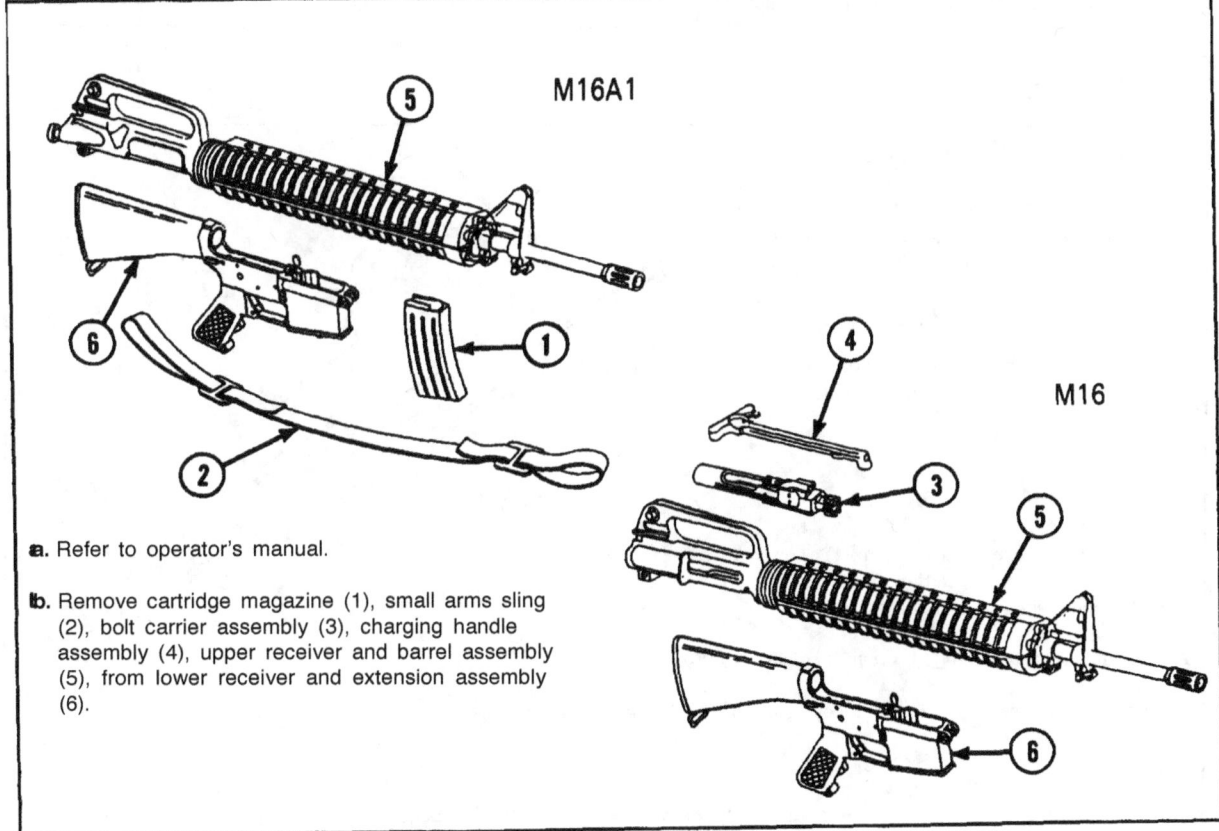

a. Refer to operator's manual.

b. Remove cartridge magazine (1), small arms sling (2), bolt carrier assembly (3), charging handle assembly (4), upper receiver and barrel assembly (5), from lower receiver and extension assembly (6).

2-15. BOLT CARRIER ASSEMBLY.

This task covers:

a. Disassembly
b. Cleaning
c. Inspection/Repair

d. Lubrication
e. Reassembly

INITIAL SETUP

Applicable Configuration
M16/M16A1   Rifle

Tools
Small Arms Repairman Tool Kit
  SC 5180-95-CL-A07 (19204)
Key tool (fig E-3, app E)

Materials/Parts
Cleaner, lubricant and preservation (CLP)
  (item 9, app D)
Cleaning compound, rifle bore (CLP)
  (item 11, app D)
Lubricating oil, weapons (LAW) (item 20, app D)
Lubricating oil, weapons (LSA)(item 21, app D)

Equipment Condition
Bolt carrier assembly removed

Reference
TM 9-1005-249-10 (Operator's manual)

General Safety Instructions
Bolt cam pin must be installed or weapon will blow
  up while firing in the first round. If the bolt cam pin
  is not installed, injury to, or death of, personnel
  may result.

Do not interchange bolt assemblies from one weapon
  to another. Doing so may result in injury to, or
  death of, personnel.

a. DISASSEMBLY

WARNING

Do not interchange bolt assemblies from
one weapon to another. Doing so may
result in injury to, or death of personnel.

CAUTION

Do not spread or close legs
of firing pin retaining pin (1).

1. Remove firing pin retaining pin (1). Lower rear
   end of key and bolt carrier assembly (2) and
   catch firing pin (3) as it drops out.

2. Rotate bolt cam pin (4) 1/4 turn and lift straight up to remove.

3. Remove bolt assembly (5) from key and bolt carrier assembly (2).

NOTE

For disassembly of bolt assembly (5), see page 2-29.

b. CLEANING

Clean all items (operator's manual). Remove carbon deposits using CLP or RBC.

c. INSPECTION/REPAIR

1

(a) Inspect carrier key (1) for dents, distortion or looseness. If dented, straighten (see step 2 on next page). If loose, evacuate to direct support maintenance.

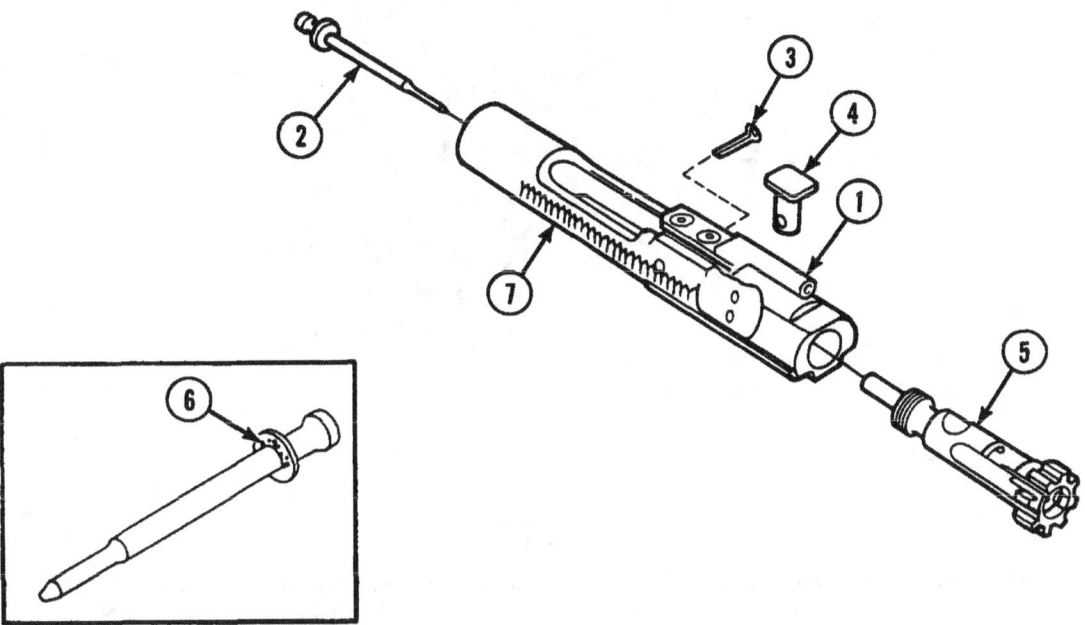

(b) Inspect firing Pin (2), retaining pin (3), and cam pin (4) for cracks, mutilation, or excessive wear. Replace if unserviceable.

(c) Inspect bolt assembly (5) for damage or excessive wear. See page 2-30 for repair procedures.

(d) Inspect firing pin (2) for breaks or if tip is mutilated. Evacuate to direct support maintenance if unserviceable. Pits or wear in area illustrated (6) is permissible.

(e) Inspect key and bolt carrier assembly (7) for damage or wear. If unserviceable, evacuate to direct support maintenance.

| 2-15. BOLT CARRIER ASSEMBLY (CONT). |

| c. INSPECTION/REPAIR (CONT) |

2

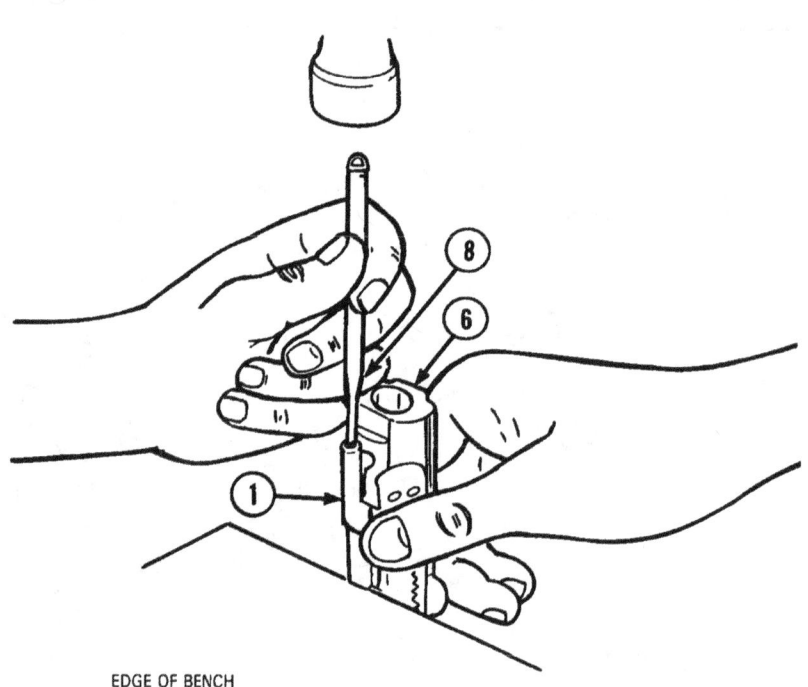

EDGE OF BENCH

CAUTION

Extreme care must be exercised during the following procedure to assure that the striking force is not directed to the attaching screws and that the tube portion is not enlarged or flared beyond original requirement. Such enlargement would permit loss of gas pressure when the key and gas tube come together during function/operation.

Straighten small dents and/or distortions in carrier key (1) using fabricated key tool (8) as follows:

(a) Place the key and bolt carrier assembly (6) in a vertical position, supported in a manner that contact is made with the rear surface of the carrier key (1).

(b) Insert the small end of the key tool (8) into the tube portion of the key.

(c) Strike the large end of the key tool (8) lightly with a 3-ounce, soft-brass hammer.

(d) Repeat striking (gently) until carrier key (1) is reformed to original configuration.

(e) If carrier key cannot be reformed to original configuration, evacuate to direct support maintenance.

d. LUBRICATION

Lubricate all items using CLP, LSA or LAW (p 2-22) or (operator's manual).

e. REASSEMBLY

1

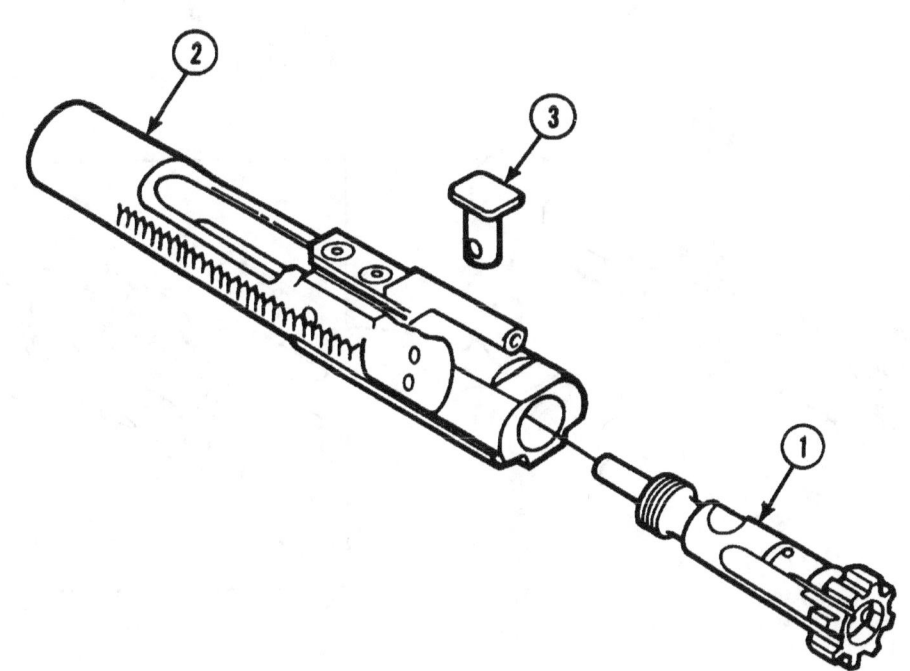

WARNING

Do not interchange bolt assemblies from one weapon to another. Doing so may result in injury to, or death of, personnel.

Bolt cam pin must be installed or weapon will blow up while firing the first round. If the cam pin is not installed, injury to, or death of, personnel may result.

NOTE

Before installing bolt assembly, check to see that the ring gaps are staggered to prevent loss of gas pressure.

(a) Install bolt assembly (1) in key and bolt carrier assembly (2).

(b) Install bolt cam pin (3) and rotate one quarter turn to secure bolt assembly (1).

2-15. BOLT CARRIER ASSEMBLY (CONT).

e. REASSEMBLY (CONT)

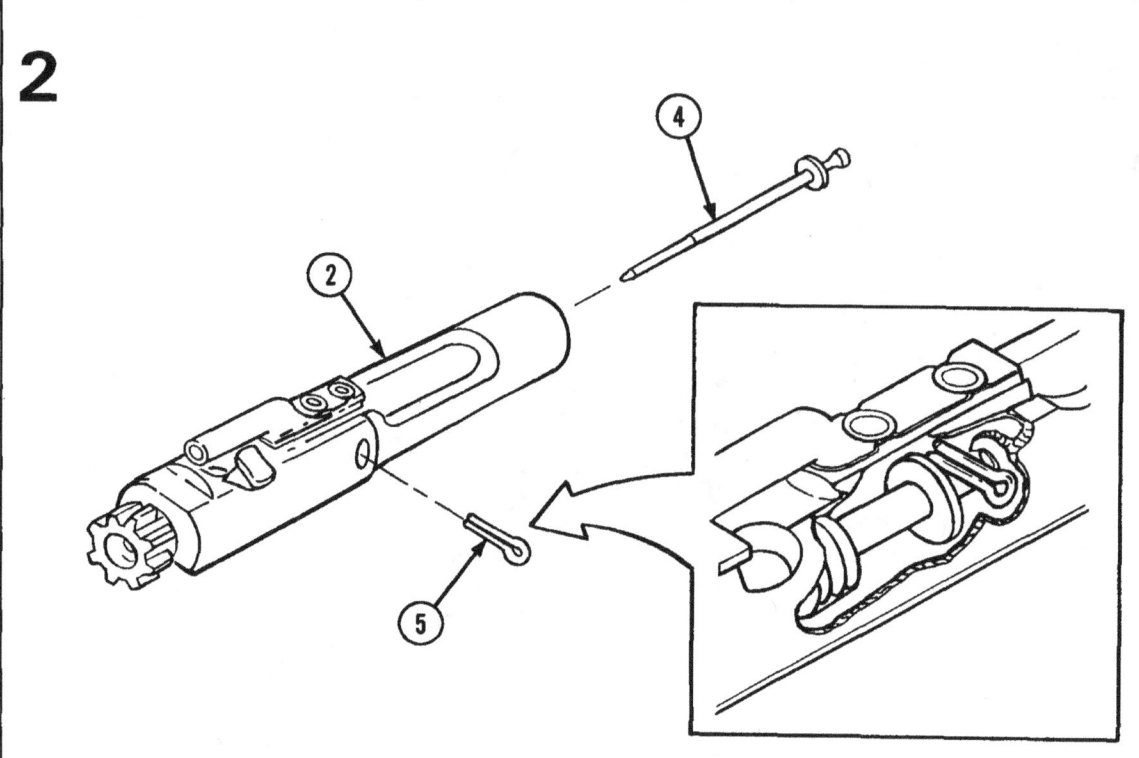

NOTE

Firing pin retaining pin must be installed from the left side only.

(a) Hold key and bolt carrier assembly (2) in vertical position and drop firing pin in position.

(b) Install firing pin retaining pin (5) from left side only. Check proper installation by attempting to shake out firing pin.

2-16. BOLT ASSEMBLY.

This task covers:

a. Disassembly
b. Cleaning
c. Inspection/Repair

d. Lubrication
e. Reassembly

INITIAL SETUP

Applicable Configuration
M16/M16A1 Rifle

Tools
Small Arms Repairman Tool Kit.
SC 5180-95-CL-A07 (19204)

Materials/parts
Cleaner, lubricant and preservative (CLP)
(item 9, app D)
Cleaning compound, rifle bore (RBC)
(item 11, app D)
Lubricating oil, weapons (LAW) (item 20, app D)
Lubricating oil, weapons (LSA) (item 21, app D)

Reference
TM 9-1005-249-10 (Operator's manual)

Equipment Condition
Bolt carrier assembly removed

General Safety Instructions
Do not interchange bolt assemblies from one
weapon to another. Doing so may result in
injury to, or death of, personnel.

To avoid injury to your eyes, use care when
removing and installing spring-loaded parts.

a. DISASSEMBLY

1

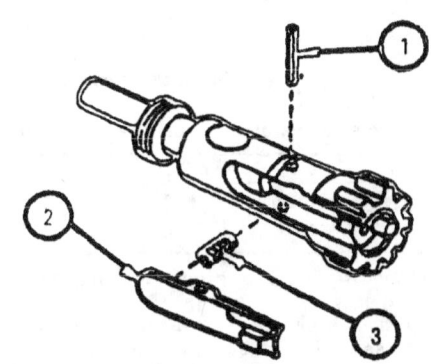

NOTE

Do not separate cartridge extractor and extractor spring assembly unless replacement
of either or both is required.

Do not remove the insert from the extractor
spring assembly.

(a) Push out extractor pin (1) using a 3/32 punch and remove cartridge extractor (2) and extractor spring
assembly (3) as a unit.

NOTE

There are two types of extractor springs. The earlier design does not contain an
insert. The latest design contains an insert. All old type extractor springs must be
replaced.

Do not remove extractor spring assembly from cartridge extractor unless either part
requires replacement.

(b) If required, twist extractor spring assembly (3) counter-clockwise while gently pulling on it, to remove from
cartridge extractor (2). Do not remove/lose rubber insert from spring assembly.

2-16. BOLT ASSEMBLY (CONT)

a. DISASSEMBLY (CONT)

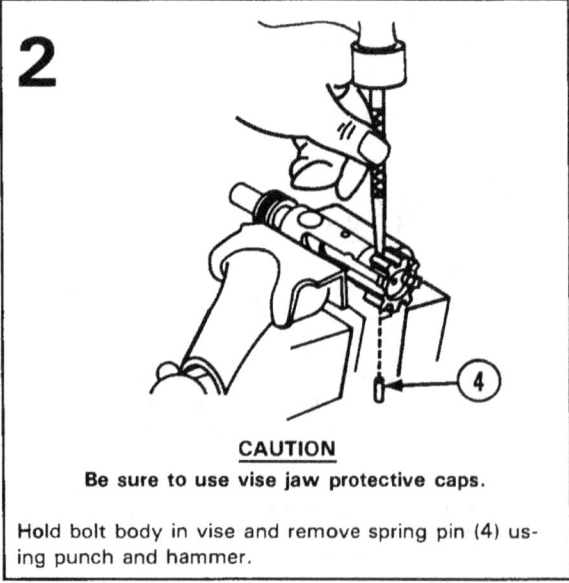

2

CAUTION

Be sure to use vise jaw protective caps.

Hold bolt body in vise and remove spring pin (4) using punch and hammer.

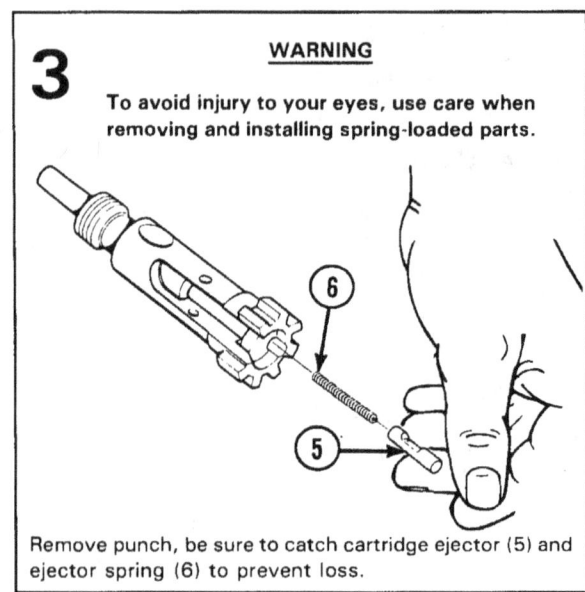

3

WARNING

To avoid injury to your eyes, use care when
removing and installing spring-loaded parts.

Remove punch, be sure to catch cartridge ejector (5) and
ejector spring (6) to prevent loss.

b. CLEANING

CAUTION

Do not distort extractor pin or spring assembly during cleaning.

Clean all items (operator's manual). Remove carbon deposits with CLP or RBC.

c. INSPECTION/REPAIR

1. Check bolt rings (1) for proper spacing, (approximately 1/3 apart).
2. With retaining pin and cam pin removed from bolt
carrier assembly (2), check for worn bolt rings (1) as
follows: Insert bolt assembly (3) all the way in bolt
carrier. Turn bolt carrier downward as illustrated. If
bolt assembly falls out, rings are worn. Evacuate to
direct support maintenance.
3. Inspect for cracks, especially around cam pin hole
(4), and locking lugs (5).
4. Inspect extractor, extractor spring assembly, and extractor pin for cracks, breaks, chips, and other
damage. Pay close attention to extractor lip.
5. Inspect ejector and ejector spring for cracks, breaks,
and chips.
6. Replace all authorized unserviceable items.
7. Repairs not authorized at this level, evacuate to direct support maintenance.
8. The inspection of the worn bolt rings can be accomplished with the bolt assembled or disassembled.

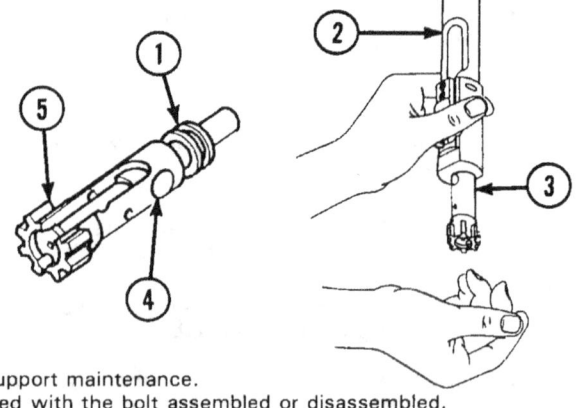

d. LUBRICATION

Lubricate all items with a light coat of CLP, LSA, or LAW (p 2-22).

e. REASSEMBLY

1

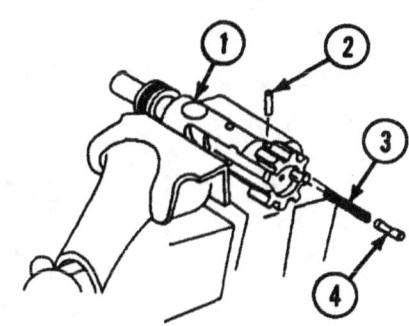

WARNING

To avoid injury to your eyes, use care when removing and installing spring-loaded parts.

Do not interchange bolt assemblies from one weapon to another. Doing so may result in injury to, or death of, personnel.

CAUTION

Be sure to use vise jaw protective caps.

(a) Hold bolt body (1) in a vise and start spring pin (2) in hole.

(b) Install ejector spring (3) and cartridge ejector (4).

(c) Align groove on cartridge ejector (4) so that spring pin (2) can be installed.

2

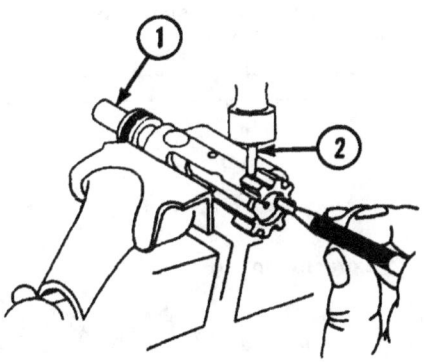

(a) Compress and hold ejector spring and cartridge ejector in place with a 3/8 inch punch. Install spring pin (2) using a hammer.

(b) Complete installation of spring pin (2) so that the ends are flush with the outside of the bolt body (1).

2-16. BOLT ASSEMBLY (CONT).

e. REASSEMBLY (CONT)

3

NOTE

There are two types of extractor springs. The earlier design does not contain an insert. The latest design (with an insert) is the only authorized repair part. All old type extractor springs must be replaced.

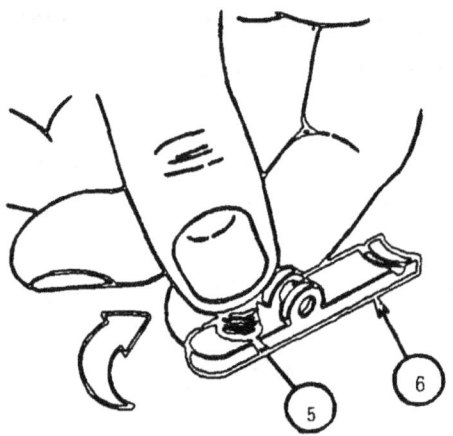

NOTE

Do not disassemble rubber insert from spring assembly.

If extractor spring was removed, insert large end of extractor spring assembly (5) into cartridge extractor (6) and seat by pushing and turning clockwise, until it is seated.

4

(a) Position cartridge extractor (6) and extractor spring assembly (5) on bolt body (1).

(b) Compress spring assembly (5) and cartridge extractor (6) to align holes.

(c) Install extractor pin (7) by hand.

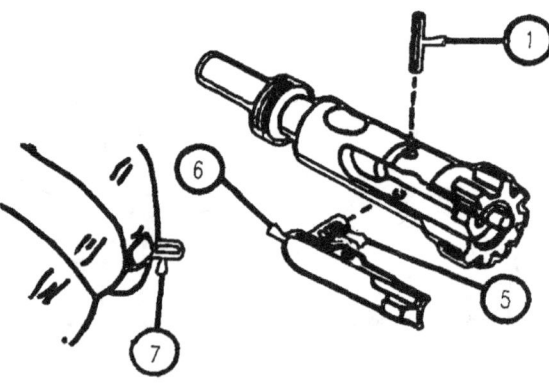

2-17. CHARGING HANDLE ASSEMBLY.

This task covers;

a. Disassembly
b. Cleaning
c. Inspection/Repair

d. Lubrication
e. Reassembly

INITIAL SETUP

Application Configuration
   M16/M16A1 Rifle

Tools
   Small Arms Repairman Tool Kit
   SC 5180-95-CL-A07 (19204)

Materials/Parts
   Cleaner, lubricant and preservative (CLP)
   (item 9, app D)

Lubricating oil, weapons (LAW) (item 20, app D)
Lubricating oil, weapons (LSA) (item 21, app D)

References
   TM 9-1005-249-10 (operator's manual)

Equipment Condition
   Charging handle removed

a. DISASSEMBLY

WARNING

To avoid injury to eyes, use care when removing and installing spring-loaded parts.

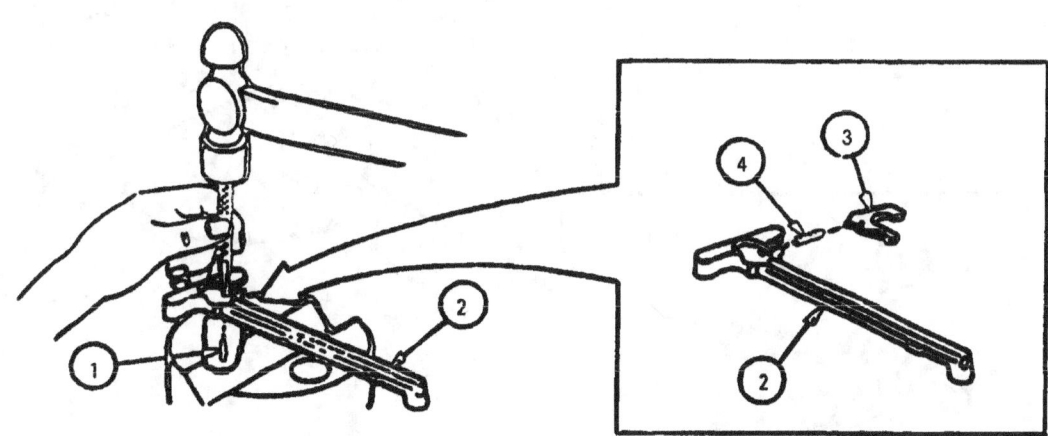

1. Remove spring pin (1) from charging handle (2) using a hammer and 1/16 inch punch.

2. As punch is withdrawn, catch charging handle latch (3) and helical spring (4) to prevent loss.

2-17. CHARGING HANDLE ASSEMBLY (CONT).

b. CLEANING

Clean all items (operator's manual).

c. INSPECTION/REPAIR

Inspect all items for breaks, cracks, or mutilation. Replace all authorized unserviceable items.

d. LUBRICATION

Lubricate all items, with a light coat of CLP, LSA, or LAW (p 2-22) (operator's manual).

e. REASSEMBLY

1. Position helical spring (1) and charging handle latch
   (2) in charging handle (3). Align holes and hold in
   position.

2. Install spring pin (4) using a hammer. Make pin
   flush.

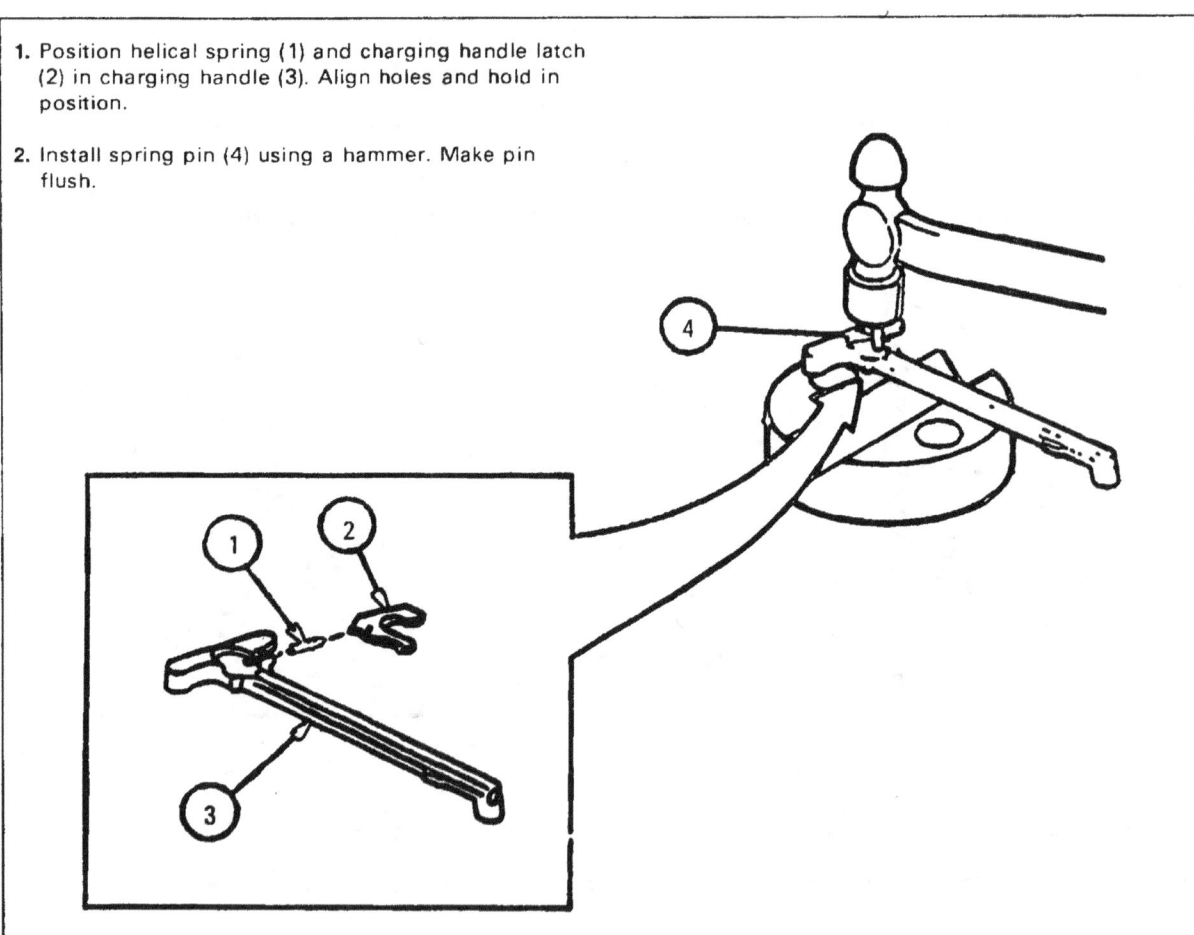

2-18. UPPER RECEIVER AND BARREL ASSEMBLY (HANDGUARD ASSEMBLY).

This task covers:

a. Disassembly
b. Inspection/Repair

c. Reassembly

INITIAL SETUP

Applicable Configuration
  M16/M16A1 Rifle

Equipment Condition
  Weapon assembled.

Reference
  TM 9-1005-249-10 (operator's manual)

a. DISASSEMBLY

1

CAUTION

Do not use a screwdriver or any other tool when removing the handguards. Doing so may damage the handguard and/or slip ring.

Do not remove heat shields from handguards. Doing so will damage the heatshield and the handguard will have to be replaced.

NOTE

Refer to operator's manual for "buddy system" procedure on removing handguards.

Push down on handguard slip ring (1) and lift the handguard (2) up and out.

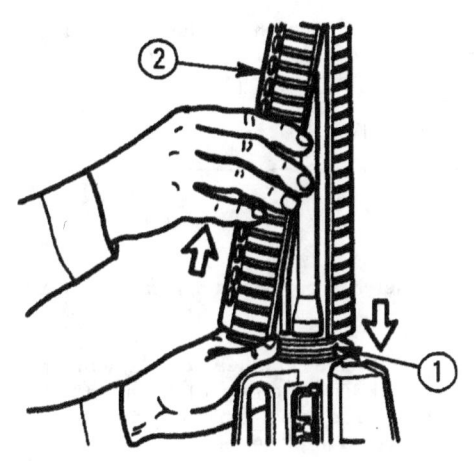

2

Push down on handguard slip ring (1) and lift the other handguard (2) up and out.

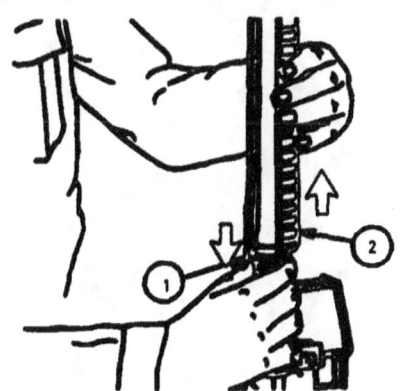

2-18. UPPER RECEIVER AND BARREL ASSEMBLY (HANDGUARD ASSEMBLY) (CONT).

b. INSPECTION/REPAIR

1. Inspect handguard assembly for breaks, separations, and cracks.

2. Breaks and separations of material which prevent proper retention or interfere with functioning of the weapon will be cause for handguard rejection and replacement.

3. Cracks up to one inch in length are acceptable provided they do not extend into the handguard retaining flange (1) (critical area).

4. Each handguard assembly may have up to two of the three front retaining tabs (2) missing. If all three front tabs are missing, the handguard assembly must be replaced.

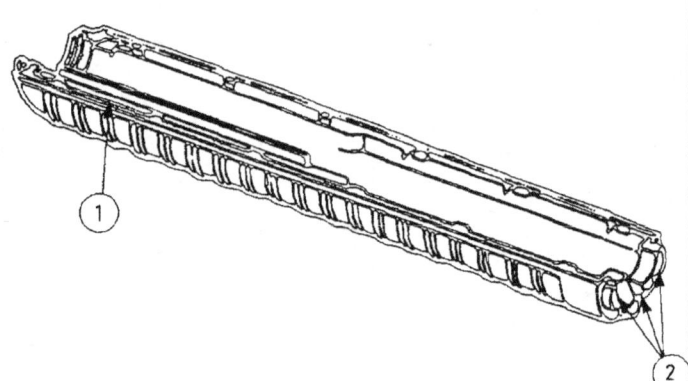

5. Replace severely cracked handguards. Handguards that have a heatshield loose enough to rattle when installed on the rifle must be replaced.

c. REASSEMBLY

1

<u>NOTE</u>

Refer to operator's manual for "buddy system" procedure on installing handguards.

Install top of handguard (1) in tube cap (2) while pushing down on handguard slip ring (3). Push bottom of handguard (1) in place and release handguard slip ring (3) to lock handguard in place.

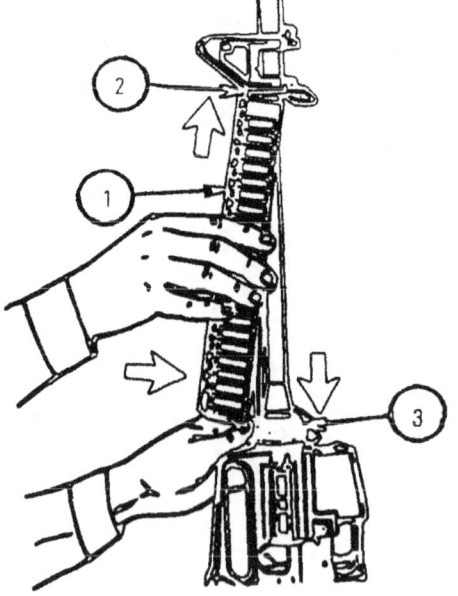

2

Install top of the other handguard (4) in handguard cap (2) while pushing down on handguard slip ring (3). Push bottom of handguard (4) in place and release handguard slip ring (3) to lock both handguards in place.

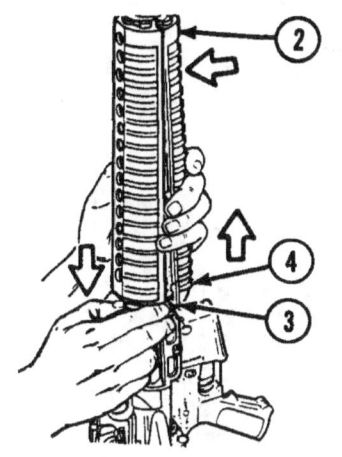

2-19. UPPER RECEIVER AND BARREL ASSEMBLY.

This task covers:

a. Disassembly
b. Cleaning
c. Inspection
d. Repair

e. Lubrication
f. Reassembly
g. Mechanical Zero Procedures (A.F. only)

INITIAL SETUP

Application Configuration
M16/M16A1 Rifle

Tools
Front sight post and low light level front sight post removal/installation tool (fig E-1, app E)
Small Arms Repairman Tool Kit SC 5180-95-CL-A07 (19204)

Materials/Parts
Cleaner, lubricant and preservative (CLP) (item 9, app D)
Cleaning compound, rifle bore (RBC) (item 11, app D)
Lubricating oil, weapons LAW (item 20, app D)
Lubricating oil, weapons LSA (item 21, app D)

Reference
TM 9-1005-249-10 (operator's manual)

Equipment condition
Handguards removed.
Upper receiver and barrel assembly removed from lower receiver.

General Safety Instructions
To avoid injury to your eyes, use care when removing and installing spring-loaded parts.
When using solid film lubricant or dichloromethane, be sure the area is well ventilated.

Barrel assembly may be equipped with a low light level sight. The low light level sight contains radioactive material. If so equipped, do not insert metal objects into the post slot or otherwise treat roughly to cause breakage of the radioactive element.

2-19. UPPER RECEIVER AND BARREL ASSEMBLY (CONT).

a. DISASSEMBLY

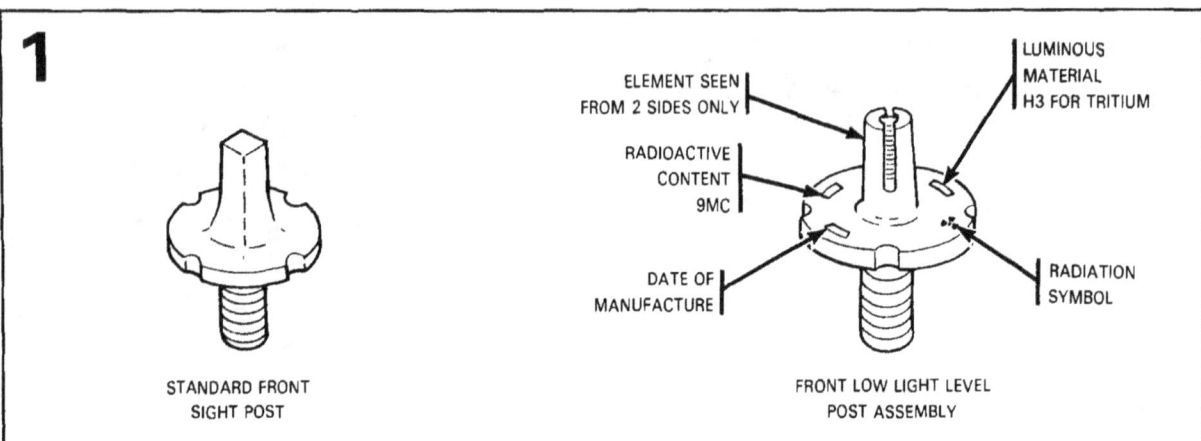

1

ELEMENT SEEN
FROM 2 SIDES ONLY

LUMINOUS
MATERIAL
H3 FOR TRITIUM

RADIOACTIVE
CONTENT
9MC

DATE OF
MANUFACTURE

RADIATION
SYMBOL

STANDARD FRONT
SIGHT POST

FRONT LOW LIGHT LEVEL
POST ASSEMBLY

Prior to disassembly, inspect upper receiver and barrel assembly to determine type of front sight installed, standard or low light level. If a radioactive low light level sight is installed and if it has been damaged, see warning page and Chapter 2, Section V.

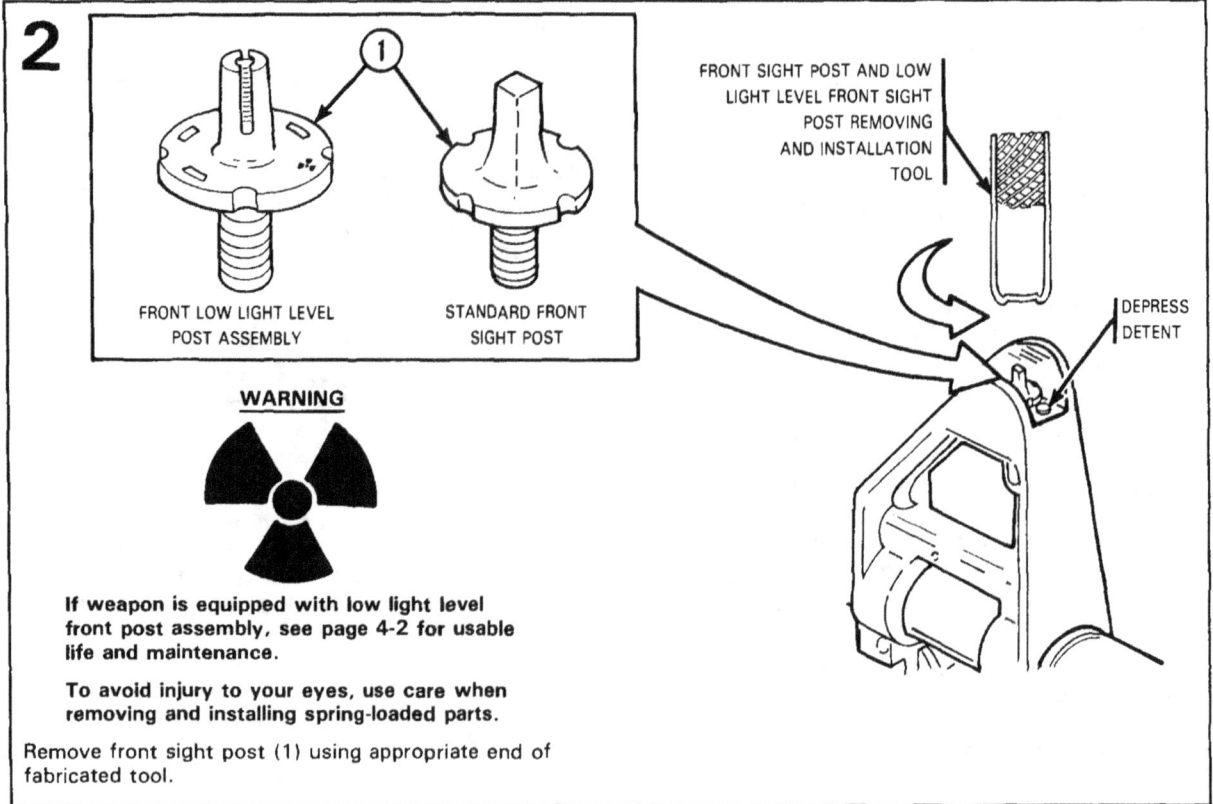

2

①

FRONT LOW LIGHT LEVEL
POST ASSEMBLY

STANDARD FRONT
SIGHT POST

FRONT SIGHT POST AND LOW
LIGHT LEVEL FRONT SIGHT
POST REMOVING
AND INSTALLATION
TOOL

DEPRESS
DETENT

WARNING

If weapon is equipped with low light level front post assembly, see page 4-2 for usable life and maintenance.

To avoid injury to your eyes, use care when removing and installing spring-loaded parts.

Remove front sight post (1) using appropriate end of fabricated tool.

3

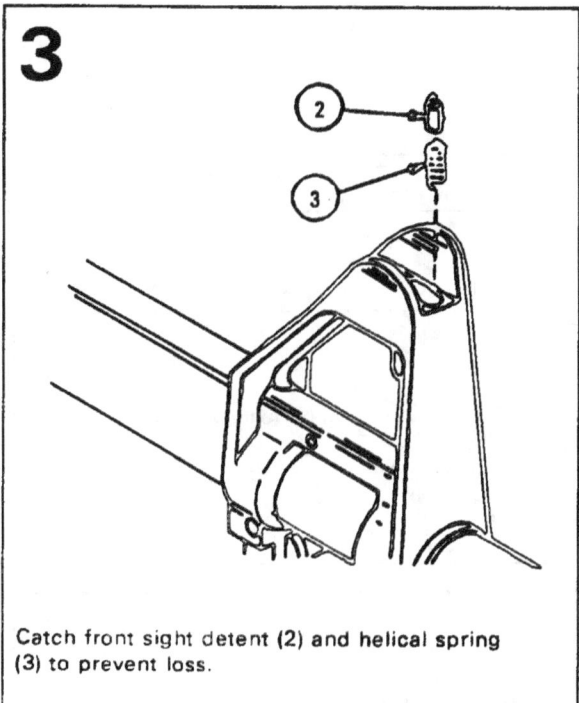

Catch front sight detent (2) and helical spring (3) to prevent loss.

4

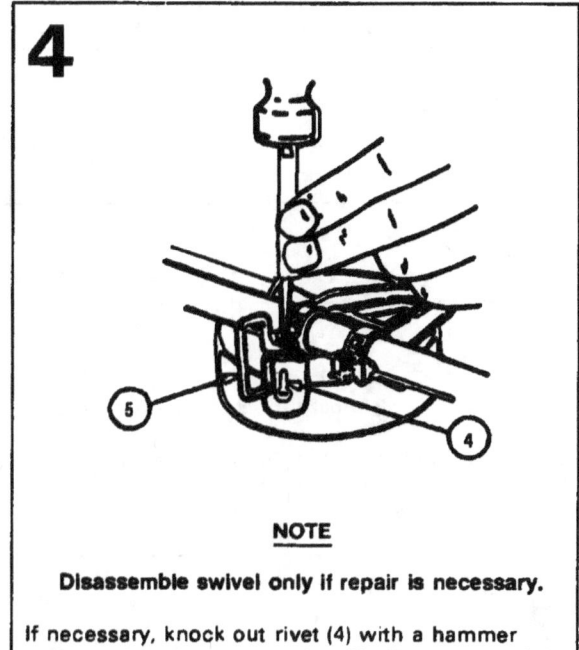

NOTE

Disassemble swivel only if repair is necessary.

If necessary, knock out rivet (4) with a hammer and punch and remove swivel (5). Discard rivet (4).

5

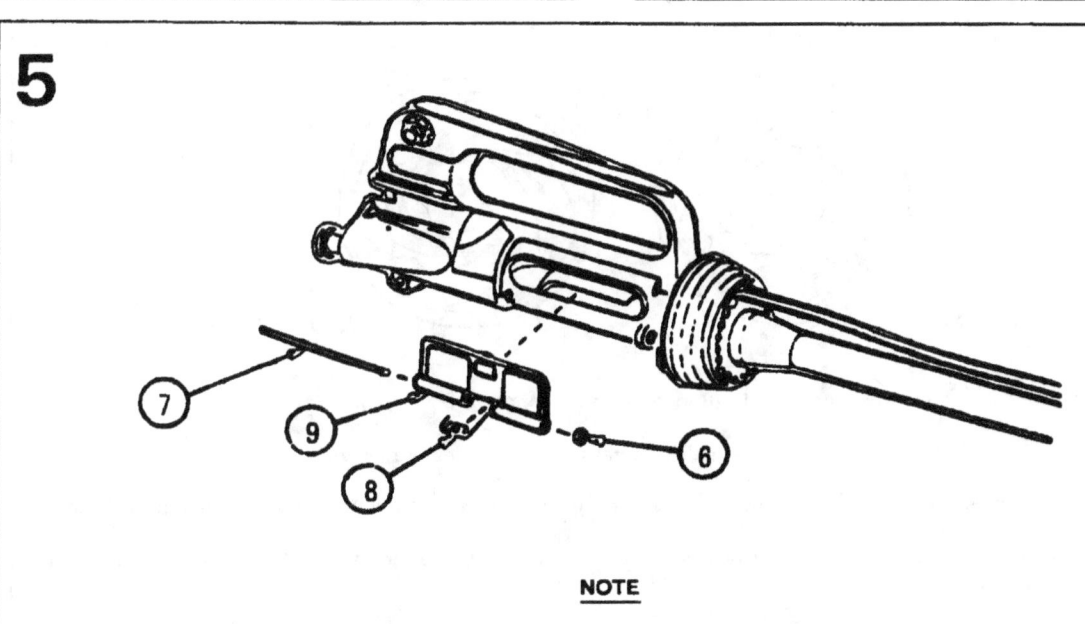

NOTE

Do not disassemble further unless repair is necessary. Ejection port cover pin (7) may bind against the forward assist housing on the M16A1 rifle and require some additional force to remove.

(a) Using two flat tip screwdrivers, remove retaining ring (6) and slide ejection port cover pin (7) out to the rear.

(b) Catch helical spring (8) and ejection port cover (9) to prevent loss.

2-19. UPPER RECEIVER AND BARREL ASSEMBLY (CONT).

b. CLEANING

Clean all items with CLP or RBC (operator's manual).

c. INSPECTION

1

(a) Inspect front sight base for chips, breaks and cracks. If damaged, evacuate to support maintenance.

(b) Inspect low light level sight (if installed) for broken sights and loss of illumination.

(c) Inspect all parts for serviceability.

2

(a) Inspect barrel for pits, dirt and rust in bore, burrs, broken or worn locking lugs, and surface cracks and defects.

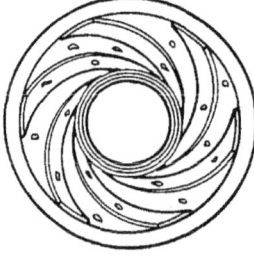 

ACCEPTABLE   NOT ACCEPTABLE

(1) Pits no wider than a land or groove and 3/8 inch or less in length are allowable in the bore.

(2) Lands that appear dark due to coating of gilding metal from projectiles are allowable.

(3) Stripping of lands and grooves shall not be cause for rejection unless so determined by barrel erosion gage.

(b) Inspect chamber for pitting. Fine pits, or fine pits in a densely pitted area, are allowable. Pits 1/8 inch in length are cause for rejection.

(c) Inspect bore for ringing. Definitely ringed bores or bores ringed sufficiently to bulge the outside surface of the barrel are causes for rejection.

(d) If the barrel is rejected in accordance with the above criteria, evacuate to support maintenance.

d. REPAIR

For touch up of M16/M16A1 Rifle, see page 2-22.

Replace all authorized unserviceable parts. If repair is not authorized at this level, evacuate to direct support maintenance.

e. LUBRICATION

Lubricate all items with a light coat of CLP, LSA, or LAW (p 2-22) or operator's manual.

f. REASSEMBLY

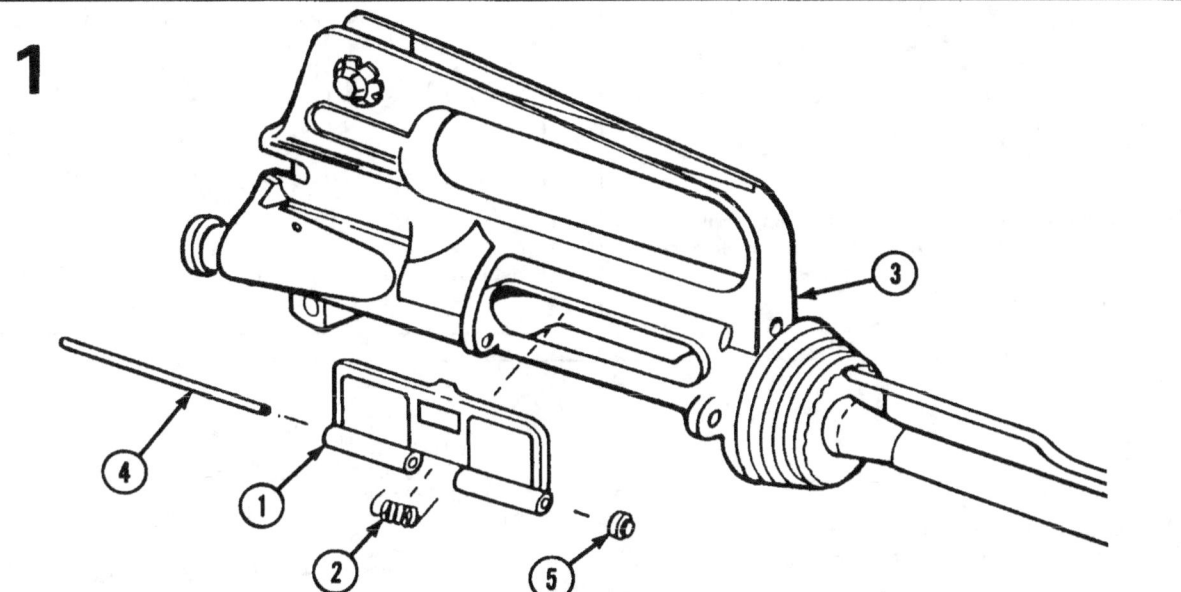

(a) If previously disassembled, position cover (1) and spring (2) on upper receiver (3) with short leg of spring to the rear pointing up toward top of receiver.

NOTE

Legs of spring must be positioned and pretensioned before the pin is installed.

(b) Hold spring (2) short leg in this position and turn long leg 1/2 turn clockwise (as viewed from front of receiver (3)) to increase spring tension.

(c) Position long leg of spring (2) to be on inside of cover (1) when it is closed. Hold spring and cover in this position and install pin (4) and retaining ring (5).

2-19. UPPER RECEIVER AND BARREL ASSEMBLY (CONT).

f. REASSEMBLY (CONT)

2

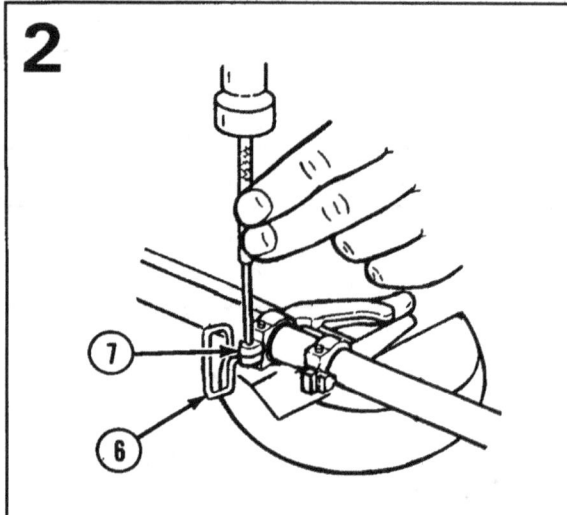

If previously disassembled, position sling swivel (6) and install new tubular rivet (7) using center punch and hammer to spread and flare the hollow head of the tubular rivet.

3

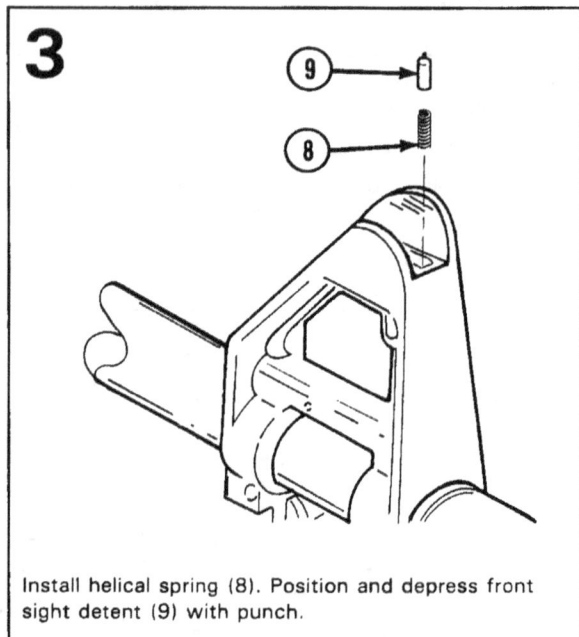

Install helical spring (8). Position and depress front sight detent (9) with punch.

4

Install front sight post (10) using appropriate end of fabricated tool.

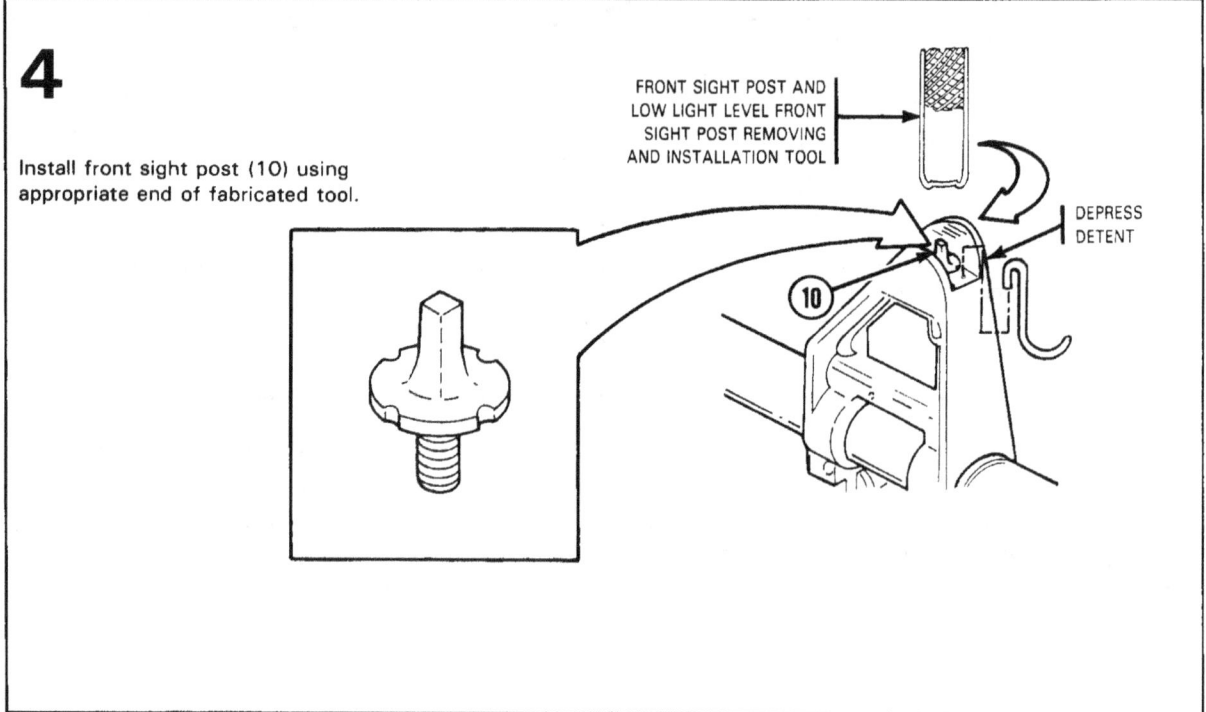

FRONT SIGHT POST AND LOW LIGHT LEVEL FRONT SIGHT POST REMOVING AND INSTALLATION TOOL

DEPRESS DETENT

g. MECHANICAL ZERO PROCEDURES

1

Mark a piece of plastic card stock or rigid paper with lines from 1 to 5mm in 1 mm increments. Set the card on the front sight frame and check the height of the top of the front sight post.

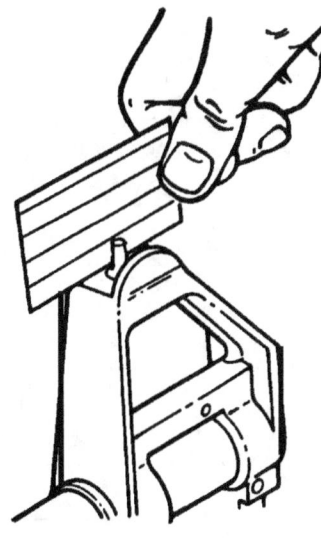

2

Adjust the front sight so the top of the front sight post is 5mm above the machined surfaces of the front sight frame.

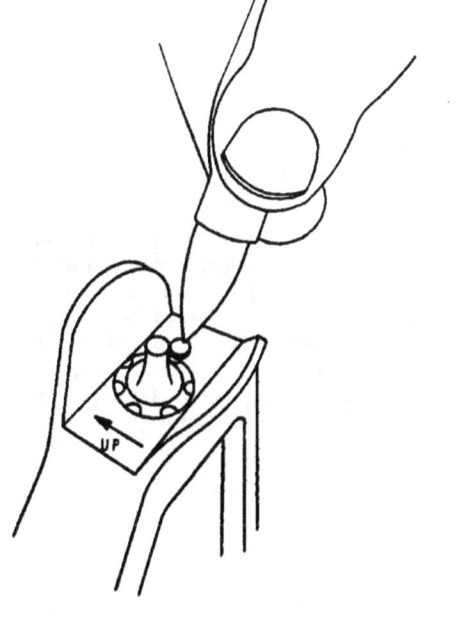

2-19. UPPER RECEIVER AND BARREL ASSEMBLY (CONT).

g. MECHANICAL ZERO PROCEDURES (CONT)

3

Visually check the front sight post top height by using the marked plastic or paper card. Card must set level on the machined surfaces of the front sight frame to obtain an accurate reading.

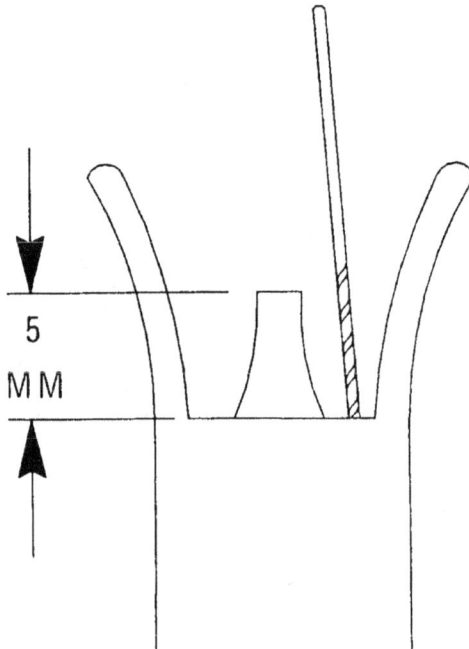

NOTE: Procedure will give an approximate battle sight zero to most M16 rifles. Once the above steps are completed, the rifle will be mechanically zeroed for 250 meters using the unmarked or short-range aperture and at 375 meters using the "L" or long-range aperture. The above steps can also be used before firing a new or newly assigned rifle. Use the procedure to check rifles stored in preferred packaging during routine inspections. This will help ensure people armed with the rifles will stand a better chance of hitting an enemy if the rifles must be used before a live fire zero can be made. Whenever possible, zeroing of the rifle should be accomplished using ball ammunition on a 25 meter zeroing target using the "L" aperture.

2-20. LOWER RECEIVER AND EXTENSION ASSEMBLY.

This tasks covers:

a. Disassembly
b. Cleaning
c. Inspection

d. Repair
e. Lubrication
f. Reassembly

INITIAL SETUP

Applicable Configuration
M16/M16A1 Rifle

Tools
Small Arms Repairman Tool Kit
  SC 5180-95-CL-A07 (19204)
Pivot Pin Removing Tool (fig E-2, app E)
Pivot Pin Installation Tool (fig E-5, app E)

Materials/parts
Cleaner, lubricant and preservative (CLP) (item 9,
  app D)
Lubricant, solid film (SLF) (item 19, app D)
Lubricating oil, weapons (LAW) (item 20, app D)
Lubricating oil, weapons (LSA) (item 21, app D)
Screw, Self-Locking (Butt-Cap Screw) (item 28,
  pg C-10)

Reference
TM 9-1005-249-10 (operator's manual)

Equipment Condition
Lower receiver and extension assembly removed.

General Safety Instructions
To avoid injury to your eyes, use care when removing and installing spring-loaded parts.

a. DISASSEMBLY

1

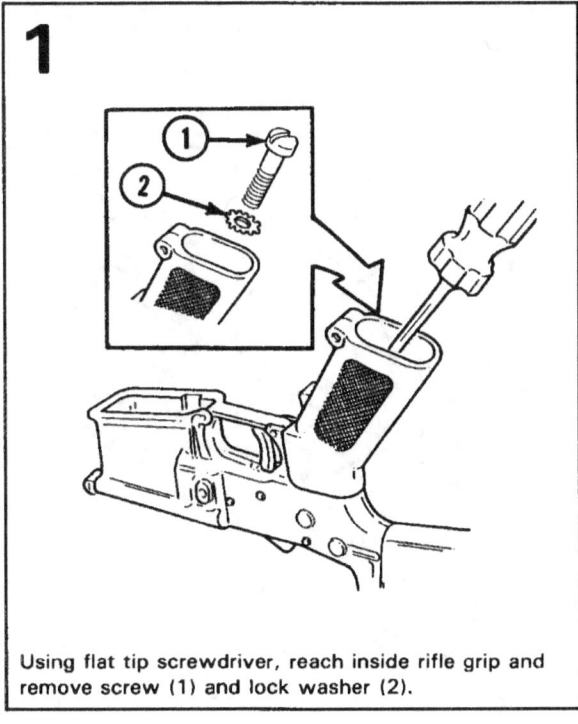

Using flat tip screwdriver, reach inside rifle grip and remove screw (1) and lock washer (2).

2

WARNING
To avoid injury to your eyes, use care when removing and installing spring-loaded parts.

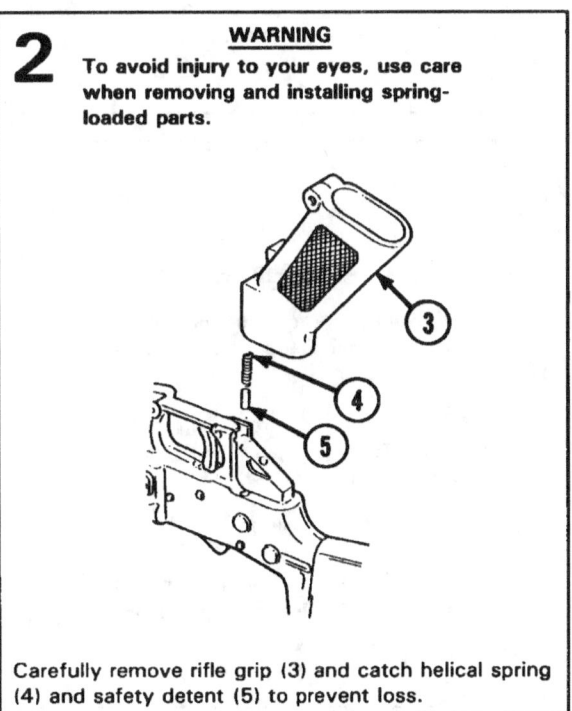

Carefully remove rifle grip (3) and catch helical spring (4) and safety detent (5) to prevent loss.

2-20. LOWER RECEIVER AND EXTENSION ASSEMBLY (CONT).

a. DISASSEMBLY (CONT)

3

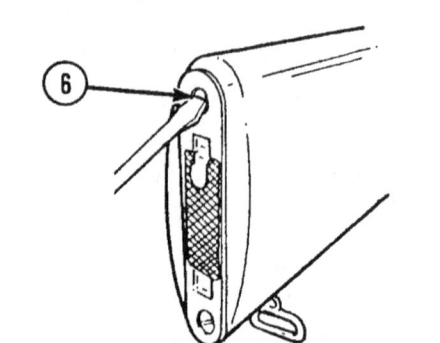

NOTE

The butt cap screw is a self-locking screw. Due to the critical nature of the parts concerned, if the butt cap screw is removed, it must be discarded and replaced with a new one.

Remove butt cap screw (6).

4

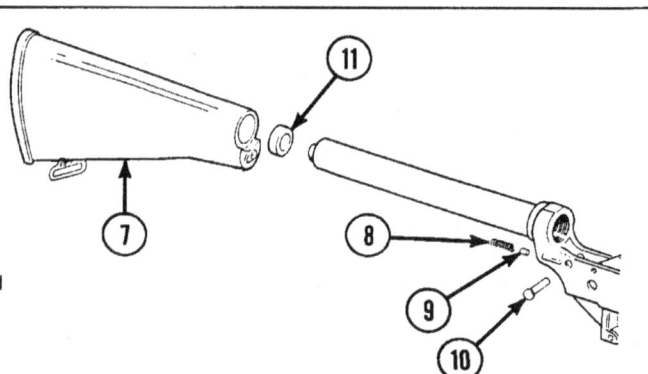

WARNING

To avoid injury to your eyes, use care when removing and installing spring-loaded parts.

Remove buttstock assembly (7) carefully and catch helical spring (8), detent (9), takedown pin (10), and stepped spacer (11) to prevent loss.

5

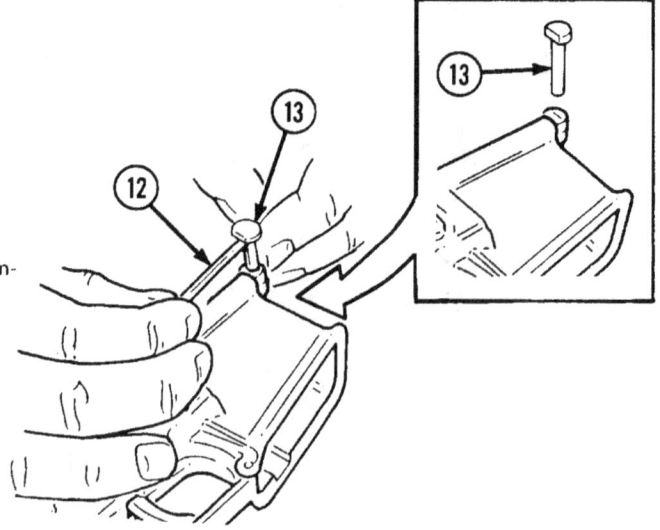

WARNING

To avoid injury to your eyes, use care when removing and installing spring-loaded parts.

Insert fabricated pivot pin removing tool (12) to compress detent. Turn pivot pin (13) a quarter-turn. Remove tool and pin.

NOTE

Catch detent and spring as pivot pin is removed (see step 6 on next page).

6

Be sure to hold cupped hand in front of detent (14) and helical spring (15) to prevent loss of detent and spring.

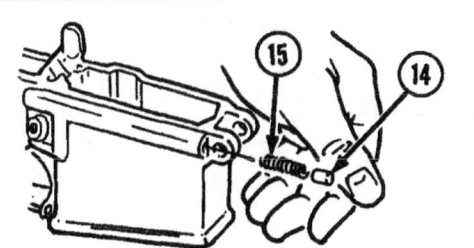

7

WARNING

To avoid injury to your eyes, use care when removing and installing spring-loaded parts.

NOTE

Make sure the hammer is cocked and the selector level is not set on AUTO before removing the buffer assembly.

Press buffer assembly (16) in. Using screwdriver, depress buffer retainer (17) and release buffer assembly (16) and action spring (18). Remove buffer assembly (16) and action spring (18) from receiver while depressing retainer (17).

NOTE

Early type buffer assembly (19) must be replaced.

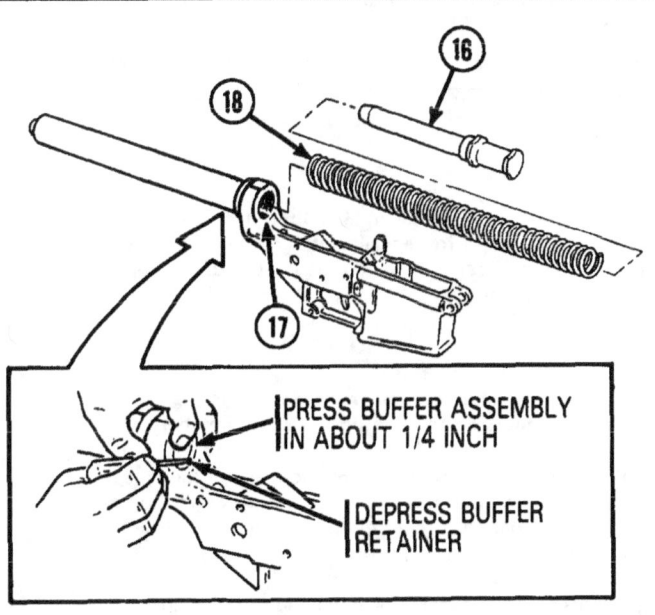

PRESS BUFFER ASSEMBLY IN ABOUT 1/4 INCH

DEPRESS BUFFER RETAINER

b. CLEANING   Clean all items (operator's manual).

c. INSPECTION

1

Inspect buffer assembly (1, 2, or 3) for cracks or damage.

(a)   Some old buffers (1) have a hole with pin installed which protrudes equally on each side approximately 1/32 inch.

(b)   Some buffers (2) have a hole in the housing but no pin.

(c)   New buffers (3) do not have a hole in buffer body or a pin.

All configurations (1, 2, or 3) may be utilized. However, if cracked or damaged, replace.

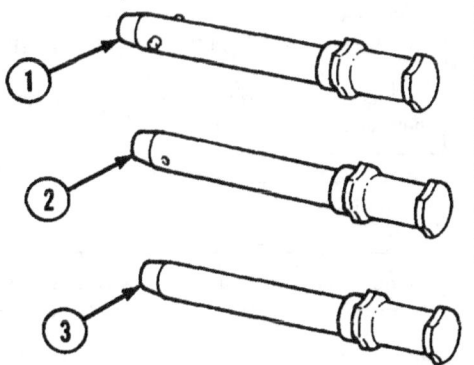

2-20. LOWER RECEIVER AND EXTENSION ASSEMBLY (CONT).

c. INSPECTION (CONT)

2

Check free length of action spring (4). The free length must be between 11 3/4 inches minimum and 13 1/2 inches maximum. Do not attempt to adjust spring length.

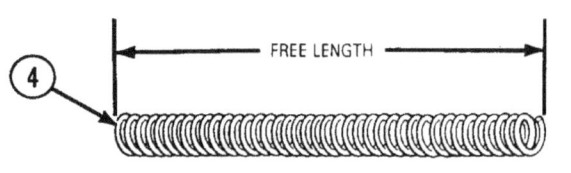

3

(a) Inspect lower receiver (5) (without further disassembly) for legibility of serial number. If the serial number is hard to read, notify direct support maintenance.

NOTE

Only direct support maintenance is authorized to restamp the serial number.

(b) Check lower receiver extension (6) for looseness and corrosion. If loose, evacuate to direct support maintenance. If corroded, clean area and touch up with solid film lubricant.

(c) Inspect for missing or damaged parts. Inspect finish of lower receiver for shiny spots. Touch up with solid film lubricant as required.

(d) Visually inspect all other parts for unserviceable or missing parts. Replace defective or missing parts.

d. REPAIR

For touch up of M16/M16A1 Rifle, use SFL (see p 2-22).

Replace all authorized unserviceable parts. If repair is not authorized at this level, evacuate to direct support maintenance.

e. LUBRICATION

Lubricate all metal components with a light coat of CLP, LSA, or LAW (p 2-22) (operator's manual).

f. REASSEMBLY

1

WARNING

To avoid injury to your eyes, use care when removing and installing spring-loaded parts.

NOTE

Make sure the hammer is cocked and the selector level is not on AUTO before installing the buffer assembly.

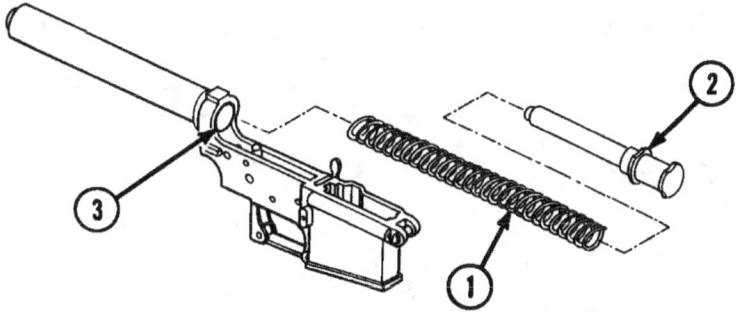

Press action spring (1) and buffer assembly (2) in until retainer (3) snaps up and holds them in place.

2

Install pivot pin installation tool (4). Insert helical spring (5) and detent (6). Compress detent in recess with punch and rotate tool.

2-20. LOWER RECEIVER AND EXTENSION ASSEMBLY (CONT)

f. REASSEMBLY (CONT)

3

NOTE

Rounded end of detent must be in the groove
of the pivot pin (7) when assembly is complete.

Position pivot pin (7) to keep detent depressed while
removing fabricated pivot pin removing tool (6). Slide pin
(7) into hole. Rotate pin and receive detent.

4

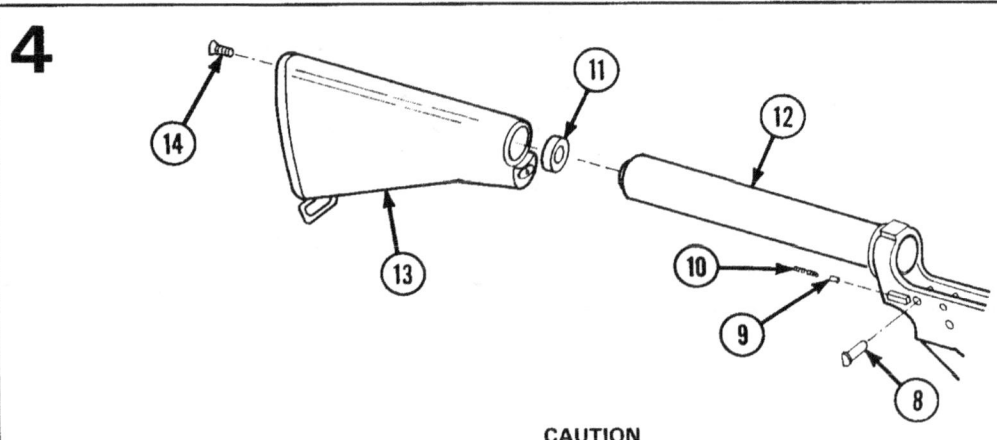

CAUTION

Do not kink the detent spring (10) during assembly.

NOTE

Pointed end of detent (9) must be in the groove of takedown pin (8) when assembly is
complete.

(a) Install takedown pin (8) with groove toward the rear. Install detent (9) and spring (10) from the rear.

NOTE

Stepped spacer (11) and butt-cap screw (14) PN 9349128 are required when using 10.103
inch long buttstock PN 9349121. When using old 9.478 in. long buttstock PN 8448651,
stepped spacer (11) is not required but butt cap screw PN 8448627, NSN
1005-00-992-6657, is required.

(b) Install spacer (11) on receiver extension (12) and carefully slide buttstock assembly (13) on to compressed
helical spring (10).

NOTE

Installing the buttstock assembly is easier if the lower receiver is held in a vertical position with the end of the lower extension pointed up.

5

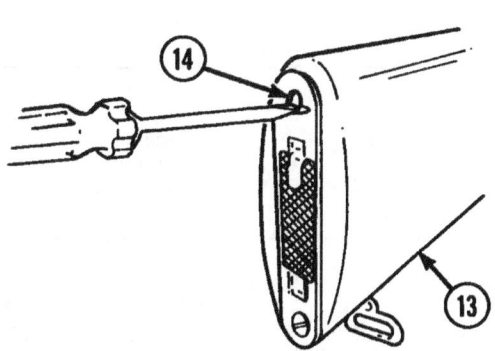

<u>NOTE</u>

The butt cap screw (14) is a self-locking screw, and if removed, it must be discarded and replaced with a new one.

Secure buttstock assembly (13) in place with a new butt cap screw (14) as follows:

Tighten the screw until the tapered screw head has seated under normal pressure and resistance is felt.

Tighten screw an additional quarter turn. If butt cap screw continues to loosen under use, it should be replaced with a new one.

6

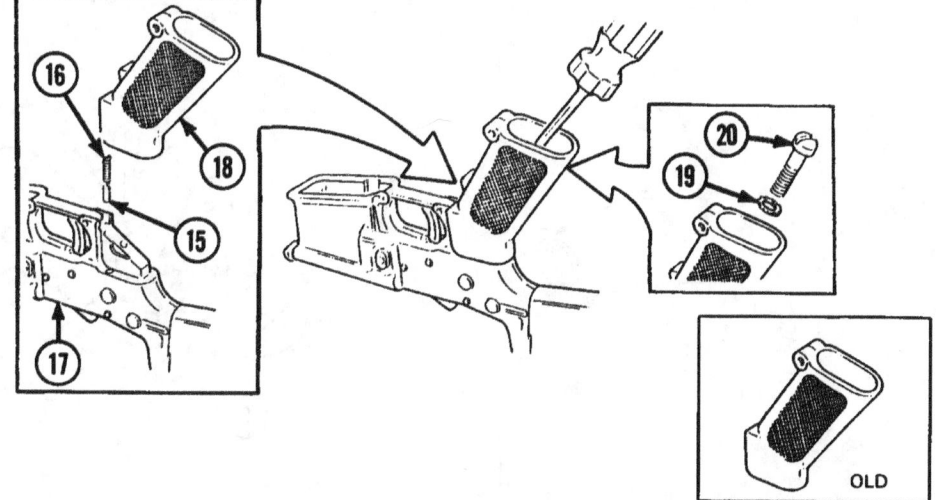

OLD

<u>WARNING</u>

When utilizing the enhanced rifle grip (it has a bump between the second and third finger for a better grip) PN 9349127, rifle grip screw, PN AN501D416-18 (1-1/8 in.) or AN501D416-16 (1 in.) are the authorized screws to be used with the enhanced grip. Any screw longer than 1-1/8 in. used with 9349127, could cause a hazardous situation. Also, ensure the washer is in place.

(a) Install detent (15), pointed end first, and spring (16) into bottom of lower receiver (17).

<u>NOTE</u>

A portion of the spring will fit in a hole in the rifle grip.

(b) Carefully install rifle grip (18) to compress spring (16). Secure grip (18) in place with lockwasher (19) and screw (20).

2-21. BUTTSTOCK ASSEMBLY.

This task covers:

a. Disassembly	**d.** Repair
b. Cleaning	**e.** Lubrication
c. Inspection	**f.** Reassembly

INITIAL SETUP

Application Configuration
  M16/M16A1 Rifle

Tools
  Small Arms Repairman Tool Kit
  SC 5180-95-CL-A07 (19204)

Materials/Parts
  Cleaner, lubricant and preservative (CLP)
    (item 9, app D)
  Lubricating oil, weapons (LAW) (item 20, app D)
  Lubricating oil, weapons (LSA) (item 21, app D)

Equipment Condition
  Lower receiver and extension assembly removed
    buttstock assembly removed.

a. DISASSEMBLY

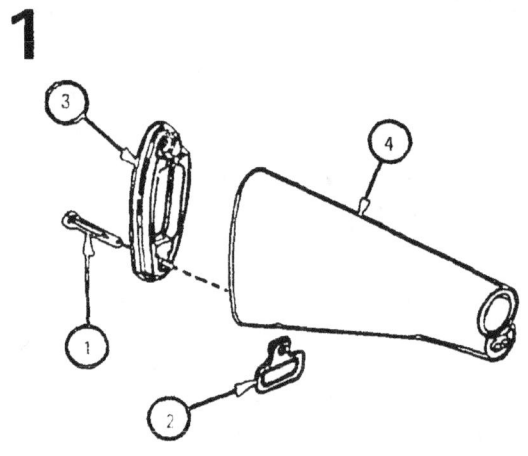

1

Using screwdriver, remove self-locking screw (1), rear sling swivel (2) and butt plate group (3) from buttstock (4).

NOTE

The buttstock assembly may utilize a buttstock (4) which is 10.103 inches long (PN 9349126) or 9.478 inches long (PN 8448654). See note on page 2-46 in reassembly for buttstock assembly part usage.

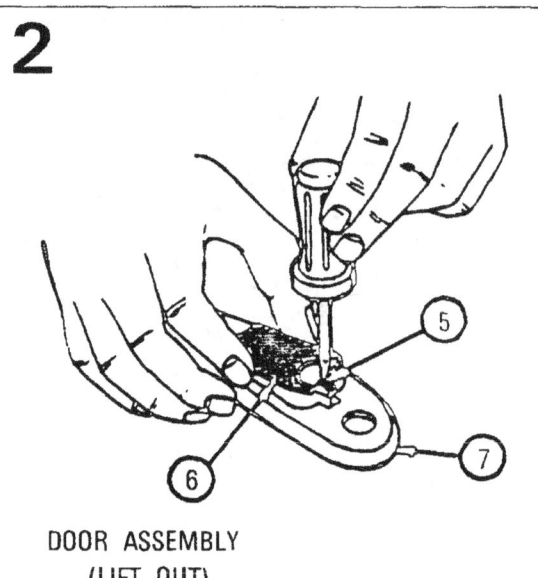

2

DOOR ASSEMBLY
(LIFT OUT)

Push down on plunger (5) with screwdriver and lift door assembly (6) out of butt plate (7).

3

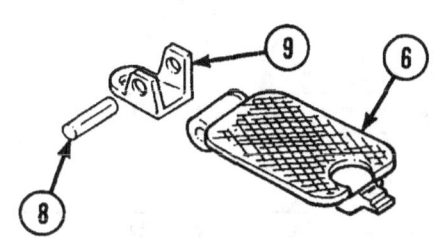

Remove straight pin (8) and separate hinge (9) and door assembly (6).

| **b. CLEANING** | Clean all items. |

c. INSPECTION

Inspect buttstock assembly for dents, cracks, and chips. Check for breaks and separation of material which could prevent proper functioning of weapon.

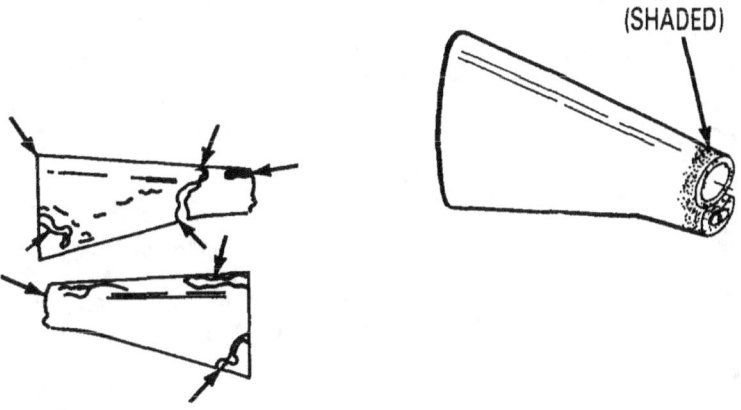

CRITICAL AREA (SHADED)

Under the following conditions, hairline cracks originating from buttplate end of buttstock are acceptable. No chipped away material is allowed.

(1) One hairline crack, not to exceed one inch in length, per side of buttstock.

(2) Two additional hairline cracks up to .22 inch in length, per side of buttstock.

(3) A total of three cracks per side of buttstock, originating from buttplate end, are allowable.

Buttstocks with unauthorized markings stamped into their surfaces will be replaced. Unauthorized markings, scratched, etched, carved, etc, are acceptable if they do not extend into the fiber of the buttstock which may weaken it. These marks may lie at any location on the buttstock.

Cracks in the critical area at the front end of the buttstock are not acceptable and these buttstocks must be replaced.

Visually inspect all other parts for unserviceable or missing parts. Replace defective or missing parts.

2-21. BUTTSTOCK ASSEMBLY (CONT).

d. REPAIR

Replace all authorized unserviceable items. Unserviceable items are those items which are damaged.

e. LUBRICATION

Lubricate all metal components with CLP, LSA, or LAW (p 2-22).

f. REASSEMBLY

1

Position hinge (1) on door assembly (2) and install straight, pin (3).

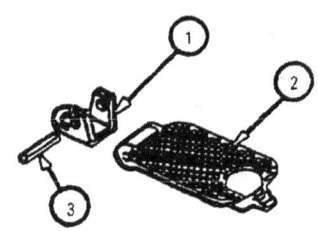

2

Install door assembly (2) into butt plate (4) and press plunger (5) to lock.

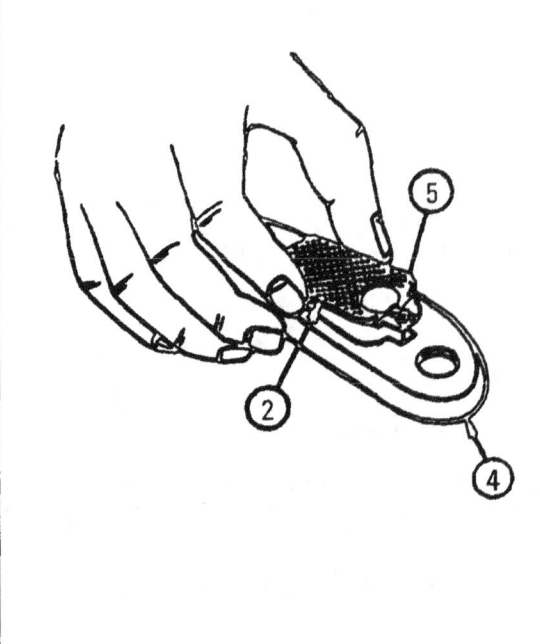

3

Position butt plate group (6) and rear sling swivel (7) to the buttstock (8) and secure with self-locking screw (9).

NOTE

See page 2-50, reassembly, for reassembly of buttstock assembly to lower receiver. 10.103 inches long (PN 9349126) 9.478 inches long (PN 8448654)

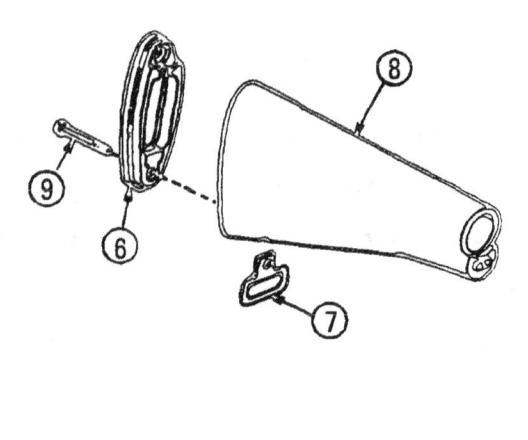

2-22. MAJOR COMPONENTS OF M16/M16A1 RIFLE.

This task covers:

a. Reassembly
b. Inspection

c. Stowage

INITIAL SETUP

Applicable Configuration
M16/M16A1 Rifle

Reference
TM 9-1005-249-10 (operator's manual)

Equipment Condition
Weapon disassembled into major components

General Safety Instructions
To avoid injury to eyes, use care when removing and installing spring-loaded parts.
Do not interchange bolt assemblies from one weapon to another. Doing so may result in injury to, or death of, personnel.
Do not keep live ammunition near the work area.

a. REASSEMBLY

NOTE

Only direct support maintenance is authorized to restamp the serial number.

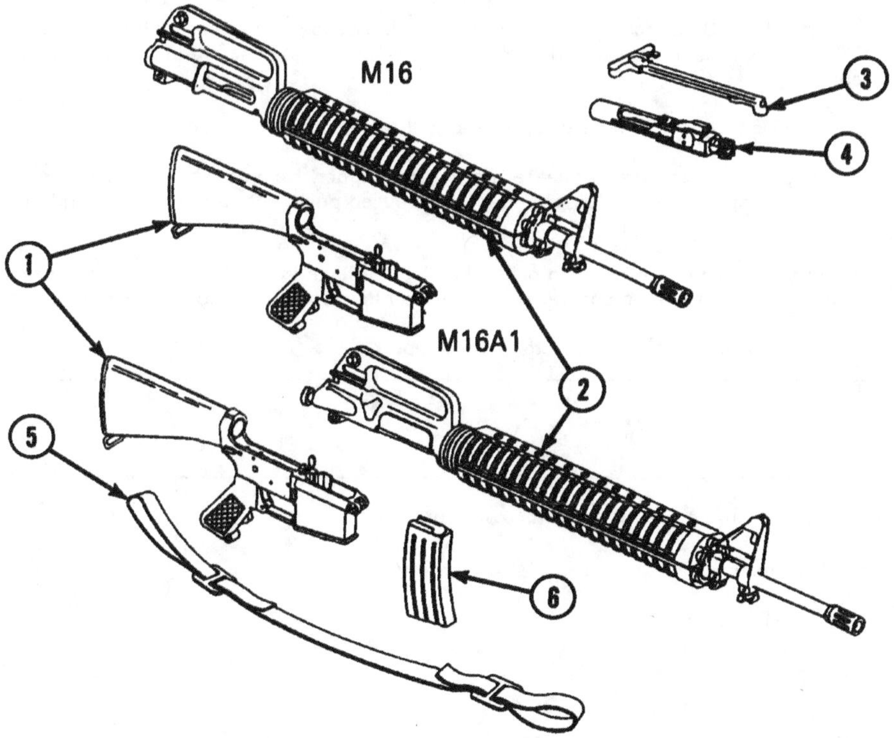

Refer to operator's manual and install lower receiver and extension assembly (1), upper receiver and barrel assembly (2), charging handle assembly (3), bolt carrier assembly (4), small arms sling (5), and cartridge magazine (6).

2-22. MAJOR COMPONENTS OF M16/M16A1 RIFLE (CONT).

b. INSPECTION

Perform the following function tests on assembled weapon:

1. Remove magazine if installed. Pull charging handle assembly to rear. Check that chamber is clear. Let bolt and bolt carrier close. Leave hammer in cocked position. Do not pull trigger.

WARNING

If weapon fails any of the following selector lever tests, continued use of the weapon could result in injury to, or death of, personnel.

2. Place selector lever in SAFE position and pull trigger. Hammer should not fall.

3. Place selector lever in SEMI position. Pull trigger. Hammer should fall.

NOTE

For the purpose of the following test ''SLOW'' is defined as 1/4 to 1/2 the normal rate of the trigger release:

4. Hold trigger to the rear, charge weapon, and release the trigger with a slow, smooth motion, without hesitations or stops, until the trigger is fully forward (an audible click should be heard). Hammer should not fall.

5. Repeat the above selector lever SEMI position test five times. The weapon must not malfunction during any of these five tests. If the weapon malfunctions during any of these five tests, evacuate it to direct support maintenance for repair.

6. Place selector lever in AUTO position. Charge weapon and pull trigger. Hammer should fall.

7. Hold trigger to the rear, charge weapon, and release trigger. Pull trigger. Hammer should not fall. Automatic sear should have released hammer while holding trigger in the pulled position before releasing and pulling the trigger.

8. With hammer in the forward position, attempt to place the selector lever in SAFE position. If the selector lever can be placed on SAFE by finger/thumb pressure, evacuate the rifle to direct support maintenance for repair.

9. If weapon fails any of the above tests, evacuate to direct support.

c. STOWAGE

Prior to stowing the rifle in arms room, perform the following procedures:

1. Clear. Refer to operator's manual.

2. Place selector lever in SEMI position.

3. Pull trigger. Hammer should fall.

4. Close ejection port (dust) cover.

5. Place rifle in rack.

CHAPTER 3

DIRECT SUPPORT MAINTENANCE INSTRUCTIONS

CHAPTER OVERVIEW

Chapter 3 contains information and instructions to help keep the weapon in good repair. This chapter contains:

a. Repair Parts, Special Tools, TMDE, and Support Equipment
b. Service Upon Receipt
c. Troubleshooting
d. Decontamination of Rifles and Shop Area
e. Maintenance Procedures for the M16 and M16A1 Rifle
f. Preembarkation Inspection of Materiel in Units Alerted for Overseas Movement

Section I. REPAIR PARTS, SPECIAL TOOLS, TMDE, AND SUPPORT EQUIPMENT

3-1. COMMON TOOLS AND EQUIPMENT. For authorized common tools and equipment refer to the Modified Table of Organization and Equipment (MTOE) applicable to your unit. Air Force and Coast Guard users must maintain the following common tools:

Flat tip screwdriver	Combination wrench	5/64-inch drive pin punch
Socket wrench handle and socket head screw socket wrench	(2) eight-inch adjustable wrenches	Retaining ring pliers
	Flat file	1/8-inch drive pin punch
Vise jaw caps	Ballpeen hammer	Torque wrench
Machinist's vise	Trigger Pull Test Fixture	1/16-inch drive pin punch
Solid center punch	Rod & Weights	3/32-inch drive pin punch
Hammer		

3-2. SPECIAL TOOLS, TMDE, AND SUPPORT EQUIPMENT. Special tools required for direct support are listed in appendix C and fabricated tools are listed and illustrated in appendix E.

3-3. REPAIR PARTS. Repair parts are listed and illustrated in appendix C.

NOTE

Bolt assemblies and/or barrel assemblies may be interchanged at the Direct Support Maintenance level from one rifle to another, under the provisions of the note at the bottom of page 3-39. If these parts are interchanged, the weapon must be checked/inspected as depicted in paragraph 3-10, 3-11, and 3-13. While performing these checks/inspections pay special attention to the headspace requirements depicted on pages 3-38 and 3-39.

Section II. SERVICE UPON RECEIPT

3-4. GENERAL.

a. Inspect the weapon for damage incurred during shipment. If the equipment has been damaged, report the damage on SF Form 364, Report of Discrepancy (ROD).

b. Check the weapon against the packing slip to see if the shipment is complete. Report all discrepancies in accordance with the instructions in DA PAM 738-750.

c. Check to see whether the equipment has been modified.

d. Check to see if all MWOs have been applied.

3-5. SERVICE UPON RECEIPT OF MATERIEL. Refer to the following table.

SERVICE UPON RECEIPT - M16/M16A1 RIFLE

LOCATION	ITEM	ACTION	REMARKS
M16, M16A1 Rifle	Charging handle	Clear the weapon.	Refer to TM 9-1005-249-10 (Operator's Manual)

WARNING

To avoid injury to eye, use care when removing and installing spring-loaded parts.

	Bolt carrier assembly and bolt assembly	Remove.	Refer to Operator's Manual
	All components	Visually inspect for proper assembly, damage, or for missing parts.	Refer to Operator's Manual
		Clean and lubricate (see p 2-22).	
	Bolt carrier assembly and bolt assembly	Reassemble.	Refer to Operator's Manual
		Hand function to assure proper operation.	
	Cartridge magazine	Insert empty magazine and pull the bolt to the rear. Check magazine for positive retention, and check functioning of bolt catch by assuring that bolt locks to the rear with empty magazine inserted.	Refer to Operator's Manual

Section III. TROUBLESHOOTING

3-6. GENERAL.

a. This section contains troubleshooting information for locating and correcting most of the operating troubles which may develop in the 5.56mm Rifle M16 and M16A1. Each malfunction for the individual component, unit, or system is followed by a list of tests or inspections which will help you to determine the corrective actions to take. You should perform the tests/inspections and corrective actions in the order listed.

b. This manual cannot list all malfunctions that may occur, nor all tests or inspections and corrective actions. If a malfunction is not listed or is not corrected by listed corrective actions, see individual repair sections for maintenance instructions on each major assembly.

3-7. TROUBLESHOOTING PROCEDURES. Refer to troubleshooting table for malfunctions, tests, and corrective actions. The symptom index is provided for a quick reference of symptoms covered in the table.

SYMPTOM INDEX

**Troubleshooting
Procedures
Page**

Failure of magazine to lock in weapon 3-4

Failure to feed 3-4

Failure to chamber 3-4

Failure to lock 3-4

Failure to fire 3-5

Failure to unlock 3-5

Failure to extract 3-6

Failure to eject 3-6

Failure to cock 3-6

Short recoil 3-7

Weapon cannot be zeroed 3-8

Failure to cycle with selector lever set on AUTO 3-8

**Fires when trigger is released with selector lever on SEMI, or fires two or more rounds in
SEMI selector position (Doubling)** 3-9

Fires with selector lever on SAFE 3-9

Bolt fails to lock to rear after firing last round 3-9

TROUBLESHOOTING

MALFUNCTION
      TEST OR INSPECTION
            CORRECTIVE ACTION

---

1. FAILURE OF MAGAZINE TO LOCK IN WEAPON.

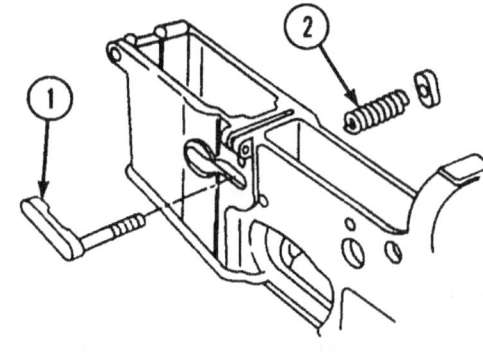

      Step 1. Dirty or corroded magazine catch (1).

          Disassemble and clean.

      Step 2. Defective magazine catch spring (2).

          Replace spring (2).

      Step 3. Worn or broken magazine catch (1).

          Replace magazine catch (1).

2. FAILURE TO FEED.

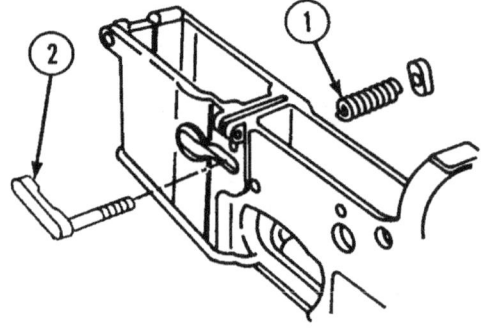

      Step 1. Magazine catch spring (1) weak or broken.

          Replace magazine catch spring (1).

      Step 2. Magazine catch (2) broken or defective.

          Replace magazine catch (2).

      Step 3. Short recoil.

          Refer to page 3-7.

3. FAILURE TO CHAMBER.

      Obstruction in bore/chamber.

          Remove obstruction. If unable to remove obstruction, rebarrel (P. 3-28).

4. FAILURE TO LOCK.

      Step 1. Damaged bolt carrier key (1).

          Repair or replace bolt carrier key (1) and check alignment.

      Step 2. Loose screws (2) on bolt carrier key (1).

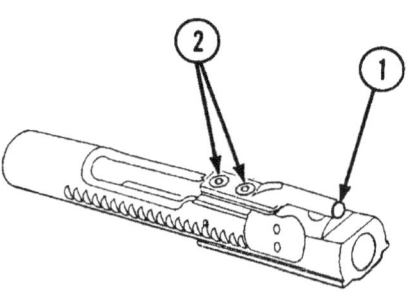

          Disassemble and repair (p 3-19).
          Reassemble using new screws.

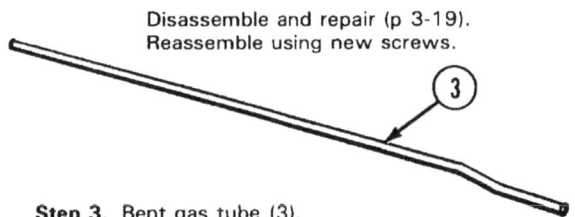

      Step 3. Bent gas tube (3).

          Adjust by bending tube in area of handguards.
          Replace gas tube (3) and check alignment.

TROUBLSHOOTING (CONT)

MALFUNCTION
    TEST OR INSPECTION
        CORRECTIVE ACTION

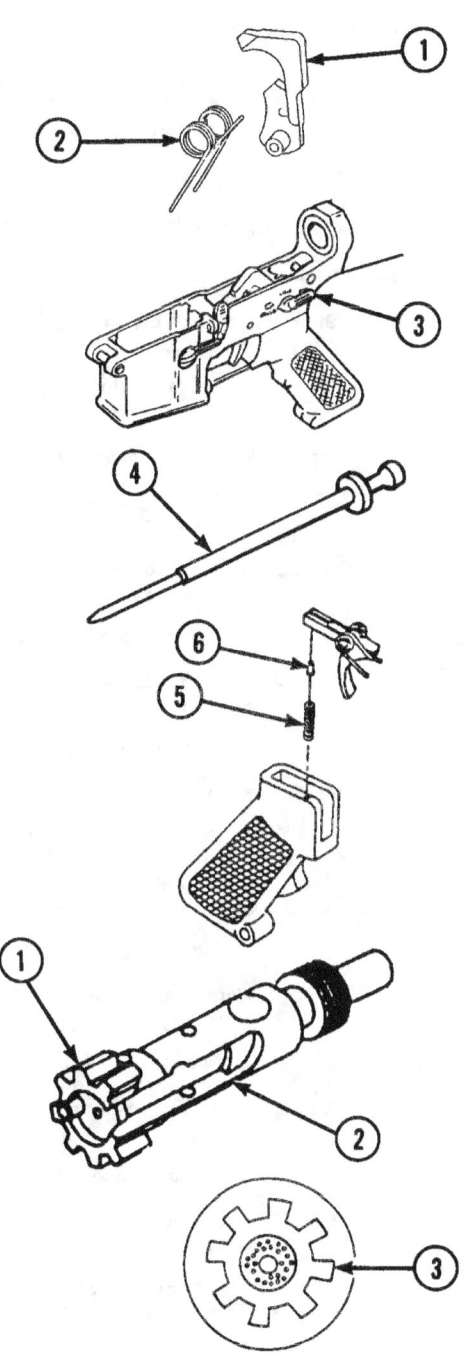

5. FAILURE TO FIRE.

    Step 1. Broken hammer (1).

          Replace hammer (1).

    Step 2. Weak or broken hammer spring (2).

          Replace spring (2).

    Step 3. Hammer spring (2) improperly assembled.

          Reassemble correctly (p 3-62).

    Step 4. Selector lever (3) frozen on SAFE position.

          Disassemble and clean.

    step 5. Broken firing pin (4) or firing pin does not meet gage protrusion requirement.

          Replace.

    Step 6. Damaged, dirty, or corroded spring (5) and detent (6).

          Clean and/or replace if necessary.

6. FAILURE TO UNLOCK.

    Step 1. Burred locking lugs (1) cm bolt assembly (2).

          Remove burrs.

    Step 2. Burred locking lugs (3) on barrel extension.

          Remove burrs.

    Step 3. See short recoil (p 3-70.

    Step 4. Broken bolt assembly (2).

          Replace bolt assembly (2).

TROUBLESHOOTING (CONT)

MALFUNCTION
>**TEST OR INSPECTION**
>>**CORRECTIVE ACTION**

7. FAILURE TO EXTRACT.

>Badly pitted chamber (1).

>>Replace rifle barrel assembly.

8. FAILURE TO EJECT.

>See short recoil (p 3-7).

9. FAILURE TO COCK.

>Step 1. Worn or broken trigger nose (1) or trigger spring (2).

>>Replace trigger (3) or defective trigger spring (2).

>Step 2. Worn or broken hammer trigger notch (4)

>>Replace hammer (5).

>Step 3. Worn or broken hammer disconnector hook (6).

>>Replace hammer (5).

>Step 4. Worn or broken hammer automatic sear hook (7).

>>Replace hammer (5].

>Step 5. Worn or broken disconnector hook (8).

>>Replace disconnector (9).

>Step 6. Weak broken, or missing trigger spring (10)

>>Replace spring (10).

>Step 7. Worn, broken, or missing automatic sear(11).

>>Replace automatic sear (11)

>Step 8. Weak or broken automatic sear spring (1 2).

>>Replace automatic sear (11).

>Step 9. Automatic sear spring (12) incorrectly assembled in receiver.

>>Remove automatic sear assembly (11) and install correctly (p 3-59).

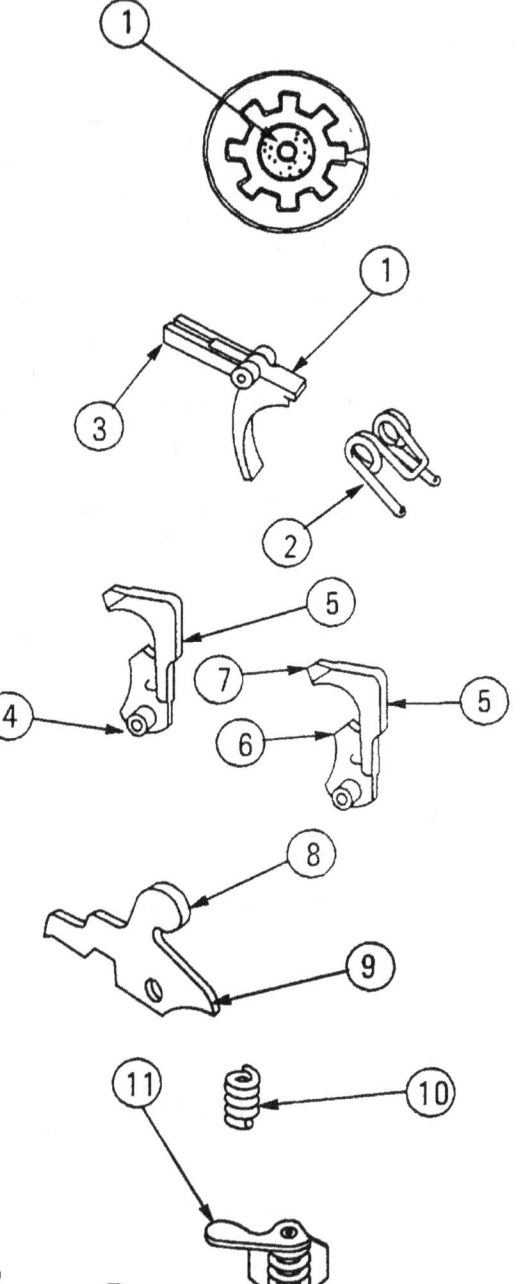

TROUBLESHOOTING (CONT)

MALFUNCTION
        TEST OR INSPECTION
                CORRECTIVE ACTION

10. SHORT RECOIL.

Step 1. Improper gap, space or worn, missing, or broken bolt rings (1).

Replace bolt rings and stagger gaps.

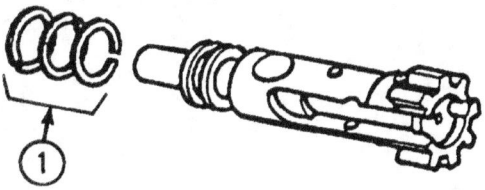

Step 2. Broken or bent gas tube (2).

Adjust by bending in area of handguards or replace gas tube.

Step 3. Gas tube spring pin (3) missing from front sight (4).

Replace spring pin (3).

Step 4. Partially plugged gas system because of carbon buildup in the gas tube (2).

Replace gas tube (2).

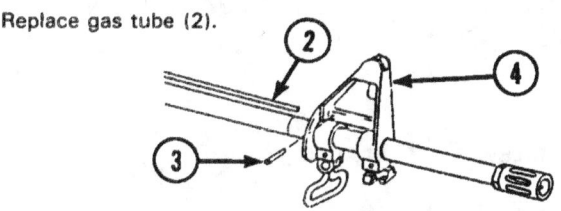

WARNING

When using P-C-111, avoid skin contact. If it comes in contact with the skin, wash off thoroughly with running water. Using a good lanolin base cream after exposure is helpful. Using rubber gloves is recommended.

Step 5. Carbon buildup in barrel gas port (5).

Remove carbon buildup by soaking in P-C-111 (item 8, app D). Wear rubber gloves (item 16, app D).

TROUBLESHOOTING (CONT)

MALFUNCTION
         TEST OR INSPECTION
                 CORRECTIVE ACTION

---

11. **WEAPON CANNOT BE ZEROED**

      Step 1. Bent or bulged rifle barrel (1).

          Replace rifle barrel
          assembly (1).

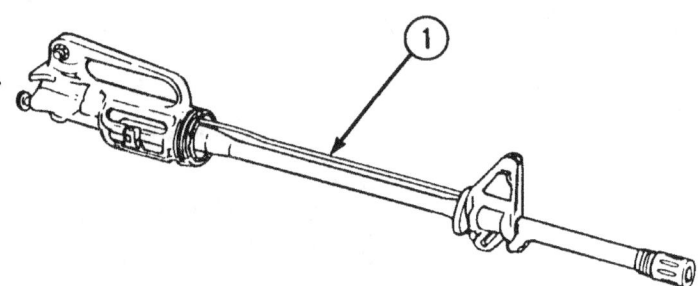

      Step 2. Barrel assembly out of alignment with rear sight on upper receiver

          Align barrel and upper receiver (p 3-33).

      Step 3. Corroded front (2) or rear (3) sights.

          Disassemble, clean, and lubricate.

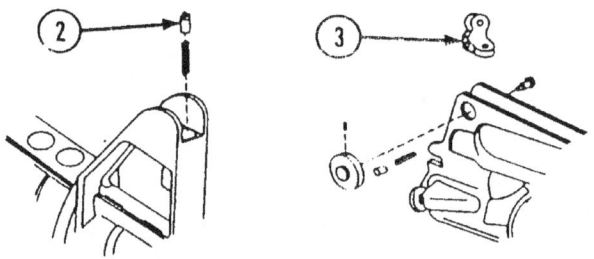

12. **FAILURE TO CYCLE WITH SELECTOR LEVER SET ON AUTO.**

      Step 1. Broken automatic sear (1) or spring (2)

          Replace automatic sear assembly (1).

      Step 2. Faulty selector lever (3).

          Replace selector lever (3).

      Step 3. Short recoil.

          See malfunction 11.

TROUBLESHOOTING (CONT)

MALFUNCTION
TEST OR INSPECTION
CORRECTIVE ACTION

13. FIRES WHEN TRIGGER IS RELEASED WITH SELECTOR LEVER ON SEMI, OR FIRES TWO OR MORE ROUNDS IN SEMI SELECTOR POSITION (DOUBLING).

Step 1. Defective disconnector (1).

Replace disconnector (1).

step 2. Worn or broken hammer trigger notch (2).
Worn or broken hammer disconnector notch (3).

Replace firing hammer (4).

step 3. Worn or broken trigger nose (5).

Replace trigger (6).

Step 4. Worn trigger or hammer pin hole. Gage trigger and hammer pin holes.

If gage 12006472 enters any of the four holes, replace weapon (p 3-57).

14. FIRES WITH SELECTOR LEVER ON SAFE.

Step 1. Defective selector lever (1).

Replace selector lever (1).

Step 2. Worn or broken trigger (rear portion (2).

Replace trigger (3).

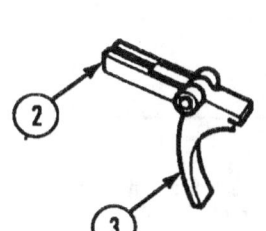
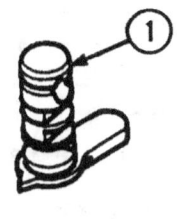

15. BOLT FAILS TO LOCK TO REAR AFTER FIRING LAST ROUND.

Step 1. Broken bolt catch (1).

Replace bolt catch (1).

Step 2. Weak or broken bolt catch spring (2).

Replace bolt catch spring (2).

Step 3. Restricted movement of bolt catch (1).

Disassemble and clean.

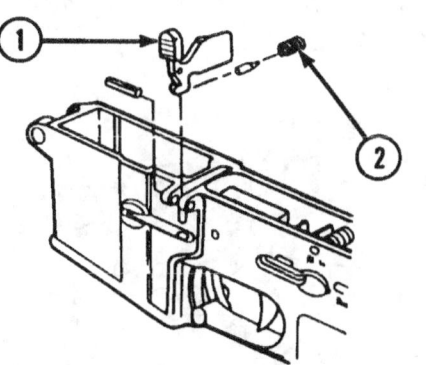

Section IV. DECONTAMINATION OF RIFLES AND SHOP AREA

3-8. DECONTAMINATION OF SIGHTS ACTIVATED WITH TRITIUM (H3). Refer to Chapter 2 Section V for procedures.

Section V. MAINTENANCE PROCEDURES FOR THE M16 AND M16A1 RIFLE

3-9. MAJOR COMPONENTS OF M16 AND M16A1 RIFLE.

This task covers disassembly.

INITIAL SETUP

Applicable Configuration
M16/M16A1 Rifle

Tools
Small Arms Repairman Tool Kit
SC 5180-95-CL-A07 (19204)

Reference
TM 9-1005-249-10 (operator's manual)

Equipment Condition
Weapon assembled

General Safety Instructions
Before starting an inspection, be sure to clear the weapon. Do not actuate the trigger until the rifle has been cleared.
Inspect the chamber to ensure that it is empty and no ammunition is in position to be chambered. Do not keep live ammunition near work area.

WARNING

Before starting an inspection on a weapon equipped with a low light level sight, check for damage to the low light level sight. See procedures listed on page 2-21.

DISASSEMBLY

---

a. Refer to TM 9-1005-249-10.
b. Remove cartridge magazine (1), small arms sling (2), bolt carrier assembly (3), charging handle (4), upper receiver and barrel assembly (5), and lower receiver and extension assembly (6).

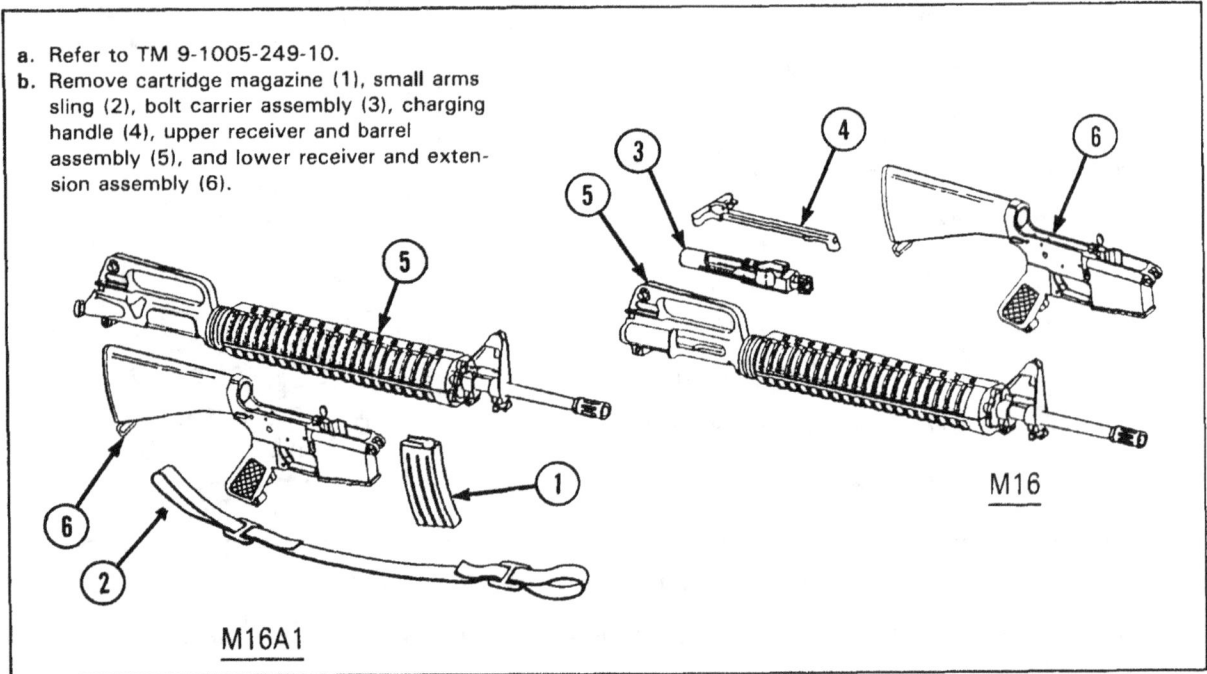

M16

M16A1

3-10. BOLT CARRIER ASSEMBLY.

This task covers:

a. Disassembly
b. Inspection
c. Test

d. Repair
e. Reassembly

INITIAL SETUP

Applicable Configuration
M16/M16A1   Rifle

Test Equipment
Tool and Gage Set 8426685

Tools
Small Arms Repairman Tool Kit
SC   5180-95-CL-A07   (19204)

Materials/Parts
Cleaner, lubricant and preservative (CLP) (item 9, app D)
Lubricating oil, weapons (LAW) (item 20, app D)
Lubricating oil, weapons (LSA) (item 21, app D)
Wiping Rag (item 24, app D)

Equipment Condition
Page Condition Description
3-10 Bolt carrier assembly removed

---

a. DISASSEMBLY

1. Remove firing pin retaining pin (1).

2. Tip key and bolt carrier assembly (2) allowing firing pin (3) to drop out. Catch the firing pin.

3. Rotate bolt cam pin (4) 1/4 turn and lift straight up to remove.

4. Remove bolt assembly (5) from key and bolt carrier assembly (2).

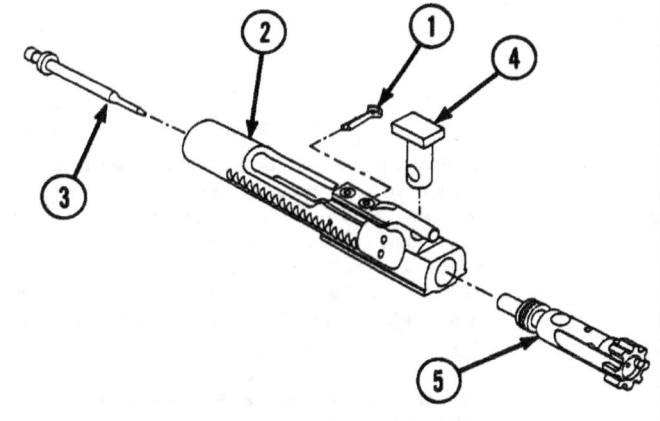

3-10. BOLT CARRIER ASSEMBLY (CONT).

b. INSPECTION

1

[a] Inspect bolt carrier assembly (1) for burrs, cracks, wear, and evidence of gas loss.

[b] Visually inspect the carrier and key screws (2) for looseness and proper staking as shown below.

NOTE

Do not attempt to retorque if there is no loosening of the screws indicated by the staking marks.

Surface "A' must not indicate distortion or damage which impairs parallelism.

IRFACE A   SURFACE A   SURFACE A

FIELD REPLACEMENT STAKING   ORIGINAL STAKING

0.025 MAX
4 PLACES

NOTE

There are bolts and bolt carriers on fielded weapons, some with chrome-plated exterior surface finishes and some with phosphate coating. Both finishes are acceptable under certain operational requirements and/or restrictions. Phosphate-coated bolt carriers are required for divisional combat units. Chrome-plated bolt carriers are acceptable for divisional noncombat units and training center units. Chrome-plated and phosphate-coated bolt assemblies, bolt carrier assemblies, and repair parts for these assemblies may be intermixed in any combination, with the following exception:

Phosphate-coated bolt carriers are required for all deployable and deploying units. Chrome-plated bolt carriers are acceptable for nondeployable and training center units.

2

Inspect firing pin (3) tip for proper contour. Inspect for pitting, wear, and burrs. Pits or wear in area (4) is permissible. Replace if unserviceable.

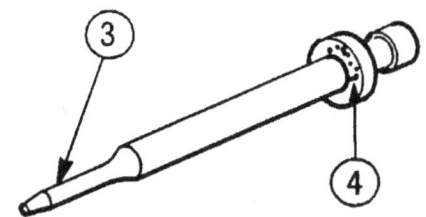

3

Prior to reassembly, insert bolt assembly (5) in to
bolt carrier assembly (1), and exercise bolt in and out
of bolt carrier assembly. Check for binding.

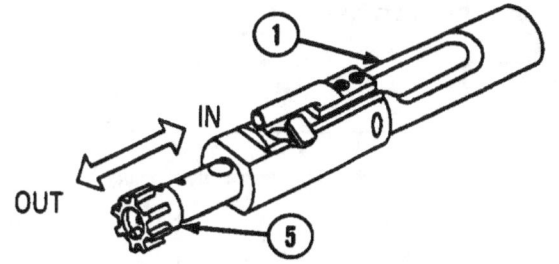

4

Check bolt assembly (5) for proper fit. Turn bolt carrier assembly (1) and suspend so the bolt assembly is
pointed down.

NOTE

The bolt assembly (5) must not drop out.
If weight of bolt assembly allows it to drop
out of carrier assembly, replace bolt rings
(p 3-18).

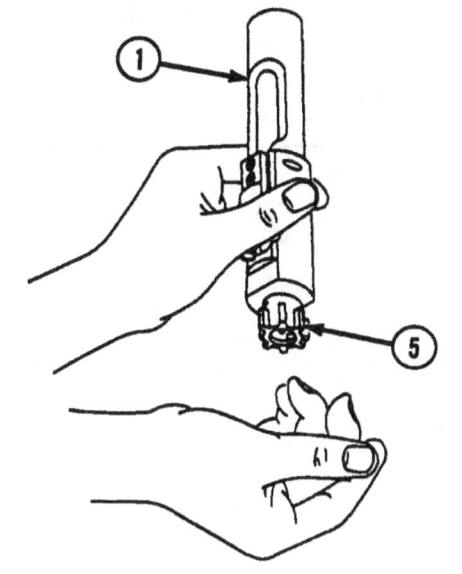

c. TEST

1. Insert firing pin (2) through bolt assembly (3).

2. Position firing pin protrusion gage (1) PN
   7799735 to check for proper firing pin (2) protrusion (minimum 0.028- maximum 0.036).

   ### NOTE

   Firing pin should touch the gage on
   minimum but should not touch on
   maximum.

3. Replace a defective firing pin.

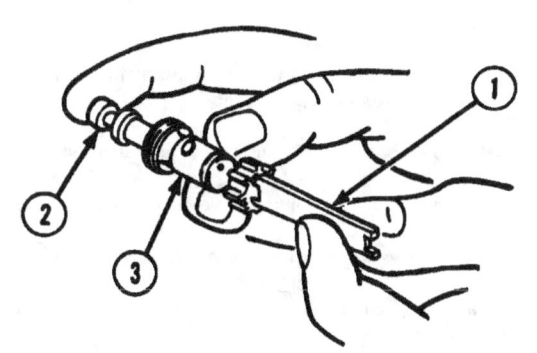

3-10. BOLT CARRIER ASSEMBLY (CONT).

d. REPAIR

1. Replace all authorized unserviceable items.

NOTE

Be sure to retest a replaced firing pin, key and bolt carrier assembly, bolt assembly, or bolt carrier assembly.

2. Lubricate all metal parts using CLP, LSA, or, LAW (see p 2-22).

e. REASSEMBLY

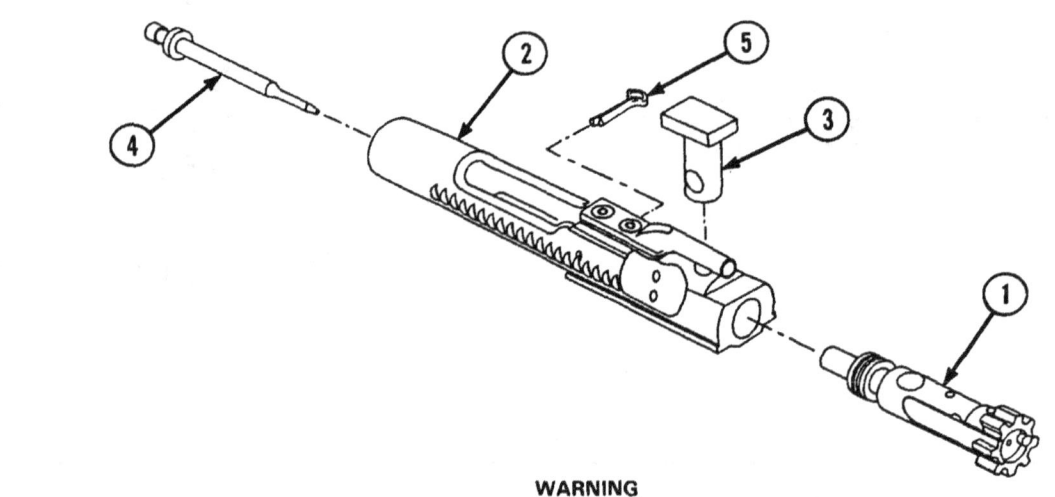

WARNING

Bolt cam pin must be installed or weapon will blow up while firing the first round. If the cam pin is not installed, injury to, or death of, personnel may result.

NOTE

Before installing bolt assembly, check to see that the ring gaps are staggered to prevent loss of gas pressure.

1. Install bolt assembly (1) into key and bolt carrier assembly (2).

2. Install bolt cam pin (3) and rotate 1/4 turn to secure bolt assembly (1).

3. Hold key and bolt carrier assembly (2) with bolt assembly (1) down and drop in firing pin (4).

4. Install firing pin retaining pin (5) from left side only to ensure proper installation. Check for proper installation by attempting to shake out firing pin.

3-11. BOLT ASSEMBLY.

This task covers:

a. Disassembly
b. Inspection/Repair
c. Test

d. Clean/Lubricate
e. Reassembly

INITIAL SETUP

Applicable Configuration
M16/M16A1 Rifle

Test Equipment
Tool and Gage Set 8426685

Tools
Small Arms Repairman Tool Kit
SC 5180-95-CL-A07 (19204)

Materials/Parts
Cleaner, Lubricant and Preservative (CLP) (item 9, app D)
Lubricating oil, weapon (LAW)
Lubricating oil, weapon (LSA)
Gloves, protective (item 16, app D)
Penetrant kit (item 23, app D)
Rag, wiping (item 24, app D)

Equipment Condition
Page Condition Description
3-10 Bolt carrier assembly removed
3-11 Bolt assembly removed

a. DISASSEMBLY

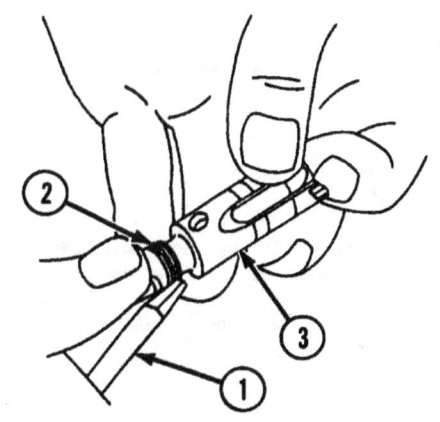

NOTE

Do not remove bolt rings unless they require re-placement.

Using flat tip screwdriver (1) remove the three bolt rings (2) from the bolt (3).

b. INSPECTION/REPAIR

1

(a) Visually inspect bolt rings for cracks, kinks, and bends.

(b) Replace all three bolt rings if one or more rings is damaged. See page 3-7 for bolt ring wear check.

3-11. BOLT ASSEMBLY (CONT).

b. Inspection/REPAIR (CONT).

2

Inspect bolt (1) for pits, burrs, and wear as follows:

[a] Bolt faces with a cluster of pits which are touching or tightly grouped, covering an area measuring approximately 1/8 inch across, will be rejected and replaced.

(b) Bolts which contain individual pits or a scattered pattern will not be cause for rejection.

(c) Bolts that contain pits extending into the firing pin hole will not be rejected unless firing pin hole gaging check determines excess wear.

(d) Rings on the bolt face (machine tool marks), grooves, or ridges less than approximately 0.010 inch will not be cause for rejection.

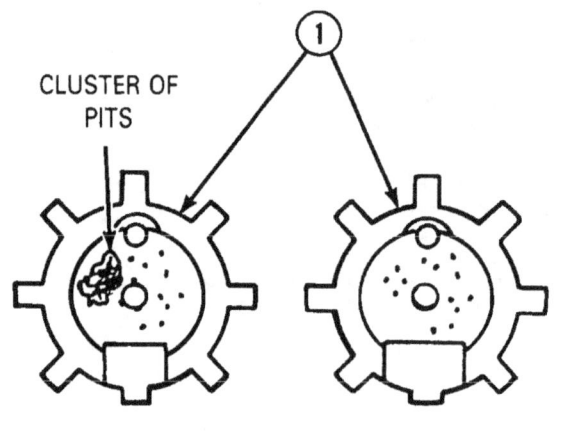

CLUSTER OF PITS

NOT ACCEPTABLE   ACCEPTABLE

3

Inspect bolt (1) for cracks especially in the locking lugs at the locking lugs base, and the cam pin hole area. Use black light if available; otherwise, use a glass of no more than 3X magnification or use a penetrant kit.

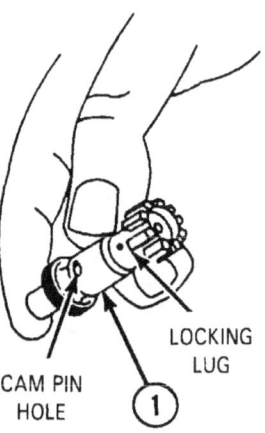

LOCKING LUG

CAM PIN HOLE

4

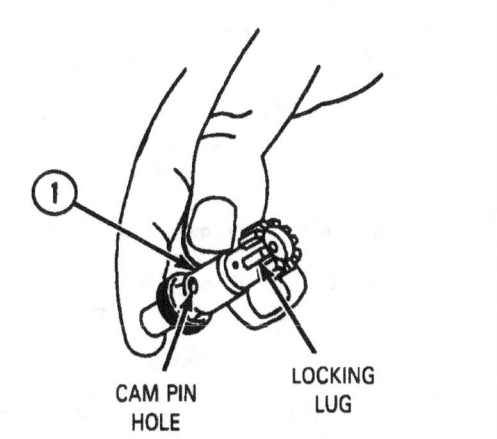

CAM PIN HOLE

LOCKING LUG

WARNING

Dry cleaning solvent is flammable and toxic and should be used in a well-ventilated area. The use of rubber gloves is necessary to protect the skin when washing rifle parts.

Use penetrant kit as follows:

The area to be inspected must be clean, free of oil, etc. Spray a small amount of remover on the area to be inspected, let dry, and wipe off with a wiping rag.

5

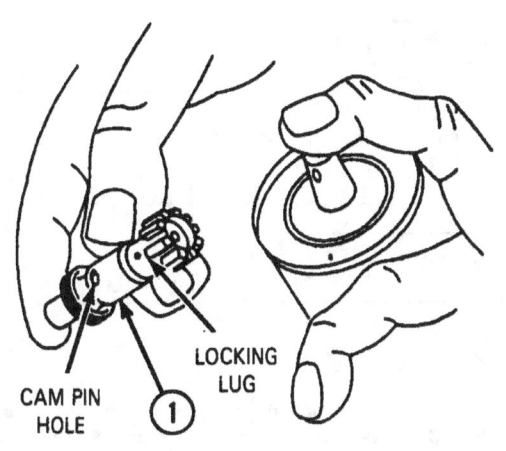

LOCKING LUG

CAM PIN HOLE

Spray penetrant (only enough to wet the area) on the area of the bolt (1) to be inspected.

Spray developer over the penetrant and let the developer work. Cracks will be indicated by a change in color where there is a crack. If there are cracks, the component is unserviceable.

Pay close attention to the area where the locking lugs meet the body.

If there are no cracks, spray remover on the area, let dry, and wipe off with a wiping rag. Oil the area to prevent corrosion.

Replace bolt assembly if bolt (1) is defective.

NOTE

Replacement of the bolt assembly will require that the headspace be tested (p 3-38, TEST).

3-11. BOLT ASSEMBLY (CONT).

c. TEST

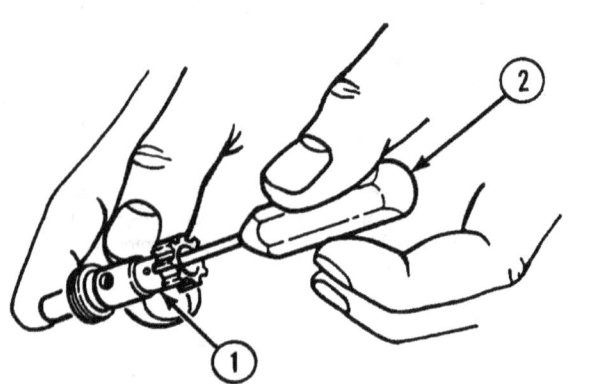

NOTE

Do not force the gage into bolt assembly.

Inspect bolt (1) for elongated or oversized firing pin hole using special no-go plug gage (2) PN 12620101.

NOTE

Bolts with firing pin hoes which permit the special no-go plug gage to fully penetrate at any position on the circumference will be rejected and replaced.

d. CLEAN/LUBRICATE

Clean all items (operator's manual). Remove carbon deposits with CLP or RBC. Lubricate all items with a light coat of CLP, LSA, or LAW.

e. REASSEMBLY

Install the three bolt rings (1) one at a time onto the bolt (2) using care not to bend them. Stagger the bolt ring gaps to prevent loss of gas pressure.

NOTE

Make certain ring gaps are staggered to prevent loss of gas pressure.

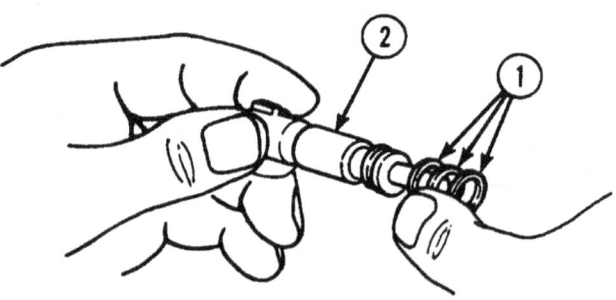

3-12. KEY AND BOLT CARRIER ASSEMBLY.

This task covers:

a. Disassembly
b. Repair

c. Reassembly

INITIAL SETUP

Applicable Configuration
  M16/M16A1 Rifle

Tools
  Field Maintenance Basic Less Power Small Arms
    Shop Set SC 4933-95-CL-A11 (19204)
  Small Arms Repairman Tool Kit
    SC 5180-95-CL-A07 (19204)
  Key tool (fig E-3, app E)

Equipment Condition
  Page Condition Description
  3-10 Key and Bolt Carrier Assembly removed
  3-11 Bolt assembly removed

a. DISASSEMBLY

<u>NOTE</u>

Do not disassemble the key and bolt carrier assembly unless the bolt carrier key or bolt carrier is defective. New screws must be used if disassembled.

1. Using socket wrench handle and socket head screw socket wrench, remove the carrier and key screws (1).

2, Remove bolt carrier key (2) from bolt carrier (3).

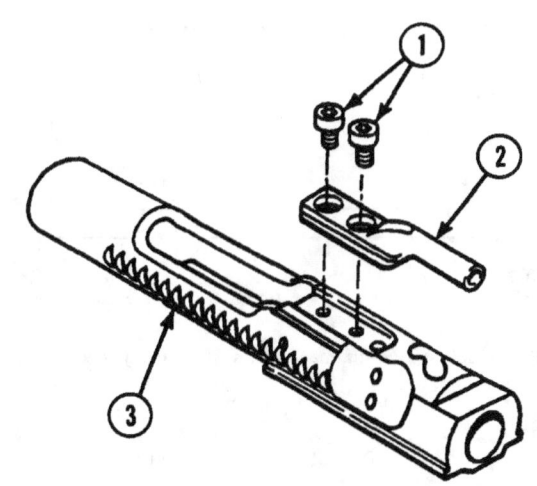

3-12. KEY AND BOLT CARRIER ASSEMBLY (CONT).

b. REPAIR

NOTE

Do not reuse old screws. New screws must be used at assembly.

Repair by cleaning mating surfaces, replacing, properly torquing, and restaking carrier and key screws

---

c. REASSEMBLY

1

(a) If disassembled, install and position bolt carrier key (1) on bolt carrier (2).

(b) Install two carrier and key screws (3). Always use new screws.

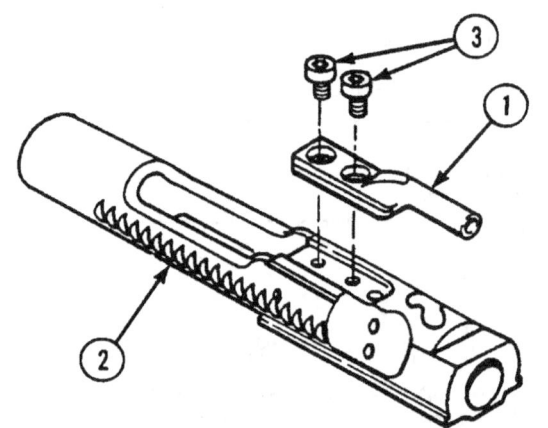

2

Place bolt carrier in machinist's vise using vise jaw caps.

NOTE

Do not reuse old screws.

Use a socket head screw wrench attachment and torque wrench to torque the carrier and key screws (3) to 35 to 40 inch-pounds.

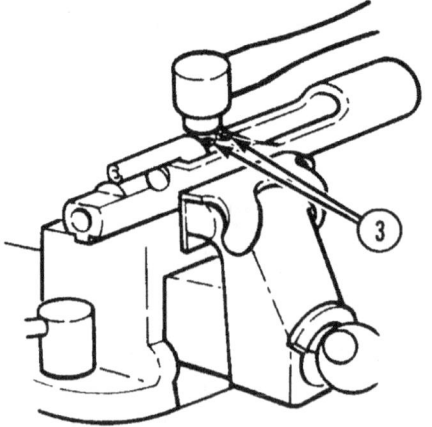

3

NOTE

The method of staking will be accomplished
as pictured below.

Use solid center punch, and hand hammer to stake the
two carrier and key screws (2) in three places.

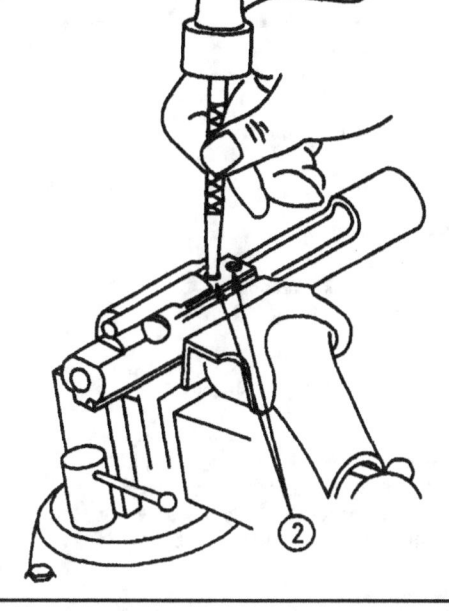

4

Stake carrier and key screws.

NOTE

A maximum of 0.025 inch protrusion in an upward direction is permissible.

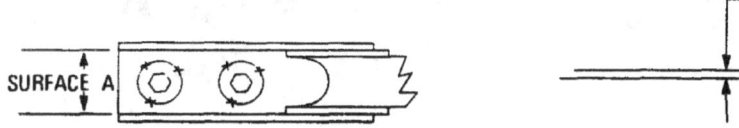

SURFACE A

0.025 MAX
4 PLACES

FIELD REPLACEMENT STAKING

NOTE

If the bolt carrier key is replaced, three to eight rounds of blank or ball ammunition
must be fired to insure a seal is created. Manual operation of the rifle may be required.
If blank ammunition is utilized, M15A2 Blank firing Attachment must be adapted.

3-13. UPPER RECEIVER AND BARREL ASSEMBLY.

This task covers:

a. Disassembly
b. Inspection/Cleaning
c. Repair

d. Reassembly
e. Test

INITIAL SETUP

Applicable Configuration
  M 16/M16A1 Rifle

Test Equipment
  Tool and Gage Set 8426685

Tools
  Small Arms Repairman Tool Kit
    SC 5180-95-CL-AO7 (19204)
  Field Maintenance Basic Less Power Small Arms
    Shop Set SC 4933-95-CL-A11 (19204)

Materials/Parts
  Carbon removing compound (P-C-111) (item 8,
    app D)
  Cleaner, lubricant and preservative (CLP) (item 9,
    app D)
  Cleaning compound, rifle bore (RBC) (item 11,
    app D)
  Cloth, abrasive (item 12, app D)
  Dichloromethane, technical (item 14, app D)
  Dry cleaning solvent (item 15, app D)
  Gloves, chemical and oil protective (item 16,
    app D)
  Grease, molybdenum disulfide (item 17, app D)
  Lubricant, solid film (item 19, app D)
  Lubricating oil, weapons (LAW) (item 20, app D)
  Lubricating oil, weapons (LSA) (item 21, app D)
  Pan, wash (item 22, app D)
  Sealing compound (item 26, app D)

References
  FM 23-9
  TM 9-1005-249-10 (operator's manual)

Equipment Condition
  Page Condition Description
  2-35 Hand guards removed
  3-10 Upper receiver and barrel assembly removed
        from lower receiver and extension assembly.

General Safety Instructions
  To avoid injury to your eyes, use care when removing
    and installing spring-loaded parts.
  When using solid film lubricant or dichloromethane, be
    sure the area is well ventilated.
  When using P-C-111, avoid skin contact. If P-C-111
    comes in contact with the skin, wash thoroughly
    with running water. Using a good lanolin base
    cream after exposure to the compound is helpful.
    Using gloves and protective equipment is
    recommended.
  Dry cleaning solvent is flammable and toxic and
    should be used in a well-ventiliated area. The use of
    rubber gloves is necessary to protect the skin when
    washing rifle parts.

WARNING

Upper receiver and barrel assembly may be
equipped with low light level front and rear sights.
The front sight contains radioactive material. If so
equipped, do not insert metal objects into the post
slot or otherwise treat roughly to cause breakage
of the radioactive element.

a. DISASSEMBLY

1

<u>WARNING</u>

To avoid injury to your eyes, use care when removing and installing spring-loaded parts.

When using solid film lubricant or dichloromethane, be sure the area is well ventilated.

When using P-C-1 11, avoid skin contact. If P-C-111 comes in contact with the skin, wash thoroughly with running water. Using a good lanolin base cream after exposure to compound is helpful. Using gloves and protective equipment is recommended.

Upper receiver and barrel assembly may be equipped with low light level front and rear sights. The front sight contains radioactive material. If so equipped, do not insert metal objects into the post slot or otherwise treat roughly to cause breakage of the radioactive element.

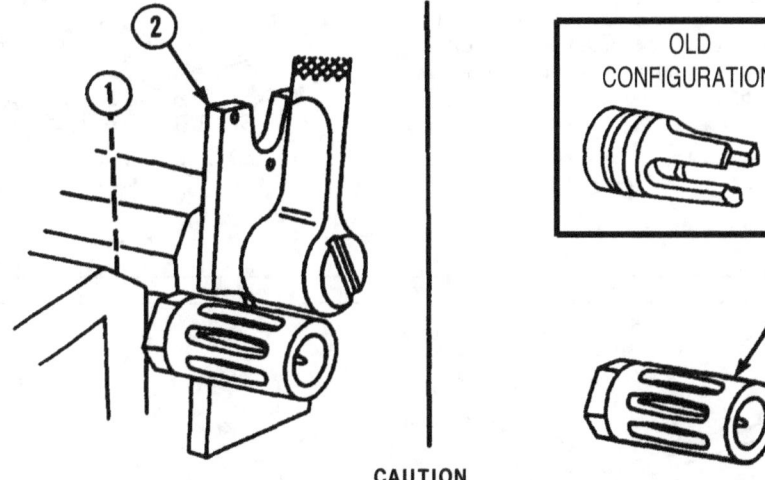

OLD CONFIGURATION

<u>CAUTION</u>

When using the barrel removal fixture, always insert the barrel from the same direction to avoid damage to the fixture.

(a) Position upper receiver and barrel assembly (1) in barrel removal fixture and secure both in machinist's vise.

(b) Using combination wrench (2) and 1/2 inch-drive handle, remove flash suppressor (3).

<u>NOTE</u>

There are two types of flash suppressors. The earliest design is open ended with three prongs. The latest is a closed-end design and is the only authorized repair part.

All M 16A1 rifles assigned to divisional combat units must be equipped with the closed end flash suppressor. M 16A1 rifles assigned to noncombat unit and training center units may be equipped with either the open or closed end type flash suppressor. If the old type flash suppressor is removed, it must be replaced with the new type flash suppressor.

3-13. UPPER RECEIVER AND BARREL ASSEMBLY (CONT).

a. DISASSEMBLY (CONT).

2

(a) Remove lockwasher.

(b) Remove upper receiver and barrel assembly (1) from barrel remover fixture and vise.

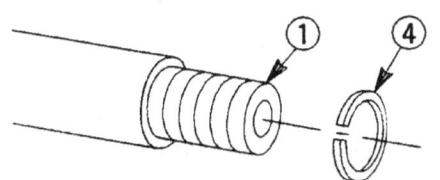

3

Using ball peen hammer and 5/64 inch-diameter drive pin punch, remove spring pin (5) (which retains the gas tube) from the front sight assembly (6).

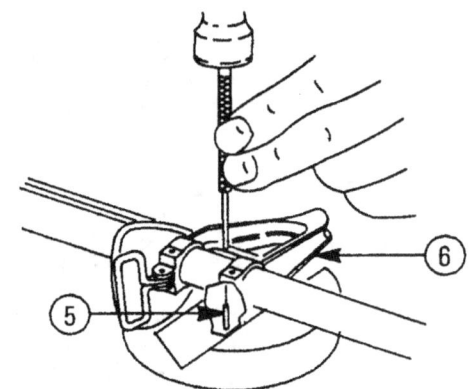

4

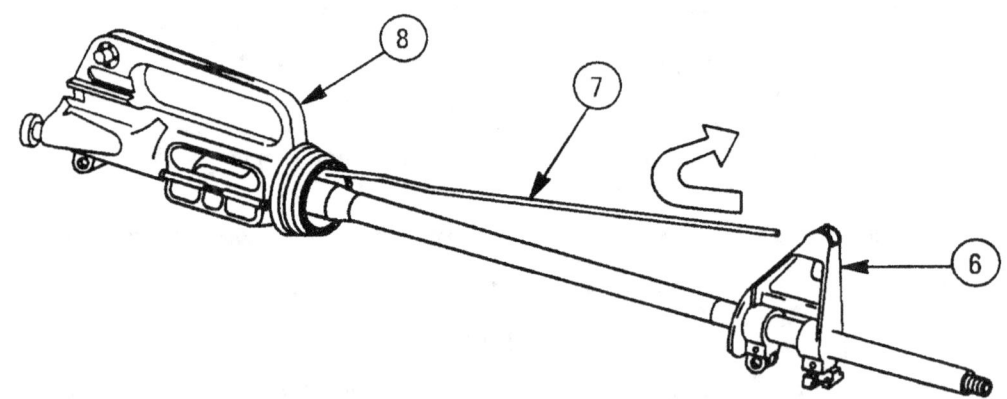

Slide gas tube (7) back into upper receiver (8) to clear front sight assembly (6). Then lift slightly, pull forward, and remove gas tube (7).

5

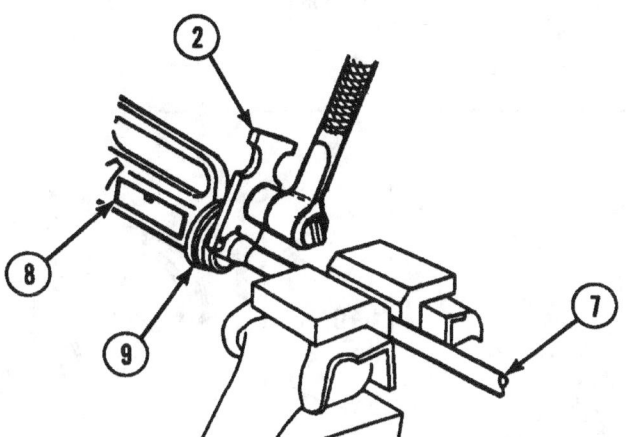

(a) Place upper receiver and barrel assembly (1) into barrel removal fixture and clamp into machinist's vise.

<u>CAUTION</u>

When using the barrel removal fixture, always insert the barrel from the same direction to avoid damage to the fixture.

<u>NOTE</u>

Be sure all three drive pins on combination wrench are engaged with barrel nut assembly (9). Wrench must be pushed toward upper receiver (8) to compress the slip ring spring in barrel nut assembly (9).

(b) Using socket wrench handle and combination wrench (2), loosen barrel nut assembly (9).

6

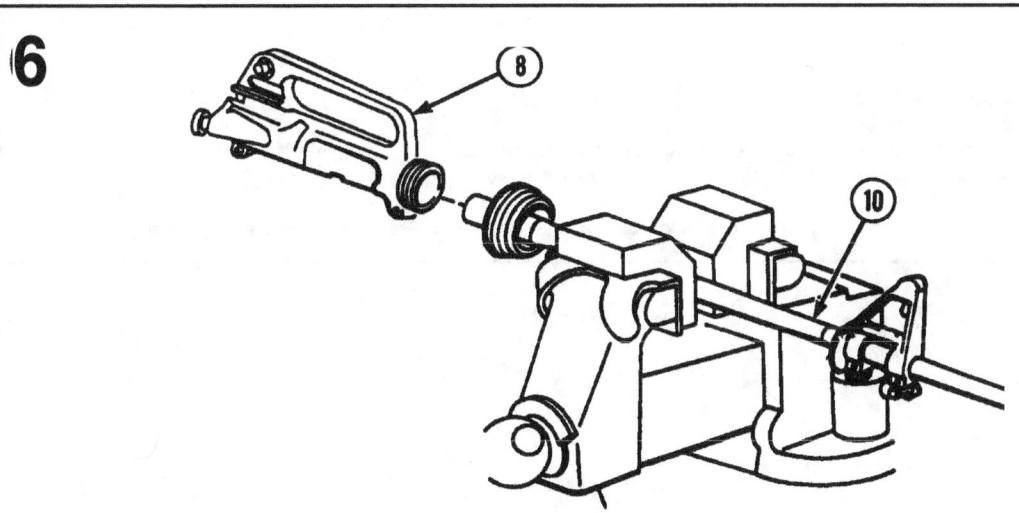

(a) Separate upper receiver assembly (8) from barrel assembly (10).

(b) Remove rifle barrel assembly (10) from vise and barrel removal fixture.

3-13. UPPER RECEIVER AND BARREL ASSEMBLY (CONT).

a. DISASSEMBLY (CONT)

7

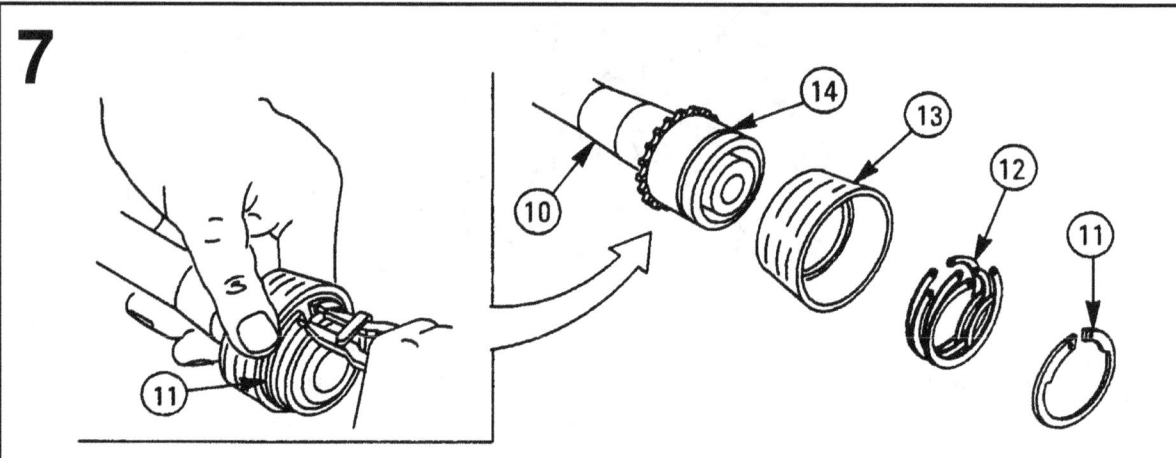

(a) Remove retaining ring (1 1) using retaining ring pliers.

(b) Remove slip ring spring (12) and handguard slip ring (13).

(c) Do not remove barrel nut (14) from rifle barrel assembly (10).

b. INSPECTION/CLEANING

1

(a) Inspect gas tube for cracks and deformities. Replace if defective.

(b) Use P-C-111 carbon removing compound to remove carbon deposits from interior and exterior of gas tube. If a large amount of carbon is found and cannot be removed, replace the gas tube.

(c) Visually inspect all other parts for unserviceable or missing parts. Replace defective or missing parts.

2

(a) Inspect rifle bore and locking lugs for burrs, cracks, rust, bulges, and pits.

   (1) Pits no wider than a land or groove and no longer than 3/8 inch are allowed in the bore.

   (2) Lands that appear dark blue due to coating of gilding metal from projectiles are allowable.

   (3) Definitely ringed bores or bores ringed sufficiently to bulge the outside surface of the barrel are cause for rejection. Replace rifle barrel assembly if defective.

NOTE

Chamber may be inspected with or without upper receiver assembled to the barrel assembly.

(b) Inspect chamber using reflector tool 1) and flashlight (2).

   Pits 1/8 inch in length are cause for rejection. Replace rifle barrel assembly if defective.

NOT ACCEPTABLE

ACCEPTABLE

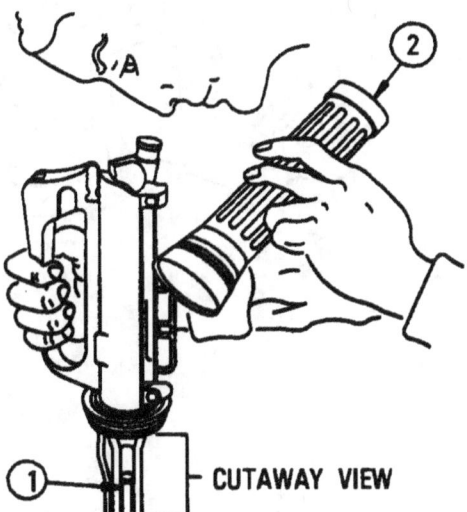

CUTAWAY VIEW

3-13. UPPER RECEIVER AND BARREL ASSEMBLY (CONT).

c. REPAIR

1. Replace all authorized unserviceable items.

2. Straighten bent front sight guards (1) as follows:

CAUTION

Remove spring before heating. (Heat will
damage spring.) The sight post and plunger
may be reused unless damaged.

(a) Remove front sight post, plunger, and spring
(see p 2-38).

(b) Place front sight base (2) in a bench vise.

Use copper or brass caps (jaw inserts) on vise to
prevent damage to sight base (2) during
clamping.

(c) Heat front sight guards (1) and bend with pliers.
The front sight guards (1) should be put back as
nearly as possible to the original position. Allow
front sight housing to air cool.

WARNING

Dry cleaning solvent is flammable and toxic
and should be used in a well-ventilated area.
The use of rubber gloves is necessary to protect skin when washing rifle parts.

(d) Roughen any damaged surface of front sight
guard with abrasive cloth and clean with dry
cleaning solvent. Wear rubber gloves and use a
wash pan to apply solvent.

CAUTION

Do not allow solid film lubricant to flow into
front sight post threaded well.

(e) Apply solid film lubricant to cover the damaged
finish.

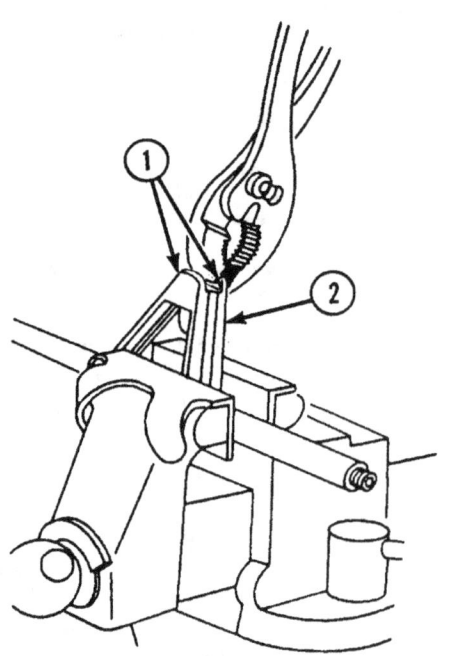

3. Slightly bent barrels may be straightened as follows.

   (a) Check straightness using straightness gage (3) 8448202 (p 3-37). If the barrel fails the straightness test, and the gage remains in the barrel in the area of the front sight, perform step (b) to determine if it may be straightened.

   (b) With the gage remaining in the bore, hold the rifle in a vertical position with the end of the barrel into which the gage was inserted pointing up. Insure that if/when the gage passes through the barrel it will not be damaged. Using hand pressure ONLY, flex the portion of the barrel between the front sight and the flash suppressor in all four directions (left, right, forward and back). If the barrel is only slightly bent, the gage will drop through when the barrel is flexed in one of these directions. Note the direction which allowed the gage to drop through the barrel.

CAUTION

Remove the gage from the barrel before continuing.

NOTE

If the gage does not pass through the barrel when it is flexed, remove the gage and replace the barrel assembly.

   (c) Place the barrel in a vise using appropriate protective jaws. Clamp the barrel between the front sight assembly and the flash suppressor approximately one inch from the front sight assembly. The barrel assembly should be in a horizontal position with the side noted in step (b) toward you.

CAUTION

Do not apply pressure to the receiver.

   (d) Grasp the BARREL near the receiver so that when force is applied the barrel will flex in the same direction as noted in step (b).

   (e) Give the barrel a sharp jerk of approximately 20 to 40 pounds of force.

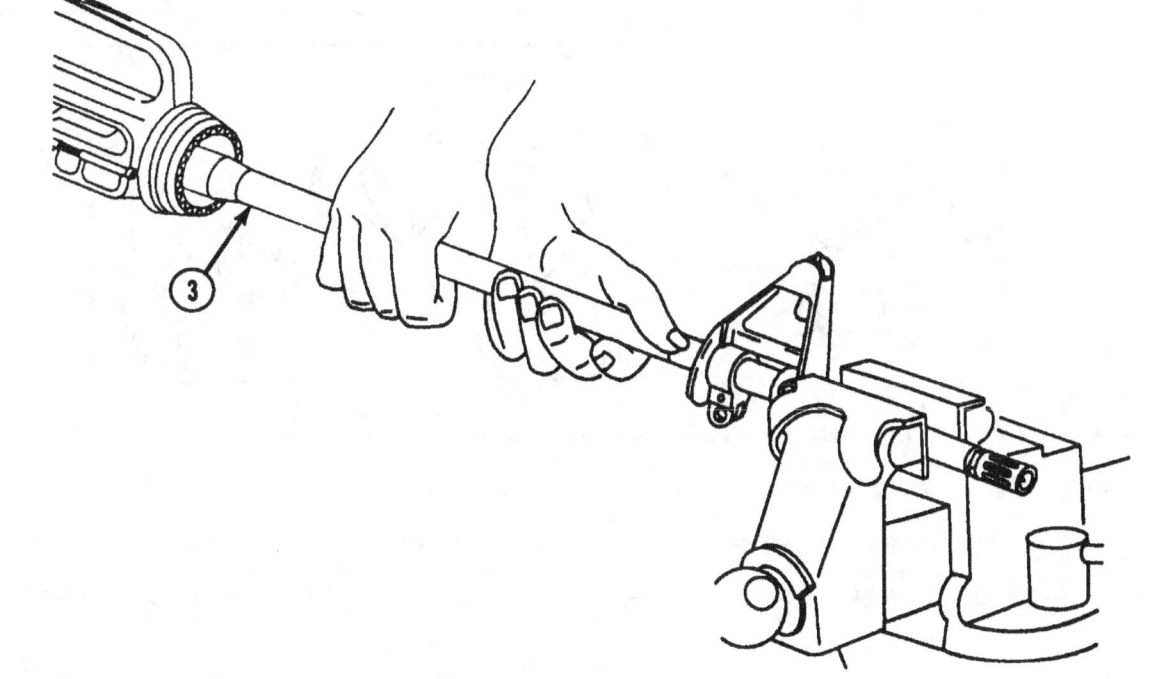

3-13. UPPER RECEIVER AND BARREL ASSEMBLY (CONT).

c. REPAIR (CONT)

(f) Remove the barrel from the vise and recheck straightness (step (a)).

(g) If gage still will not pass through the barrel, perform step (b) to determine direction of bend. If the barrel is still bent in the same direction as before, perform steps (c) through (f) using slightly more force. If the barrel is now bent in the opposite direction, replace the barrel.

(h) If the gage passes freely through the barrel, the barrel shall be considered straight and continue in service.

(i) If the barrel has been straightened, the rifle must be targeted (p 3-39).

d. REASSEMBLY

1

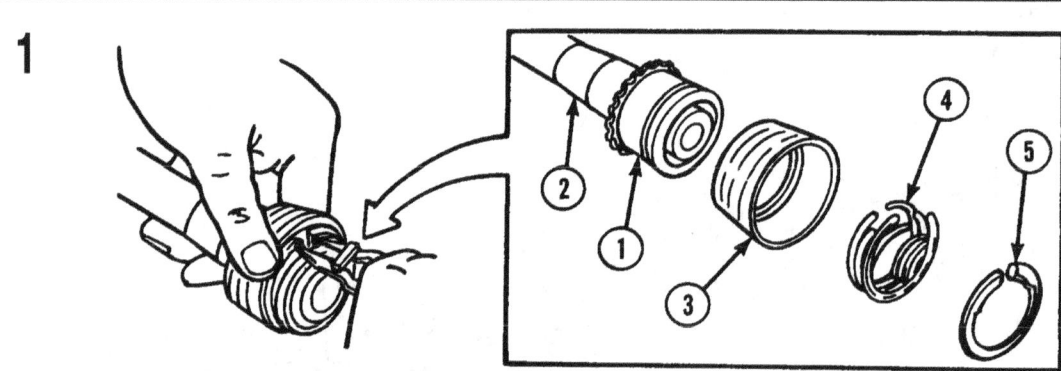

(a) Position barrel nut (1) by sliding it to the rear of barrel assembly (2) as far as possible.

(b) Slide handguard slip ring (3) over barrel nut (1).

(c) Press slip ring spring (4) from both sides and insert it into handguard slip ring (3).

(d) Install retaining ring (5) against slip ring spring (4) using retaining ring pliers. Snap retaining ring (5) to barrel nut (1).

2

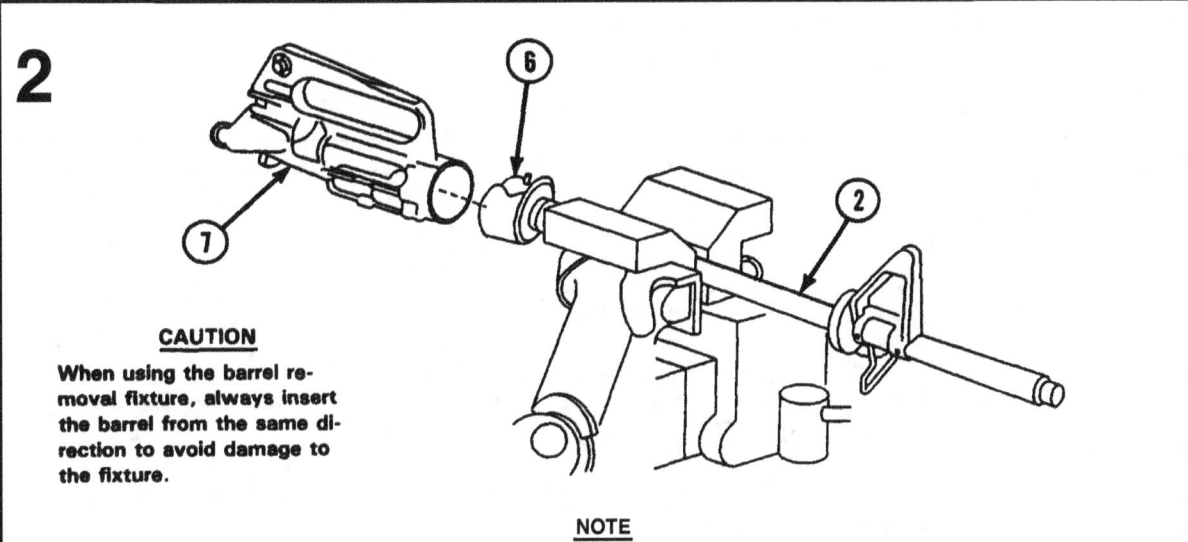

CAUTION

When using the barrel removal fixture, always insert the barrel from the same direction to avoid damage to the fixture.

NOTE

Wipe upper receiver thread clean and ensure there are no burrs. Apply molybdenum disulfide grease to the threads before installation. This operation must be done in order to make later removal of the barrel easier.

(a) Position rifle barrel assembly (2) with alignment pin (6) up. Using barrel removal fixture, clamp barrel assembly (2) in vise.

(b) Align upper receiver assembly (7) using barrel alignment pin (6) and the slot in upper receiver assembly (7). Install over end of barrel assembly (2).

3

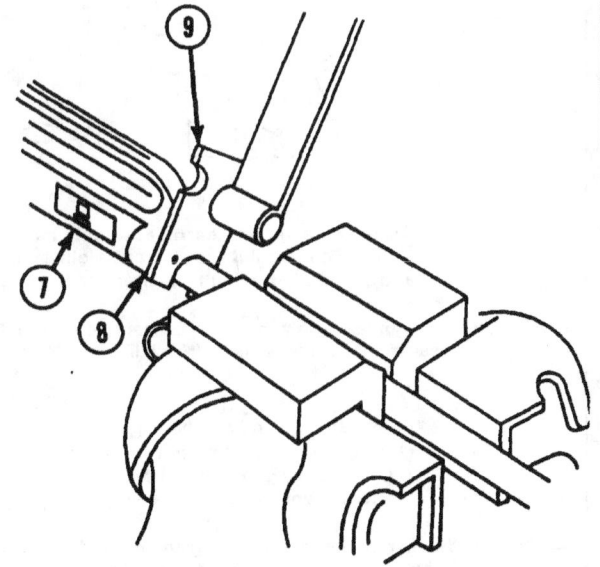

(a) Engage threads of barrel nut assembly (8) with upper receiver assembly (7).

(b) Using combination wrench (9) and torque wrench, torque barrel nut assembly (8) to 30 ft-lb. Torque is measured when both wrenches are used together.

NOTE

Two time torquing (three times total) procedures provide for a better thread fit and prevents barrel nuts from becoming loose. Do not use the torque wrench for loosening.

[c] Make certain all three drive pins on combination wrench are engaged with barrel nut assembly (8). Loosen and repeat torque operation. Then loosen the barrel nut again.

3-13. UPPER RECEIVER AND BARREL ASSEMBLY (CONT).

d. REASSEMBLY (CONT)

4

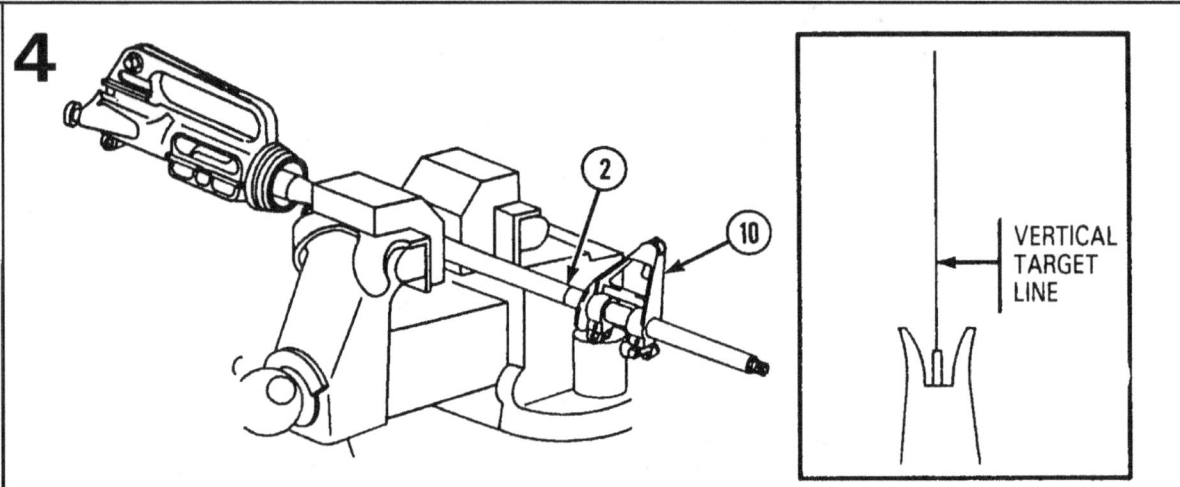

Loosen the vise and align the front sight assembly base (10) in a vertical position (use a vertical line on the wall to check this) then tighten vise to hold t-he barrel assembly (2) in that position.

5

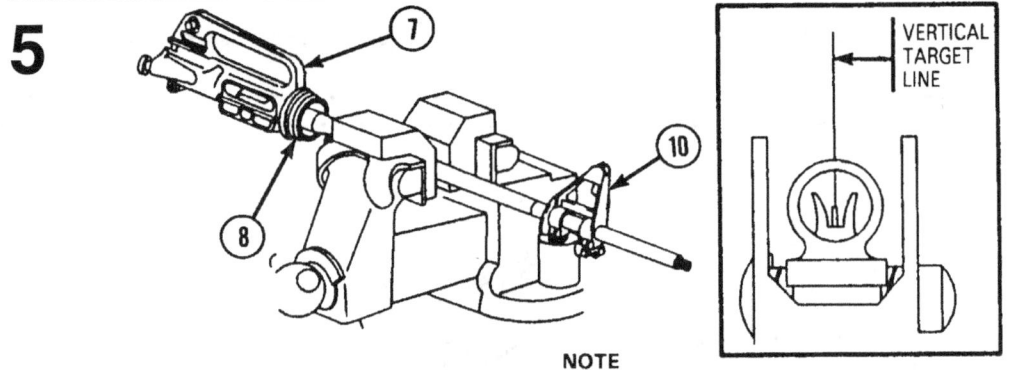

NOTE

Upper receiver and barrel assembly may be equipped with low light level front and rear sights. The low light level front sight must be removed, shipped in its original container and reinstalled at unit maintenance.

(a) With front sight assembly base (1 O) centered, view from the rear and rotate the upper receiver (7 right or left to align rear sight to the same vertical line as front sight.

NOTE

Do not attempt to hold the upper receiver (7) with a pry bar; however, if the barrel assembly (2) turns in the holding fixture, a pry bar may be used in the front sight assembly base (10) to help prevent the barrel from turning in the holding fixture. Use care not to distort or bend front sight or retaining pins.

(b) Torque the barrel nut assembly again to 30 ft-lb while maintaining sight alignment. The barrel nut may be tightened beyond 30 ft-lb to align the barrel nut serrations for gas tube clearance. Never loosen the barrel nut assembly (8) to align for gas tube clearance.

6

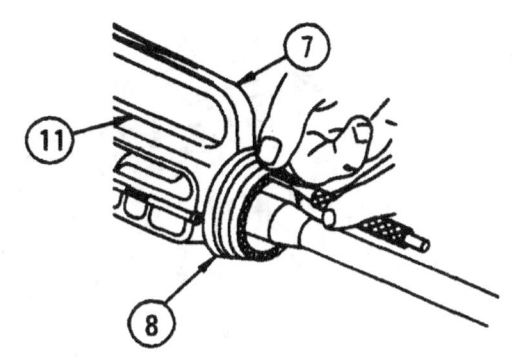

CAUTION

Do not torque over 80 ft-lb while tightening the barrel nut to next hole, to allow for proper alignment.

(a) Align barrel nut assembly (8) with hole in the upper receiver assembly (7) using 1/8 inch drive pin punch. If necessary, tighten nut to next hole to allow proper alignment.

(b) Remove drive pin punch from upper receiver and barrel assembly (11). Remove upper receiver and barrel assembly (1 1) from barrel remover fixture and vise.

7

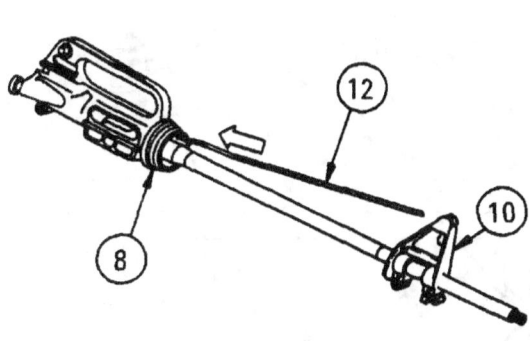

Slide gas tube (12) through the barrel nut assembly (8) and then slide forward inserting gas tube into hole in the front sight assembly base (10).

8

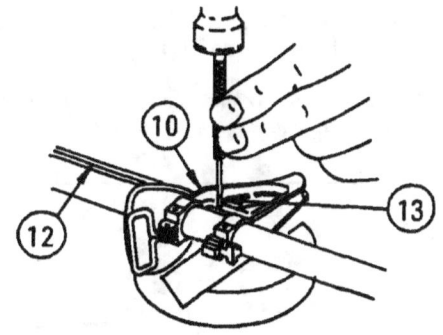

(a) Align the holes in gas tube (12) and front sight assembly base (1 O).

(b) Using ball peen hammer and 5/64-inch diameter drive pin punch, drive spring pin (13) into front sight assembly base (10) to secure gas tube (12).

3-13. UPPER RECEIVER AND BARREL ASSEMBLY (CONT).

d. REASSEMBLY (CONT)

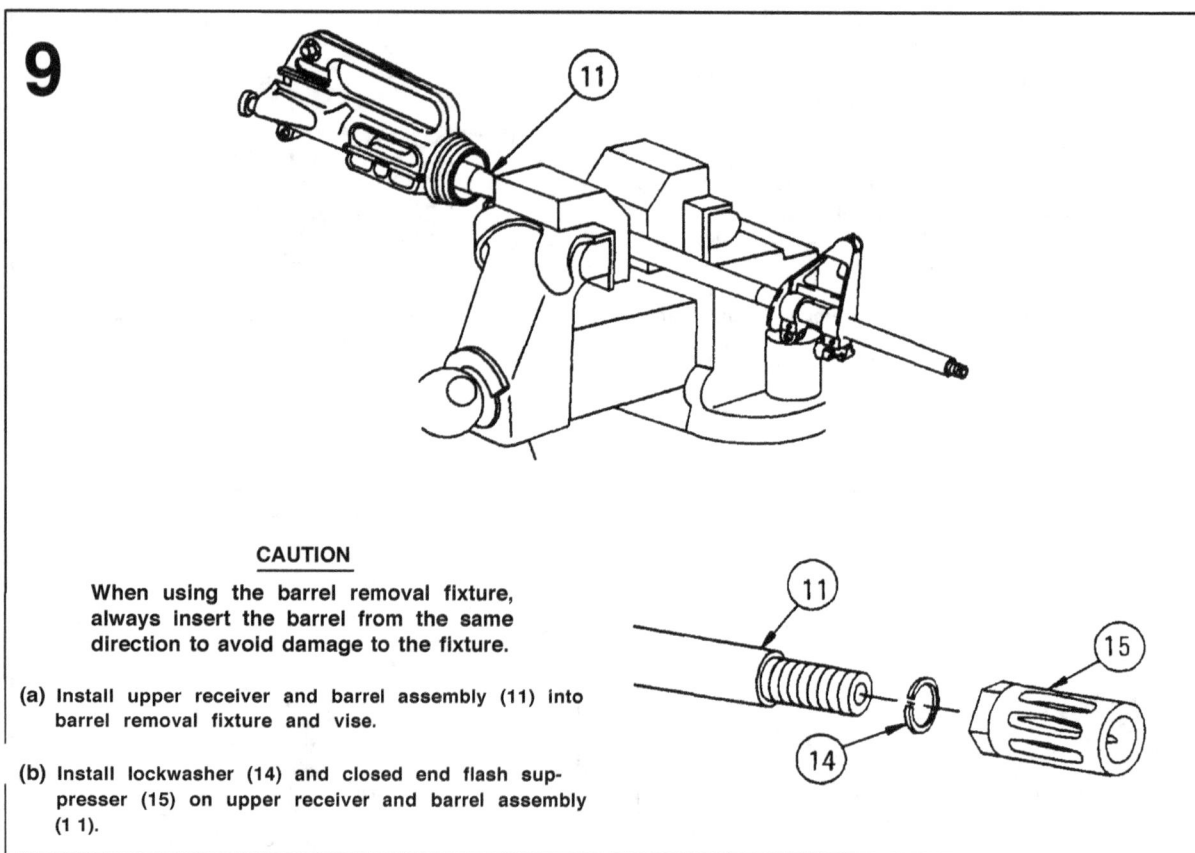

9

CAUTION

When using the barrel removal fixture, always insert the barrel from the same direction to avoid damage to the fixture.

(a) Install upper receiver and barrel assembly (11) into barrel removal fixture and vise.

(b) Install lockwasher (14) and closed end flash suppresser (15) on upper receiver and barrel assembly (11).

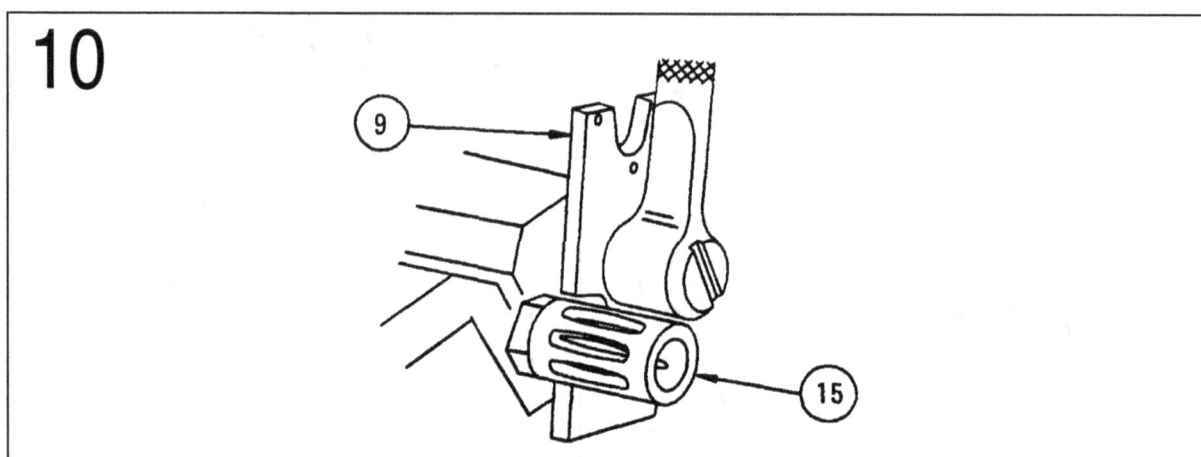

10

Torque flash suppressor (15) to 15-20 ft-lb using combination wrench (9) and torque wrench. Torque is measured when both wrenches are used together.

11

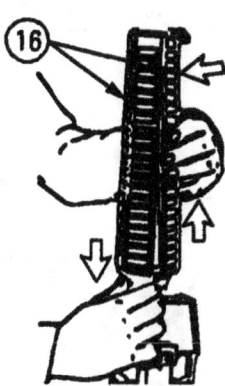

NOTE

Refer to Operator's Manual for "buddy system" procedures for installing handguards.

Install upper and lower handguards (16).

---

e. TEST

1

Determine the type of bore and chamber to be gaged.

NOTE

The following is the way to identify chromed barrels from unchromed barrels. Stampings on the barrel approximately one inch rearward from the flash suppressor are as follows

(a) (SAK MP C) SAK is the manufacturer's stamp, MP indicates magnetic partical inspection, C indicates chrome chamber only, or (C MP C) C = Colt Manufacturer, MP = magnetic partical inspection, and C = chrome chamber only.
(b) Other markings which indicate chrome chamber only are "C" alone or "RUC" or "RNC" alone. A "C" stamped on the barrel between the rings of the front sight base also indicates chromed chamber only.
(c) Markings the same as in (a) above with the last letter "B" indicate a fully chromed bore and chamber.
(d) Other markings such as "CB" alone indicate a fully chromed chamber and bore.
(e) The latest configuration is identified with the words "Chrome Bore" written out.
(f) Barrel that does not meet the above criteria is non-chrome.

2

NOTE

To insure proper operation of the gages, the barrel must be clean prior to performing the tests.

The following information pertains to the gages required for the upper receiver and barrel assembly.

(a) Barrel erosion gage, P/N 7799792, is to be used to check barrels that are not chromed. Instructions for its use are on the tag attached to the gage. The first line from the end of the gage is the reject line. The second line is no longer used.
(b) Barrel erosion gage, P/N 8448496, is to be used only on fully chromed barrels. Instructions for its use are on the tag attached to the gage.
(c) The muzzle erosion gage, P/N 8446677, is used on the unchromed barrel only. It is not required for use on chromed bore barrels. Instructions on its use are on the tag attached to the gage.
(d) The bore straightness gage, P/N 8448202, is required for use on all barrels. The gage must pass through the barrel without force.

3- 13. UPPER RECEIVER AND BARREL ASSEMBLY (CONT).

e. TEST (CONT)

3

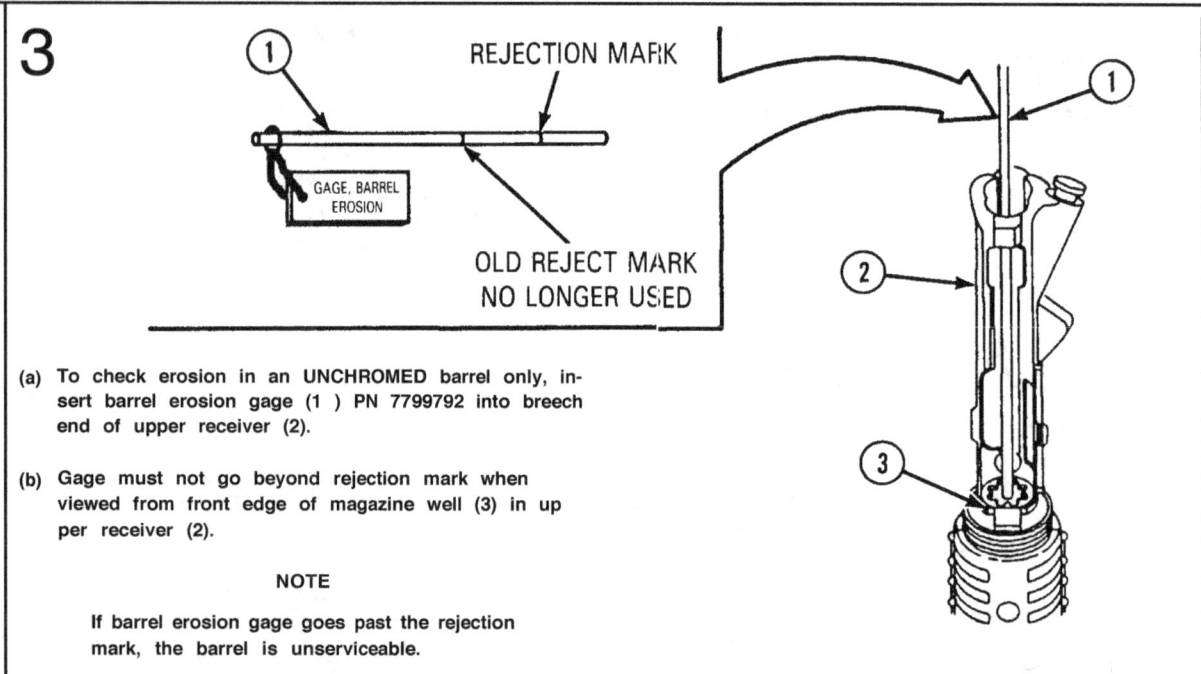

(a) To check erosion in an UNCHROMED barrel only, in- sert barrel erosion gage (1) PN 7799792 into breech end of upper receiver (2).

(b) Gage must not go beyond rejection mark when viewed from front edge of magazine well (3) in up per receiver (2).

NOTE

If barrel erosion gage goes past the rejection mark, the barrel is unserviceable.

4

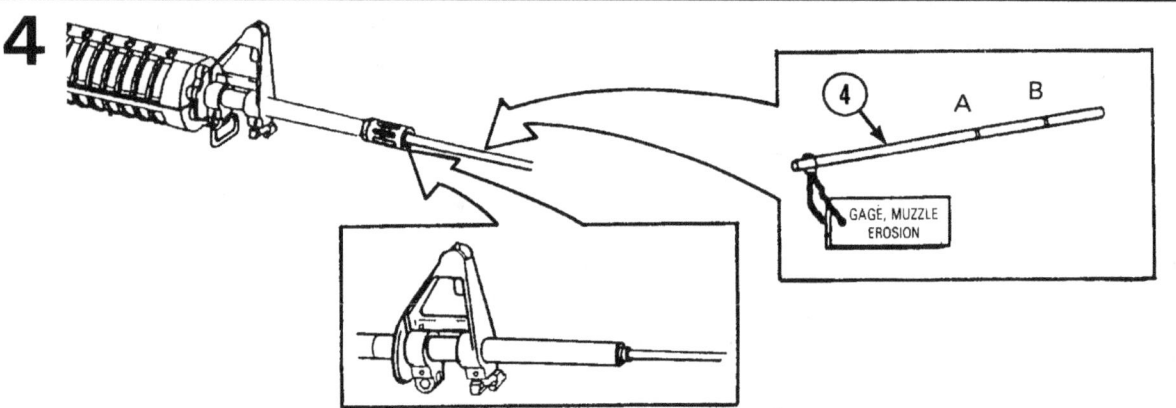

(a) To check muzzle erosion in an unchromed barrel only, insert muzzle erosion gage (4), PN 8448677, into muz- zle. Do not check muzzle erosion on chrome barrels.

(b) Gage must not go beyond applicable rejection mark or the barrel is unserviceable.

NOTE

There are two rejection marks, "A" and "B". Use rejection mark "A" when the barrel is being gaged without the flash suppressor assembled. Use rejection mark "B" when the barrel is being gaged with the flash suppressor installed.

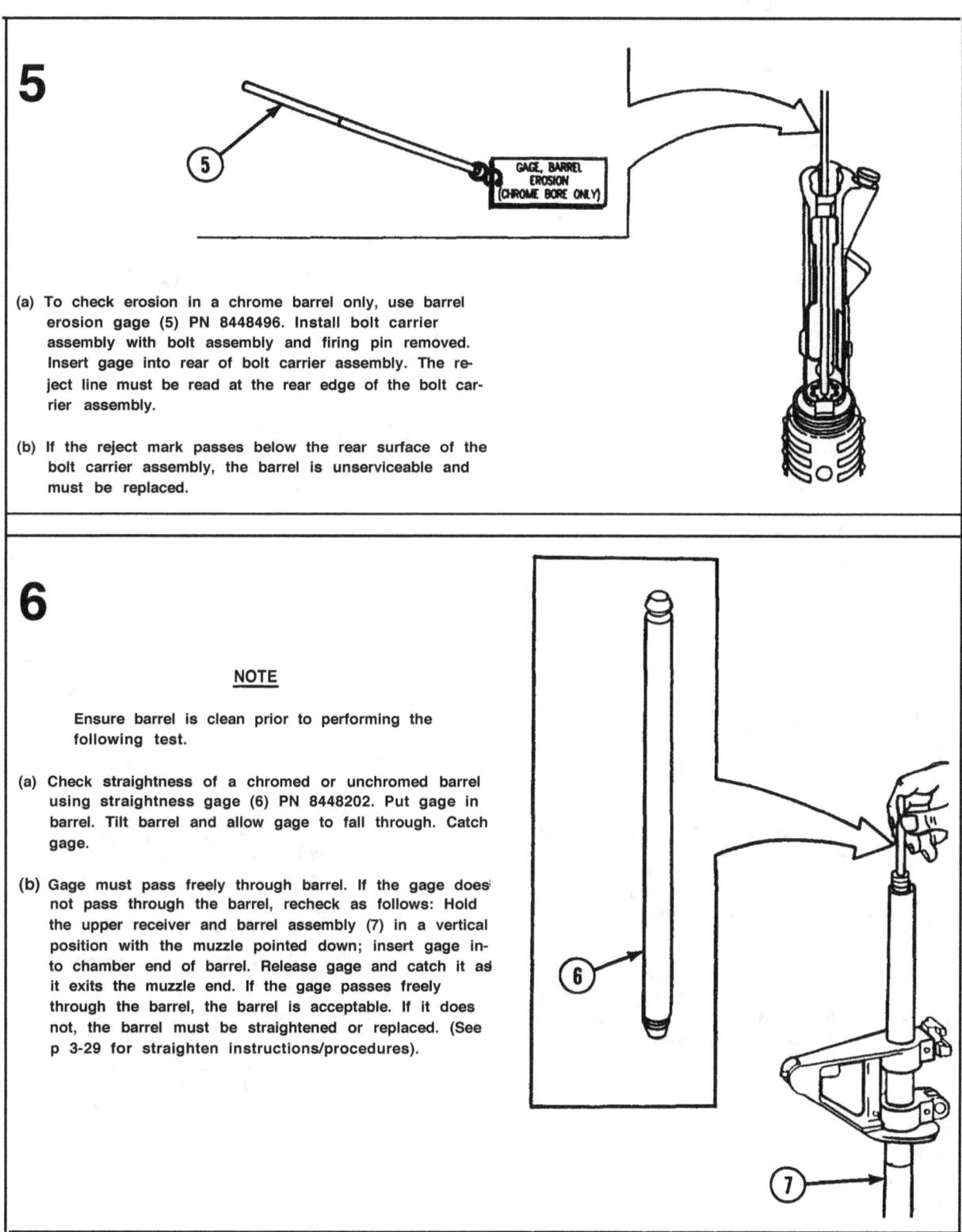

5

(a) To check erosion in a chrome barrel only, use barrel
erosion gage (5) PN 8448496. Install bolt carrier
assembly with bolt assembly and firing pin removed.
Insert gage into rear of bolt carrier assembly. The reject line must be read at the rear edge of the bolt carrier assembly.

(b) If the reject mark passes below the rear surface of the
bolt carrier assembly, the barrel is unserviceable and
must be replaced.

GAGE, BARREL
EROSION
(CHROME BORE ONLY)

6

<u>NOTE</u>

Ensure barrel is clean prior to performing the
following test.

(a) Check straightness of a chromed or unchromed barrel
using straightness gage (6) PN 8448202. Put gage in
barrel. Tilt barrel and allow gage to fall through. Catch
gage.

(b) Gage must pass freely through barrel. If the gage does
not pass through the barrel, recheck as follows: Hold
the upper receiver and barrel assembly (7) in a vertical
position with the muzzle pointed down; insert gage into chamber end of barrel. Release gage and catch it as
it exits the muzzle end. If the gage passes freely
through the barrel, the barrel is acceptable. If it does
not, the barrel must be straightened or replaced. (See
p 3-29 for straighten instructions/procedures).

3-13. UPPER RECEIVER AND BARREL **ASSEMBLY** (CONT).

---

e. TEST (CONT)

7

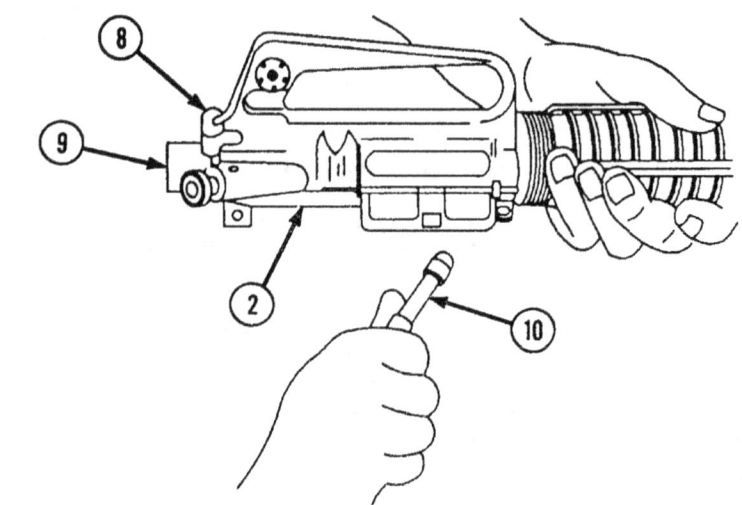

(a) Install charging handle (8), and bolt carrier assembly (9) into upper receiver (2).

(b) Insert headspace gage (10) PN 7799734 in chamber.

8

<u>NOTE</u>

For the purpose of this test "light finger pressure" is defined as 8 1/2 to 8 3/4 pounds.

(a) Check headspace by pressing bolt carrier assembly (9) and charging handle (8) forward using light finger pressure.

(b) Bolt carrier assembly (9) must protrude from rear of receiver (2) for proper headspace. If bolt carrier assembly is flush with or indented to rear surface, this indicates excessive headspace.

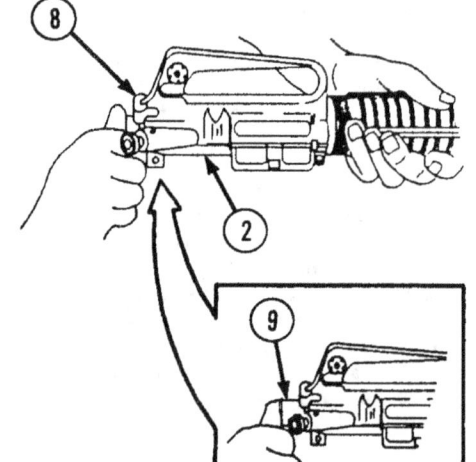

9

ARMY ONLY

(a) If the test fails using finger pressure, remove the gage and perform the test again as follows: With the muzzle down, stack 8 1/2 to 8 3/4 pounds of trigger weights (1 1) on a locally fabricated spacer/weight (12) on the bolt carrier assembly (9). Insert headspace gage (10) and test per above instructions.

(b) Remove trigger weights (11), spacer/weight (1 2), bolt carrier assembly (9), charging handle (8), and headspace gage (10).

(c) If excessive headspace, first replace bolt assembly and then recheck. if headspace is not corrected, replace barrel assembly; then recheck with the original bolt to determine if the bolt is still good or if the bolt should be replaced also.

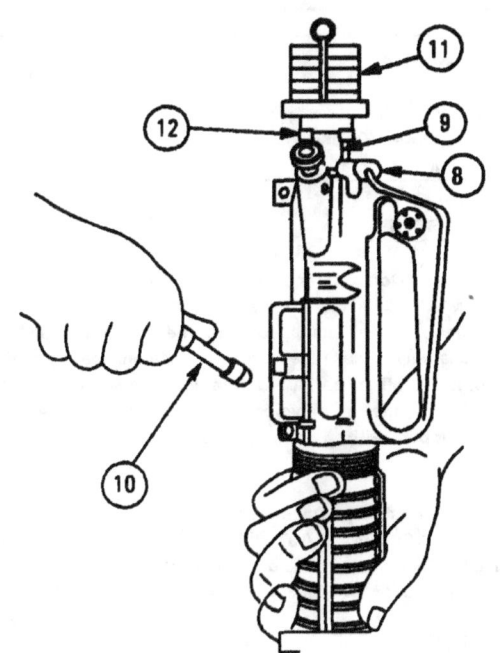

NOTE

Rifles which have been rebarreled must be function-fired with seven rounds 5.56mm of ball ammunition. After rebarreling, the rifle must be targeted with three rounds 5.56mm of ball ammunition at 25 meter range. using target. Refer to TM 9-1005-249-10 and FM 23-9.

3-14. UPPER RECEIVER ASSEMBLY.

This task covers:

a. Disassembly
b. Inspection/Repair
c. Clean

d. Lubrication
e. Reassembly
f. Mechanical Zero Procedures (A. F. only)

INITIAL SETUP

Applicable Configuration
All M16/M16A1 rifles except as noted. The M 16
rifles are not equipped with the forward assist
assembly. The receivers are different part numbers
but all other parts are interchangeable. Only the
M16A1 rifle is depicted. Some rifles may be
equipped with a low light level rear sight.

Tools
Small Arms Repairman Tool Kit
SC 5180-95-CL-A07
Field Maintenance Basic Less Power Small Arms
Shop Set SC 4933-95-CL-A11 (1 9204)

Materials/Parts
Cleaner, lubricant and preservative (CLP) (item 9,
app D)

Cloth, abrasive (item 12, app D)
Lubricant, solid film (item 19, app D)
Lubricating oil, weapons (LAW) (item 20,
app D)
Lubricating oil, weapons (LSA) (item 21,
app D)

Equipment Condition
Page   Condition Description
3-23 Upper receiver removed

General Safety Instructions
To avoid injury to your eyes, use care when removing
and installing spring-loaded parts. When using solid
film lubricant or dichloromethane, be sure the area
is well ventilated.

a. DISASSEMBLY

1

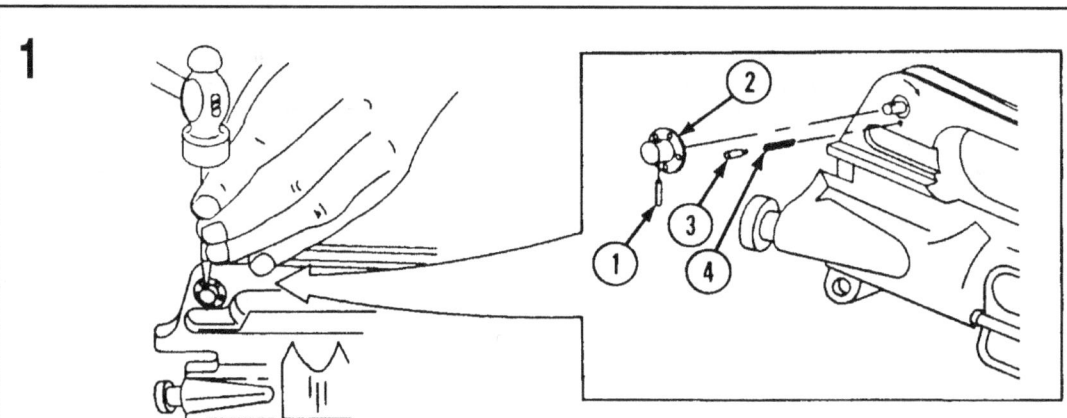

WARNING

To avoid injury to your eyes, use care when removing and installing spring-loaded parts.

CAUTION

Be sure to catch small parts (1, 2, 3, and 4)

(a) Drive out spring pin (1) using a hammer and 1/16-inch punch.

(b) Catch rear sight windage drum (2), rear sight detent (3), and helical spring (4).

2

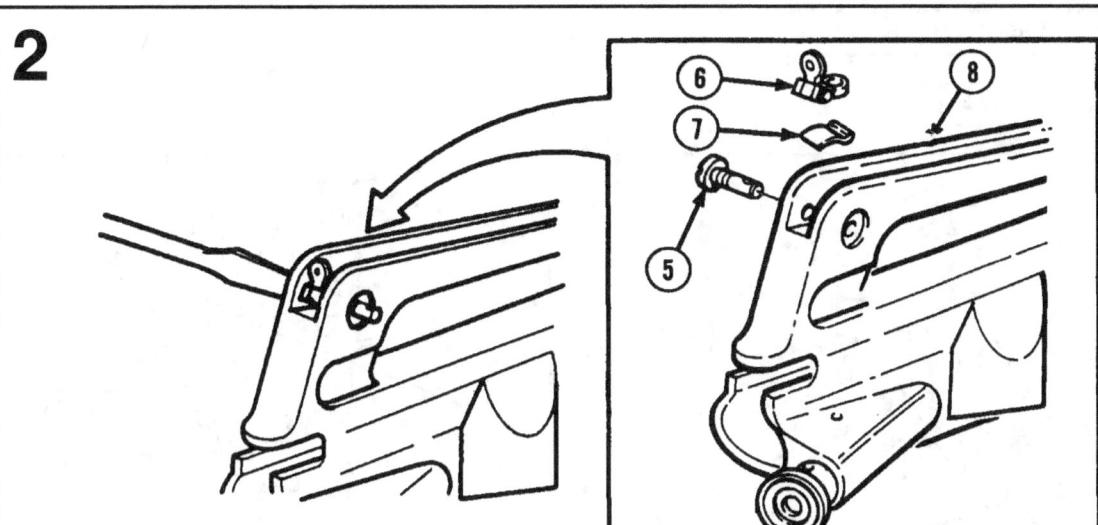

(a) Using a flat-bladed screwdriver, remove rear sight windage screw (5).

(b) Remove aperture sight (6), flat spring (7), from upper receiver (8).

NOTE

There is no further disassembly for M16 rifle upper receiver assembly. (M16 does not have forward assist assembly.)

3

NOTE

This applies to M16A1 Rifles only.

Drive out spring pin (9) using a 3/32-inch drive pin punch and hand hammer.

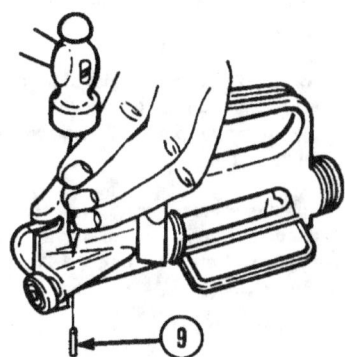

4

Remove forward assist assembly (10) and helical spring (11) from upper receiver (8).

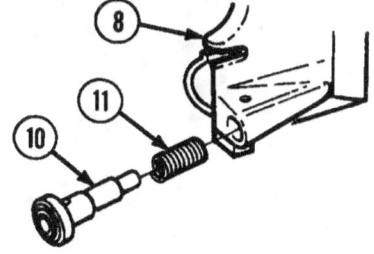

3-14. UPPER RECEIVER ASSEMBLY (CONT).

b. inspection/REPAIR

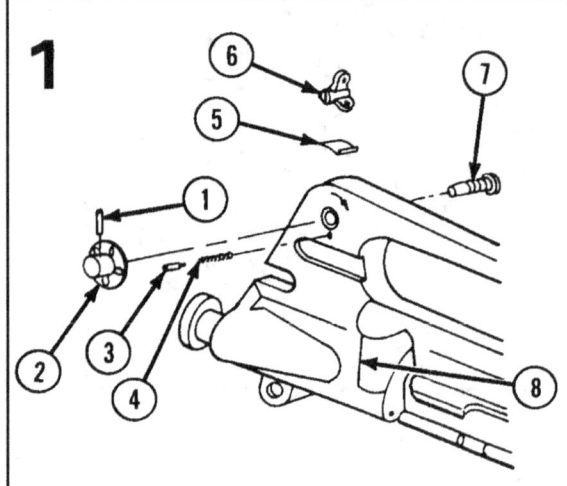

(a) Visually inspect rear sight parts (1 thru 7) for broken, bent, unserviceable condition or missing parts. Replace defective or missing parts.

b) Check helical spring (4) for serviceability, prior to disassembly and after reassembly. Replace if defective.

(c) Prior to disassembly and after reassembly, check that the flat spring (5) retains aperture sight (6) firmly in either position. Replace flat spring (5) if sight is not firm.

d) Check upper receiver (8) for cracks, corrosion, or mutilation. Repair or replace upper receiver if defective. Refer to page 3-26, inspection/ CLEANING.

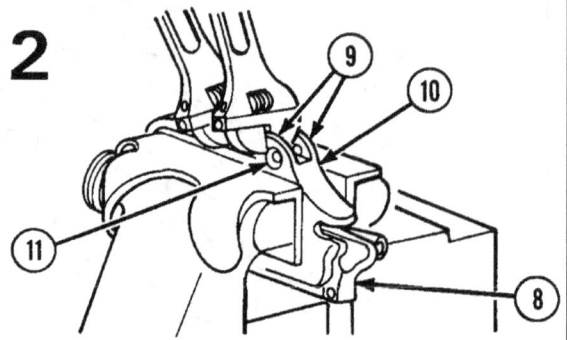

(a) To straighten bent rear sight guards (9), remove rear sight components. Place carrying handle (10) in a vise with top edge of vise at a point just below the windage screw hole (1 1). Tighten vise (11) to firmly hold upper receiver (8).

(b) Using two eight-inch adjustable wrenches, gradually bend guards (9) to straighten. When bending the guards (9), gradually bend beyond the straight point, as the guard will partially return when bending pressure is stopped.

(c) After straightening, use a flat file to remove any nicks, kinks, or burrs that remain on the inside of guards (9).

CAUTION

Do not use wire brush on aluminum surfaces.

(d) Apply solid film lubricant to brightened area for final protective coating.

(e) Replace rear sight components and check that sight functions properly. If sight functions check out, return upper receiver to service.

3

(a) Inspect upper receiver for cracks, corrosion, mutilation, wear, or damage.

    (1) Small dents or gouges that do not affect functioning will not be cause for rejection.

    (2) If receiver contains cracks or holes, the receiver will be replaced.

(b) Inspect springs for breaks, deformation, and rust.

(c) Repair corroded upper receiver surfaces as follows:

    (1) Sand corroded area with abrasive cloth and make sure all corrosion has been removed.

    (2) Wash area with technical dichloromethane (methylenechloride) to remove all dirt, grease, and foreign material.

    (3) Apply sealing compound, mixed in accordance with manufacturer's directions, to areas to be filled.

    (4) Spread sealing compound as smoothly as possible into defective area using a putty knife or similar tool.

NOTE

Do not feather edges.

    (5) Place a sheet of polyethylene, cut to size, over filled area. Rub by hand or smooth using small roller.

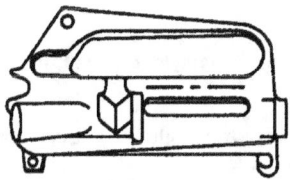

A - SHINY SURFACES
(REPARABLE)

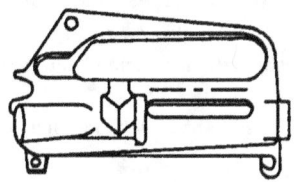

B - CORRODED
(REPARABLE)

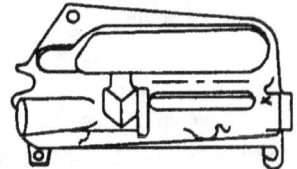

C - CORRODED
(NONREPARABLE)

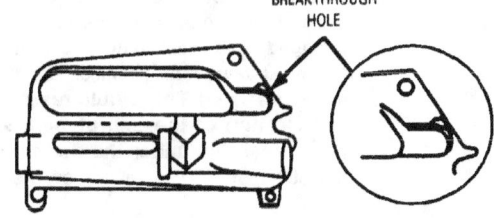

BREAKTHROUGH HOLE

D - BREAKTHROUGH HOLE
(ACCEPTABLE)

3-14. UPPER RECEIVER ASSEMBLY (CONT).

b. INSPECTION/REPAIR (CONT)

4

(a) After curing, remove polyethylene sheet in accordance with manufacturer's instructions.

WARNING

When using solid film lubricant or dichloromethane, be sure the area is well ventilated.

CAUTION

Solid film lubricant is to be used only as an exterior surface protective finish and touch up. If solid film lubricant comes in contact with recoiling parts or functional surfaces of the rifle, remove immediately by washing with technical dichloromethane.

(b) Wash area with technical dichloromethane (methylenechloride) to remove all dirt, grease, and foreign material.

(c) Roughen area to be refinished with abrasive cloth and clean surface again. Do not touch the area with fingers.

CAUTION

Do not use a wire brush on aluminum surfaces.

(d) Repair shiny surfaces by spraying a coat of solid film lubricant in accordance with manufacturer's instructions. Dry 24 hours before handling

NOTE

Solid Film Lubricant (SFL) is the authorized touch up for the M16/M16A1 Rifle and may be used on up to one third of the exterior finish of the weapon.

FOR CONUS USE ONLY: Solid Film Lubricant may be used as a touch up without limitation on the upper receiver and barrel assembly. This is to say that units which DO NOT fall under the category of Divisional Combat Units or rapid deployment type units may have up to 100% of the exterior surface of the Upper Receiver and Barrel Assembly protected with SFL. Prior to application of SFL the surface must be thoroughly clean and inspected for corrosion and/or damage. If corroded or damaged, the part must be repaired prior to application of SFL, or replaced. Continued use under combat conditions would result in an unprotected surface when the SFL wears off. This would result in a large light reflecting surface and accelerated deterioration of the unprotected surface. Therefore, Divisional Combat Units and units which fall under the definition of Rapid Deployment type must adhere to the limitation of NOT over 1/3 of their exterior surface covered by SFL

(e) Inspect all parts for damage and wear. Replace all defective parts.

c. CLEAN

Clean rear sight and forward assist portions of upper receiver and all components.

d. LUBRICATION

Lubricate upper receiver assembly. Apply CLP, LSA, or LAW (see p 2-22) to helical springs, threaded portion of screws, forward assist and sight before installation.

e. REASSEMBLY

1

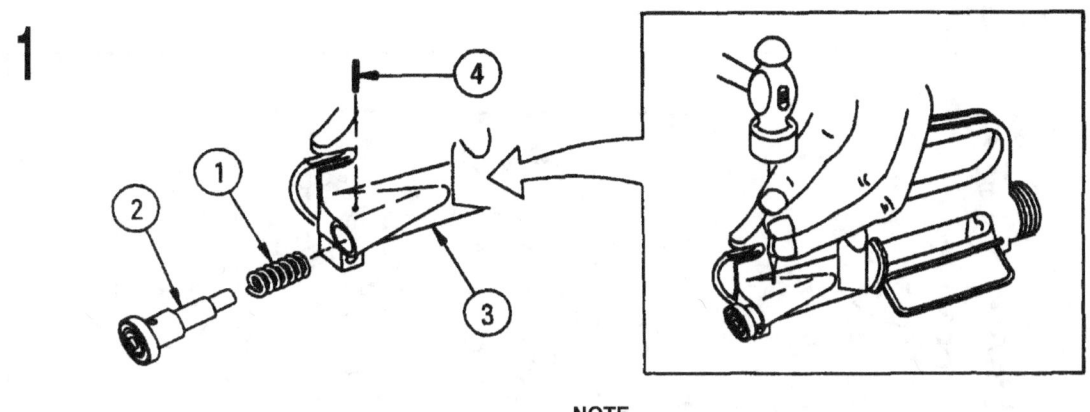

NOTE

M16A1 rifles only.

(a) Apply CLP LSA, or LAW (see p 2-22) to helical spring (1) and forward assist assembly (2) and install them into upper receiver assembly (3).

(b) Install spring pin (4) using 3/32-inch drive pin punch and hand hammer.

2

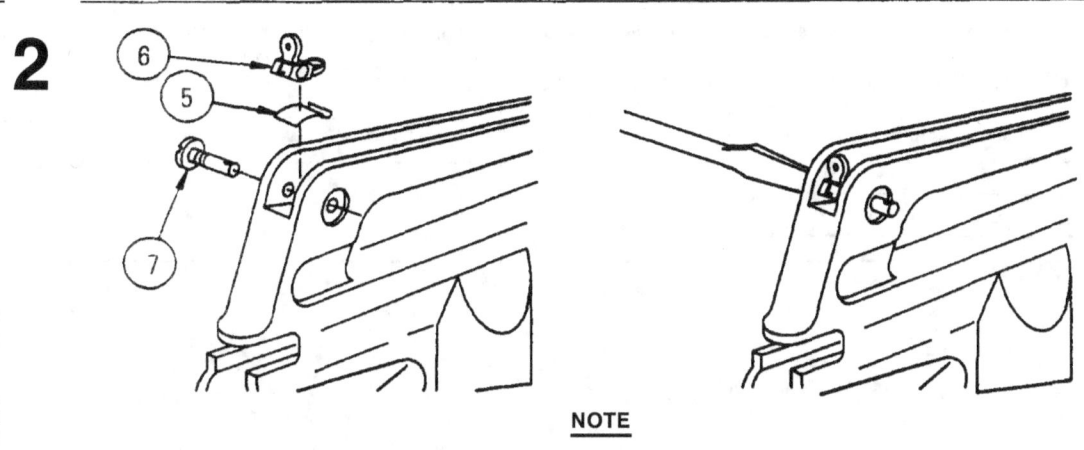

NOTE

All M16 rifles.

(a) Apply CLP, LSA or LAW (see p 2-22) to flat spring (5), aperture sight (6), and threaded portion of rear sight windage screw (7).

(b) install flat spring (5) and aperature sight (6) with letter "L" to rear.

(c) Install rear sight windage screw (7) using flat tip screwdriver. Tighten screw.

3-14. UPPER RECEIVER ASSEMBLY (CONT).

e. REASSEMBLY (CONT)

3

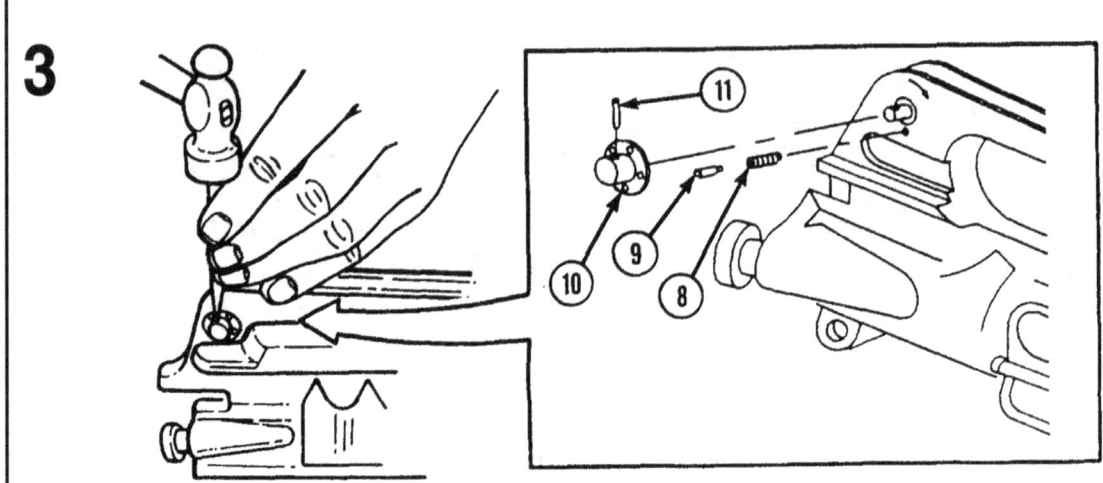

WARNING

To avoid injury to your eyes, use care when removing and installing spring-loaded parts.

(a) Install helical spring (8), rear sight detent (9), and rear sight windage drum (10).

(b) Secure by installing spring pin (1 1) using 1/16-inch drive pin punch and hand hammer.

f. MECHANICAL ZERO PROCEDURES

1

Center rear sight by moving rear sight drum in the appropriate direction.

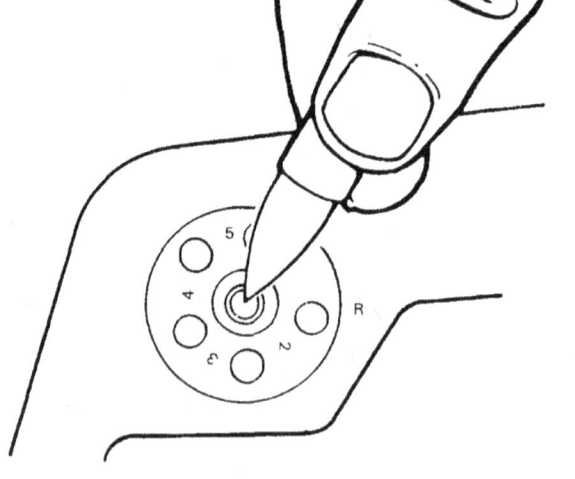

2

Always push in on bolthead after making rear sight adjustments.

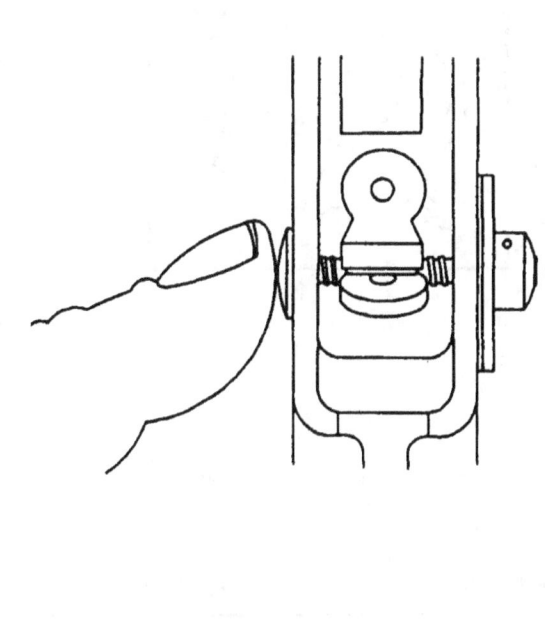

3

Visually check rear sight to ensure it is centered after making adjustments. Also, ensure the rear sight is set in the short-range (unmarked aperture) position.

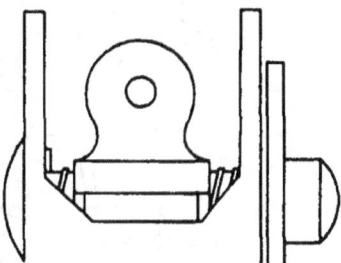

NOTE: Procedure will give an approximate battle site zero to most M 16 rifles. Once the above steps are completed, the rifle will be mechanically zeroed for 250 meters using the unmarked or short-range aperture and at 375 meters using the "L" or long-range aperture. The above steps can also be used before firing a new or newly assigned rifle. Use the procedure to check rifles stored in preferred packaging during routine inspections. This will help ensure people armed with the rifles will stand a better chance of hitting an enemy if the rifles must be used before a live fire zero can be made. Whenever possible, zeroing of the rifle should be accomplished using ball ammunition on a 25 meter zeroing target using the "L" aperture.

3-15. FORWARD ASSIST ASSEMBLY.

This task covers:

  a. Disassembly
  b. Inspection
  c. Clean

  d. Lubricate
  e. Repair
  f. Reassembly

INITIAL SETUP

Applicable Configuration
  M16A1 rifle only

Tools
  Small Arms Repairman Tool Kit
    SC 5180-95-CL-A07 (19204)
  Field Maintenance Basic Less Power Small Arms
    Shop Set SC 4933-95-CL-A11 (19204

Materials/Parts
  Cleaner, lubricant and preservative (CLP) (item 9,
    app D)

Lubricating oil, weapons (LAW) (item 20, app D)
Lubricating oil, weapons (LSA) (item 21, app D)

Equipment Condition
  Page Condition Description
  3-40 Forward assist assembly removed

General Safety Instructions
  To avoid injury to your eyes, use care when removing
    and installing spring-loaded parts.

3-15. FORWARD ASSIST ASSEMBLY (CONT).

a. DISASSEMBLY

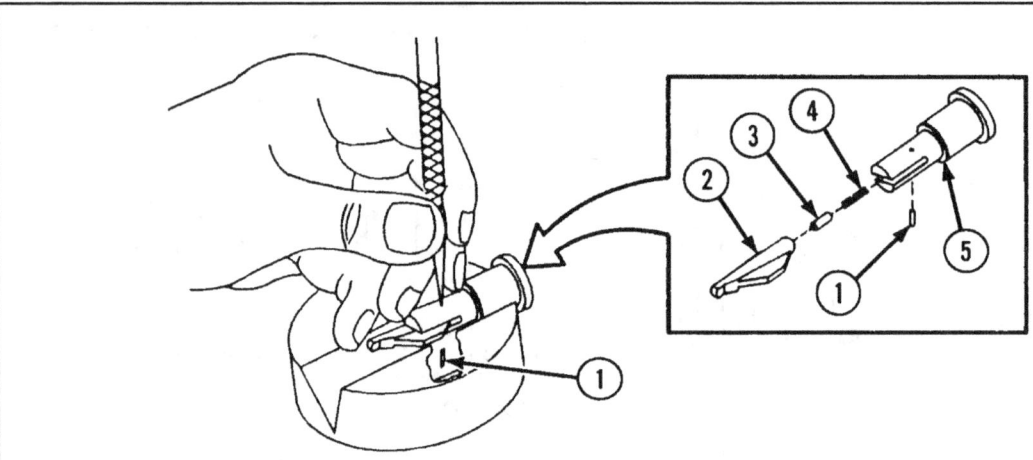

WARNING

To avoid injury to your eyes, use care when removing and installing spring-loaded parts.

1. Drive out spring pin (1) using 1/16-inch drive pin punch and hammer.

2. Remove forward assist pawl (2), pawl detent (3), helical spring (4), from plunger assembly (5).

b. INSPECTION

1. Inspect forward assist pawl (1) for deformities, burrs, chips, and cracks. Minor burrs may be removed using fine files or stones, as required. Replace pawl if defective.

2. Inspect pawl detent (2) for deformities. Replace detent if defective.

3. Inspect helical spring (3) for kinks, breaks, and wear. Replace spring if defective.

4. Inspect plunger assembly (4) for wear, burrs, chips, and breaks. Minor burrs may be removed using fine files or stones, as required. Replace if plunger assembly is defective.

5. Inspect spring pin (5) for wear or deformities. Replace if defective.

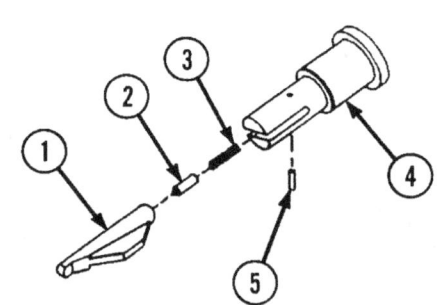

c. CLEAN

Clean all parts of the forward assist assembly.

d. LUBRICATE

Lubricate helical spring, pawl detent, and forward assist pawl with CLP, LSA, or LAW (see p 2-22) before installation.

e. REPAIR

1. Repair forward assist pawl using fine files or stones, as required, to smooth burrs. Do not deform forward assist pawl.

2. Repair plunger assembly using fine files or stones, as required, to smooth burrs. Do not deform plunger assembly.

3. Replace unrepairable parts.

f. REASSEMBLY

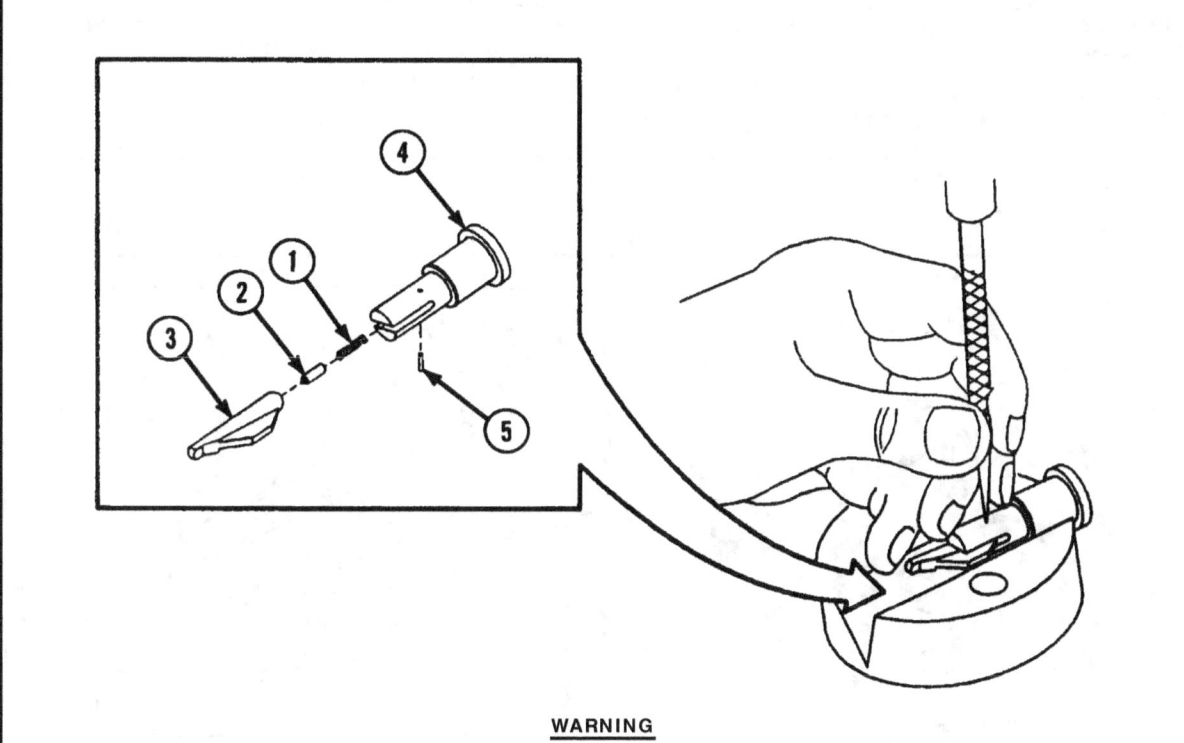

WARNING

To avoid injury to your eyes, use care when removing and installing spring-loaded parts.

1. Install helical spring (1), pawl detent (2), and forward assist pawl (3) into plunger assembly (4).

2. Align holes and install spring pin (5) using 1/16-inch drive pin punch and hammer.

3-16. LOWER RECEIVER AND EXTENSION ASSEMBLY.

This task covers:

a. Disassembly
b. Inspection
c. Repair
d. Test

e. Clean
f. Lubricate
g. Reassembly

INITIAL SETUP

Applicable Configuration
All M 16/M16A1 rifles. All parts are the same except for lower receiver body which is different only in that it specifies the different models and the serial numbers.

Test Equipment
Tool and Gage Set 8426685 (1 9204)

Tools
Small Arms Repairman Tool Kit
SC 5180-95-CL-A07 (19204)
Field Maintenance Basic Less Power Small Arms Shop Set SC 4933-95-CL-A11 (19204)
Pivot pin removing tool (locally fabricated tool) (fig E-2, app E)

Materials/Parts
Cleaner, lubricant and preservative (CLP) (item 9, app D)

Cleaning compound, rifle bore (RBC) (item 11, app D)
Dichloromethane, technical (item 14, app D)
Lubricant, solid film (item 19, app D)
Lubricating oil, weapons (LAW) (item 20, app D)
Lubricating oil, weapons (LSA) (item 21, app D)
Screw, self-locking (butt-cap screw) (item 28, p C-10)

Equipment Condition
Page Condition Description
3-10 Lower receiver and extension assembly.

General Safety Instructions
To avoid injury to your eyes, use care when removing and installing spring-loaded parts.
When using solid film lubricant or dichloromethane, be sure the area is well ventilated.

a. DISASSEMBLY

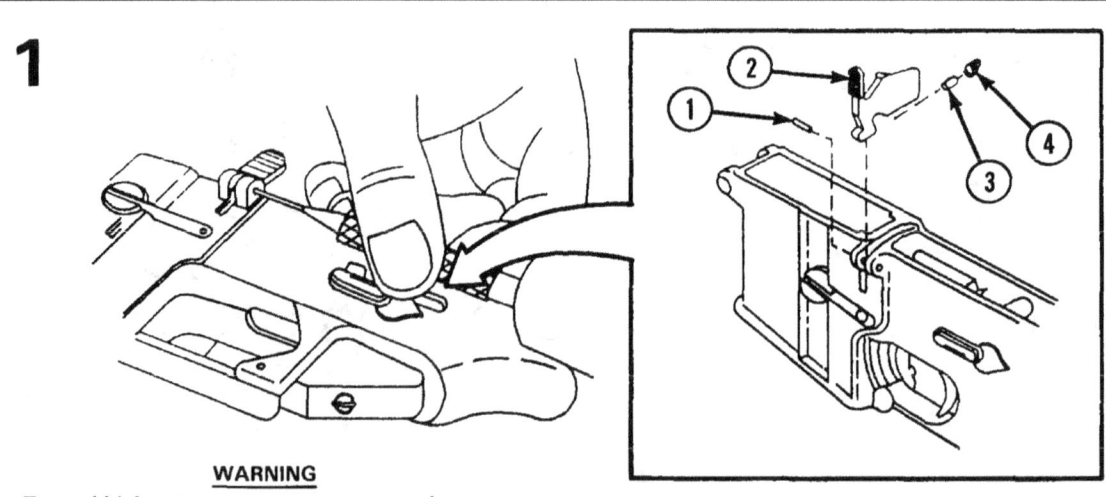

1

WARNING
To avoid injury to your eyes, use care when removing and installing spring-loaded parts.

(a) Remove spring pin (1) using 3/32-inch drive pin punch and hammer.

(b) Remove bolt catch (2), bolt catch plunger (3), and bolt catch spring (4).

2

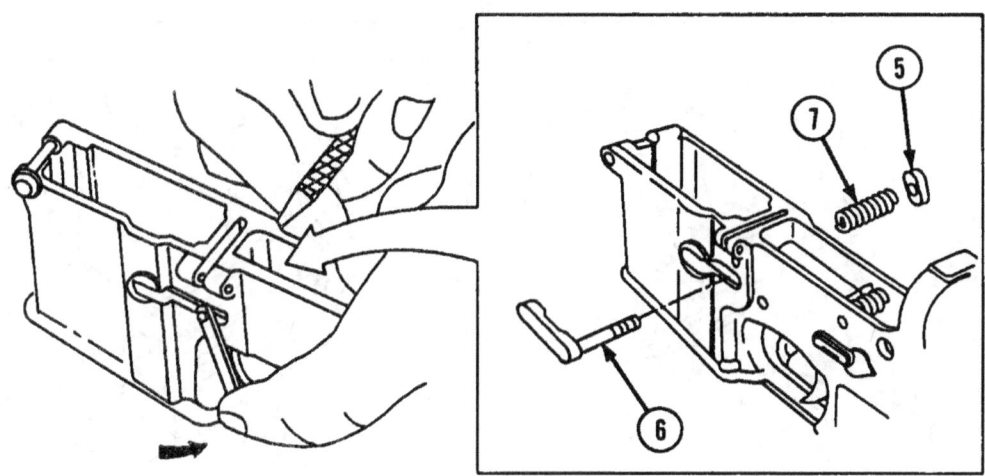

<u>WARNING</u>
To avoid injury to your eyes, use care when removing and installing spring-loaded parts.

(a) **Using drive** pin punch, press in on magazine button (5) and turn magazine catch (6) counterclockwise to unscrew and remove.

(b) Remove magazine button (5) and magazine catch spring (7)

3

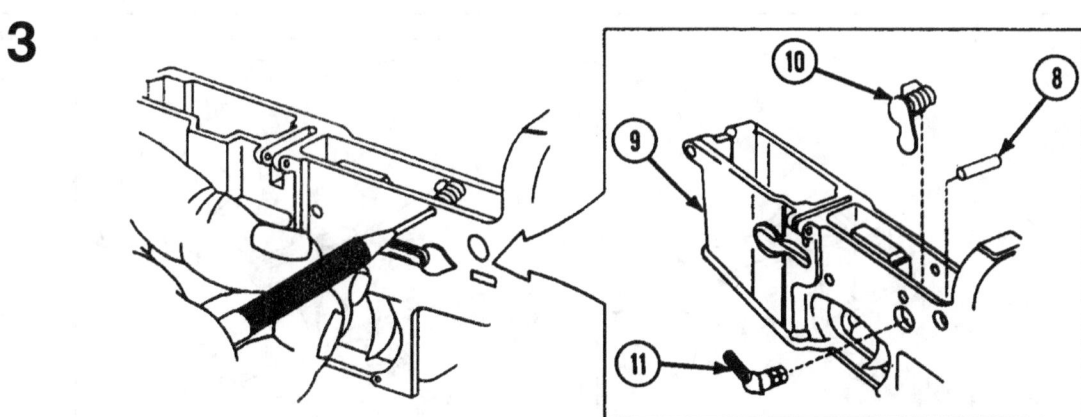

(a) **Use** a drive pin punch to push automatic sear pin (8) out of lower receiver (9).

<u>NOTE</u>
To remove sear, safety selector lever must be positioned to automatic (if installed).

(b) Remove automatic sear (10) and safety selector lever (11).

3-16. LOWER RECEIVER AND EXTENSION ASSEMBLY (CONT).

a. DISASSEMBLY (CONT)

4

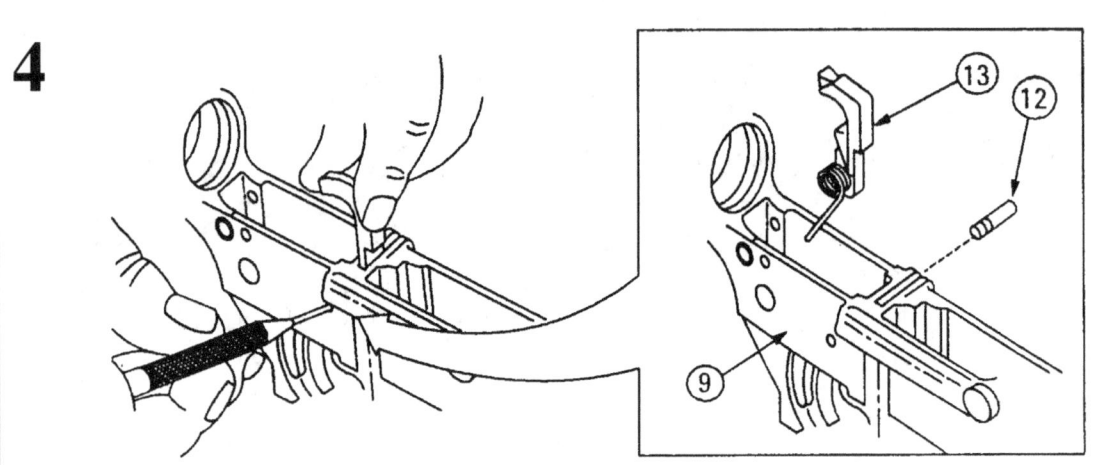

WARNING

To avoid injury to your eyes, use care when removing and installing spring-loaded parts.

NOTE

To remove (hammer should be forward), place safety selector lever (if installed) to SEMI position.

(a) Use drive pin punch to push hammer pin (12) from lower receiver (9).

(b) Remove hammer assembly (13).

5

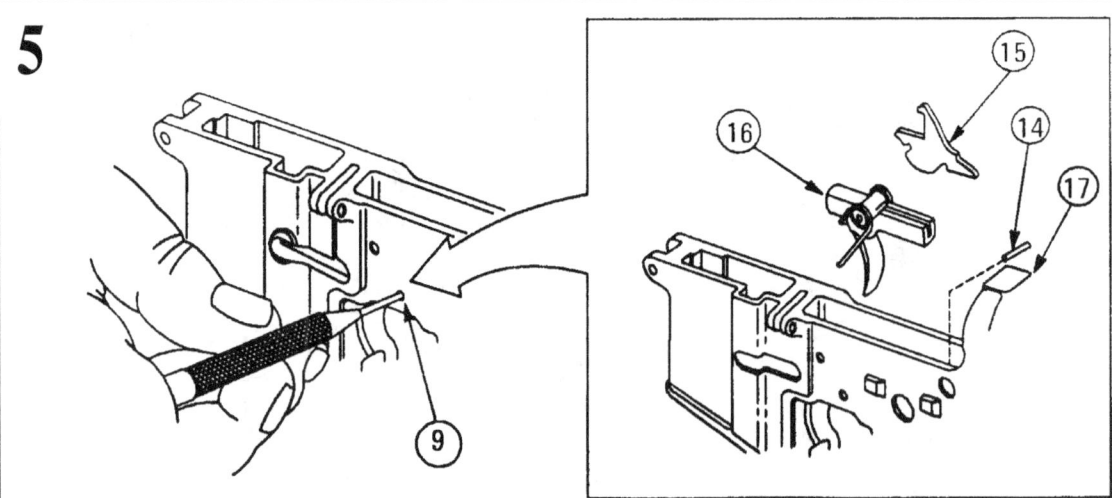

(a) Remove trigger pin (14) by pushing from the left side of lower receiver (9) with a drive pin punch.

(b) Remove disconnector (15) and trigger assembly (16) from lower receiver and extension subassembly (1 7).

b. INSPECTION

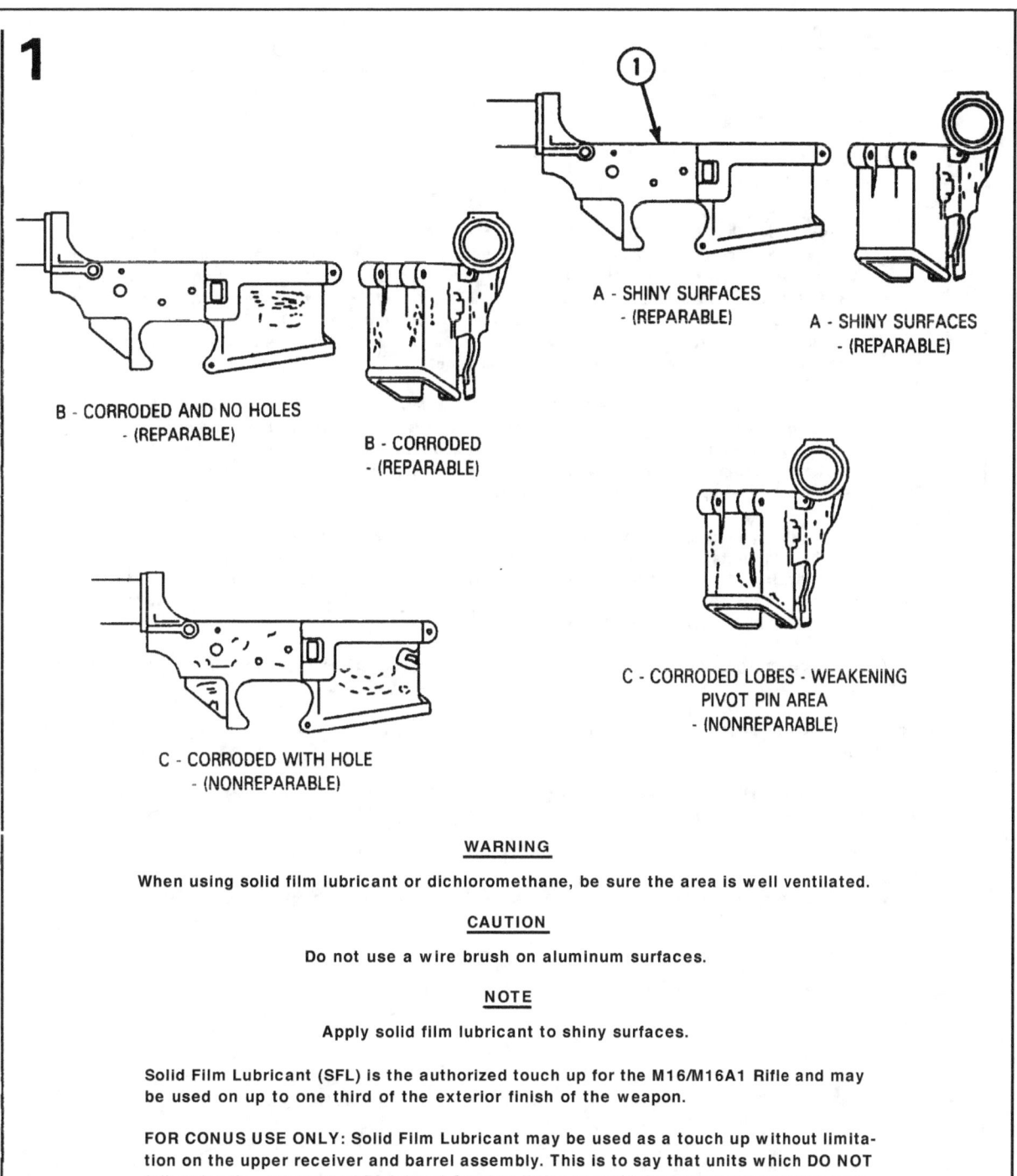

1

A - SHINY SURFACES
- (REPARABLE)

A - SHINY SURFACES
- (REPARABLE)

B - CORRODED AND NO HOLES
- (REPARABLE)

B - CORRODED
- (REPARABLE)

C - CORRODED WITH HOLE
- (NONREPARABLE)

C - CORRODED LOBES - WEAKENING
PIVOT PIN AREA
- (NONREPARABLE)

WARNING

When using solid film lubricant or dichloromethane, be sure the area is well ventilated.

CAUTION

Do not use a wire brush on aluminum surfaces.

NOTE

Apply solid film lubricant to shiny surfaces.

Solid Film Lubricant (SFL) is the authorized touch up for the M16/M16A1 Rifle and may be used on up to one third of the exterior finish of the weapon.

FOR CONUS USE ONLY: Solid Film Lubricant may be used as a touch up without limitation on the upper receiver and barrel assembly. This is to say that units which DO NOT fall under the category of Divisional Combat Units or rapid deployment type units may have up to 100% of the exterior surface of the Upper Receiver and Barrel Assembly

3-16. LOWER RECEIVER AND EXTENSION ASSEMBLY (CONT).

b. INSPECTION (CONT)

1 (CONT)

NOTE (CONT)

protected with SFL. Prior to application of SFL the surface must be thoroughly clean and inspected for corrosion and/or damage. If corroded or damaged, the part must be repaired or replaced prior to application of SFL. Continued use under combat conditions would result in an unprotected surface when the SFL wears off. This would result in a large light reflecting surface and accelerated deterioration of the unprotected surface. Therefore, Divisional Combat Units and units which fall under the definition of Rapid Deployment type must adhere to the limitation of NOT over 1/3 of their exterior surface covered by SFL.

If a M16/M16A1 Rifle LOWER RECEIVER is missing one third or more of its exterior protective finish, resulting in an unprotected/light reflecting surface, it is candidate for overhaul. This missing finish will be considered a shortcoming. This shortcoming requires action to obtain a replacement weapon. Once a replacement has been received, evacuate the original weapon to depot for overhaul.

Once the missing exterior protective finish of the lower receiver has exceeded one third of its total surface the probability of reclaiming the receiver during overhaul diminishes rapidly. In order to extend the life of the lower receiver, which is the serial numbered item, it is necessary to evacuate the weapon to depot once the missing finish reaches one third of the total surface of the receiver.

(a) Inspect lower receiver and extension subassembly (1) for corrosion in the lower receiver lobes of the pivot area or hinge pin area.

(b) If extensive corrosion appears in these areas the receiver will not be repaired and rifle will be turned in for replacement.

(c) Inspect selector lever stops. If either is missing or damaged/worn to the point of being nonfunctional, the rifle will be turned in for replacement.

NOTE

Refer to page 3-53, INSPECTION/CLEANING for repair procedures for corroded surfaces

2

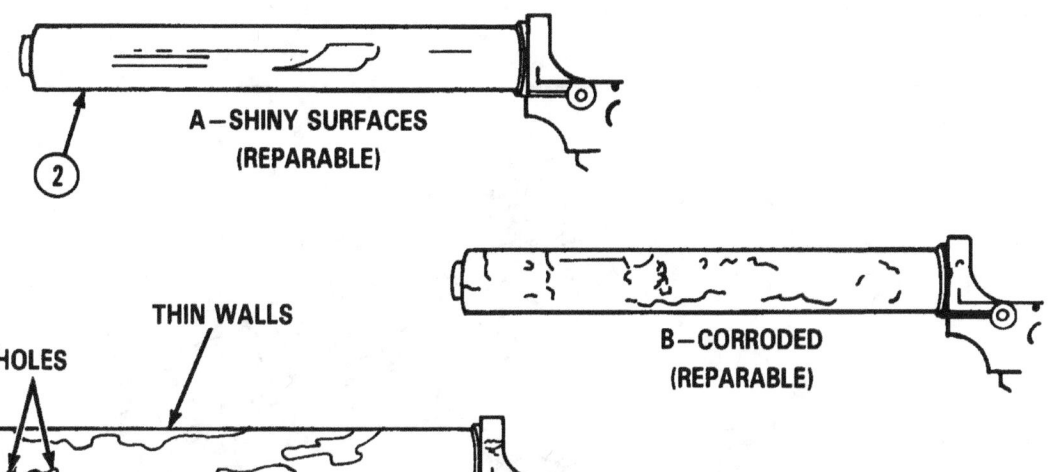

A—SHINY SURFACES
(REPARABLE)

B—CORRODED
(REPARABLE)

THIN WALLS

HOLES

C—HOLES AND THIN WALLS
(NONREPARABLE)

Inspect extension (2) portion of lower receiver and extension subassembly for corrosion. Repair or replace if defective.

<u>NOTE</u>

Refer to page 3-53, INSPECTION/CLEANING for repair procedures for corroded surfaces.

3

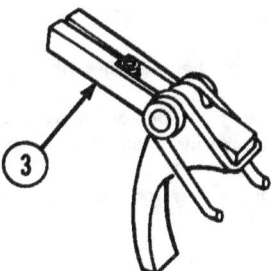

Inspect trigger assembly (3) for cracks or deformities. Inspect trigger for wear, cracks or deformities. Replace all defective components.

c. REPAIR

Repair or replace all parts of lower receiver and extension assembly if defective.

3-16. LOWER RECEIVER AND EXTENSION ASSEMBLY (CONT)

d. TEST

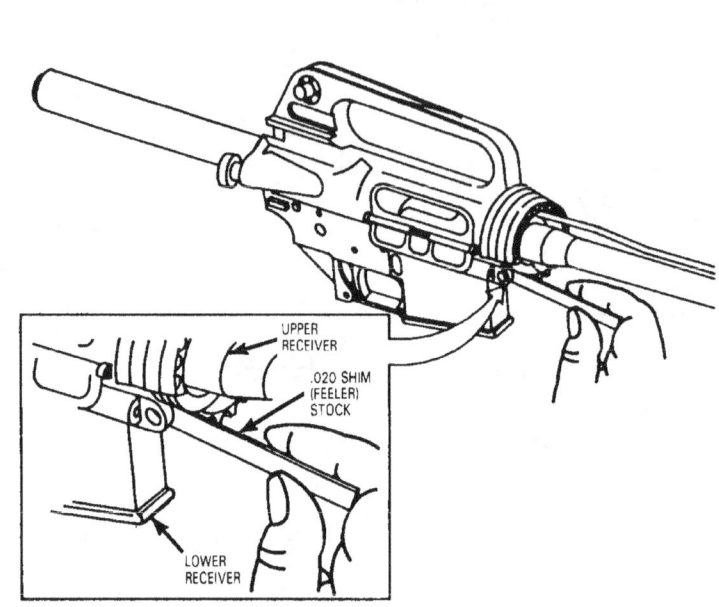

1. With the upper receiver attached to the lower receiver, and the pivot pin and takedown pin in place, perform the following test:

(a) Apply hand pressure to push the upper receiver as far to one side as possible

(b) Attempt to insert a .020" thickness gage between the pivot pin lugs of the upper and lower receivers

(c) If the thickness gage penetrates to the pivot pin at all accessible locations, repair by replacement of the upper receiver (see para 2 below) or replacement of weapon is required.

2. If the rifle fails the above test, remove the upper receiver and install a "NEW" upper receiver and perform the test again.

3. If the rifle now passes the above test, it shall be considered serviceable and continue in use

4. If the rifle fails the test with a new upper receiver, this failure shall be considered a shortcoming. This shortcoming requires action to obtain a replacement weapon, Once a replacement has been received, evacuate the original weapon to depot for overhaul.

NOTE

Failure of any portion of this test is considered a shortcoming until such time as a replacement weapon or repair parts are received.

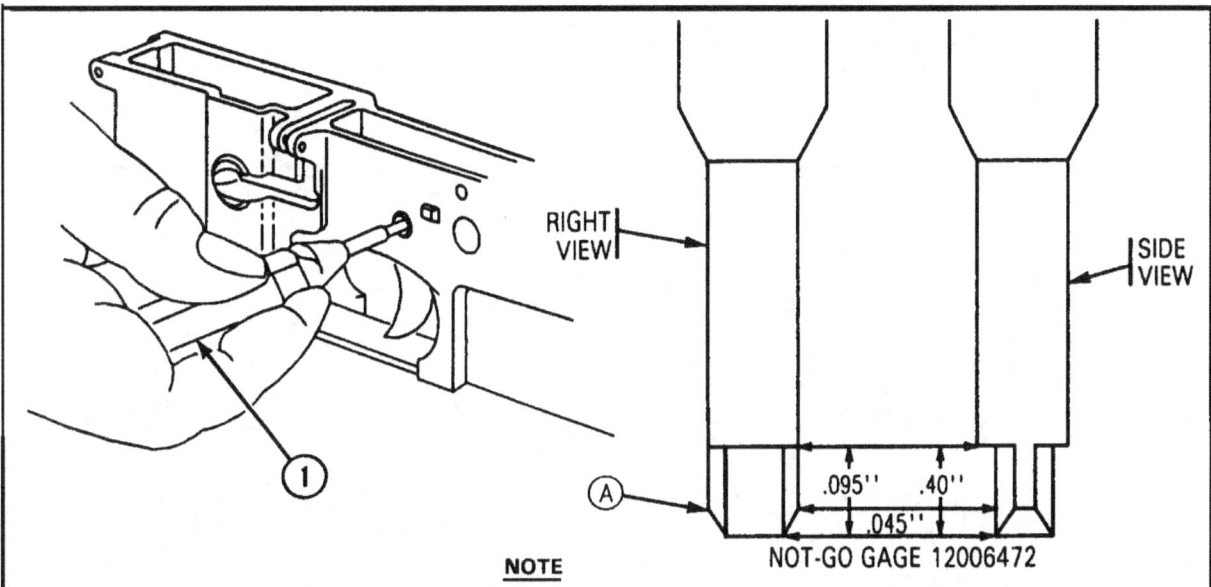

RIGHT VIEW

SIDE VIEW

.095'' .40''
.045''

NOT-GO GAGE 12006472

NOTE

If the lower receiver is not disassembled, visually inspect for broken or damaged parts, and insure that the hammer and trigger springs are correctly installed before beginning this test. It is not necessary to disassemble the lower receiver for the sole purpose of this visual inspection. If broken or damaged parts are found, disassemble (p 3-50) and repair as authorized.

5. Test two hammer pin holes and two trigger pin holes using not-go plug gage (1) P/N 12006472. This test may be conducted by disassembly of the lower receiver (p 3-50) or by pushing the pin far enough to disengage the end of the pin from the side of the receiver which is being tested. If the lower receiver is not disassembled and the not-go plug gage enters any hole to first shoulder (A) the lower receiver must be disassembled and all four holes must be tested again.

6. Gently insert the not-go plug gage and rotate it 180 degrees. If the no-go plug gage passes through any of the four pin holes, the rifle is unserviceable and will be turned in for replacement. The gage must penetrate through the wall thickness to be unserviceable.

---

e. CLEAN

WARNING

When using technical dichloromethane, be sure the area is well ventilated.

Clean lower receiver and extension assembly with technical dichloromethane.

---

f. LUBRICATE

WARNING

When using solid film lubricant be sure the area is well ventilated.

Lubricate all items with CLP, LSA, or LAW (p 2-22) before reassembly.

3-16. LOWER RECEIVER AND EXTENSION ASSEMBLY (CONT).

g. REASSEMBLY

1

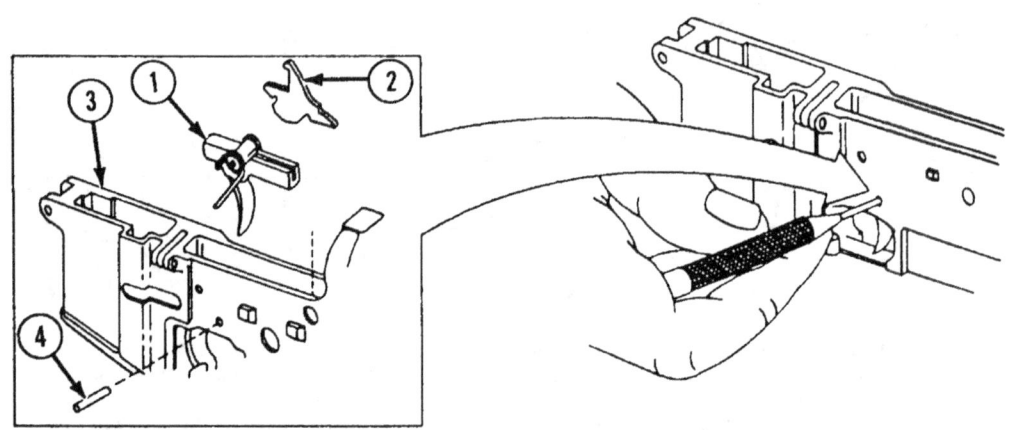

(a) Install trigger assembly (1) and disconnector (2) into lower receiver and extension subassembly (3).

(b) Install trigger pin (4) using drive pin punch. Push in until flush.

2

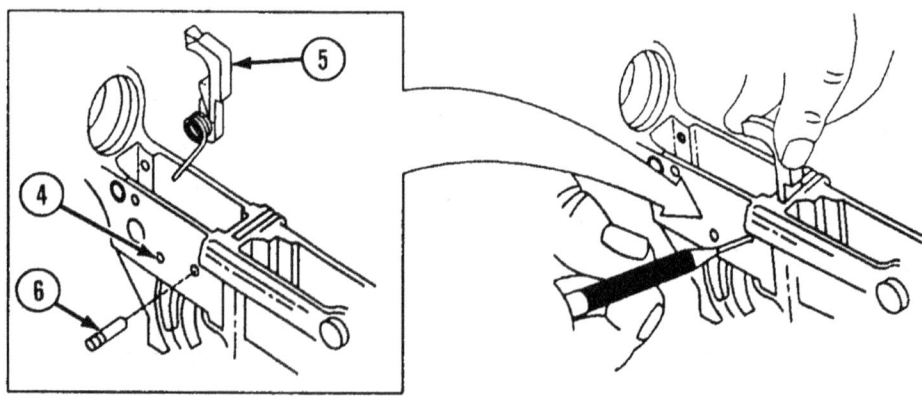

<u>NOTE</u>

Ends of hammer spring are installed to rear of trigger pin (4), resting in the annular groove on upper surface of trigger pin (4).

(a) Install hammer assembly (5).

(b) Install hammer pin (6) using drive pin punch. Push in until flush.

3

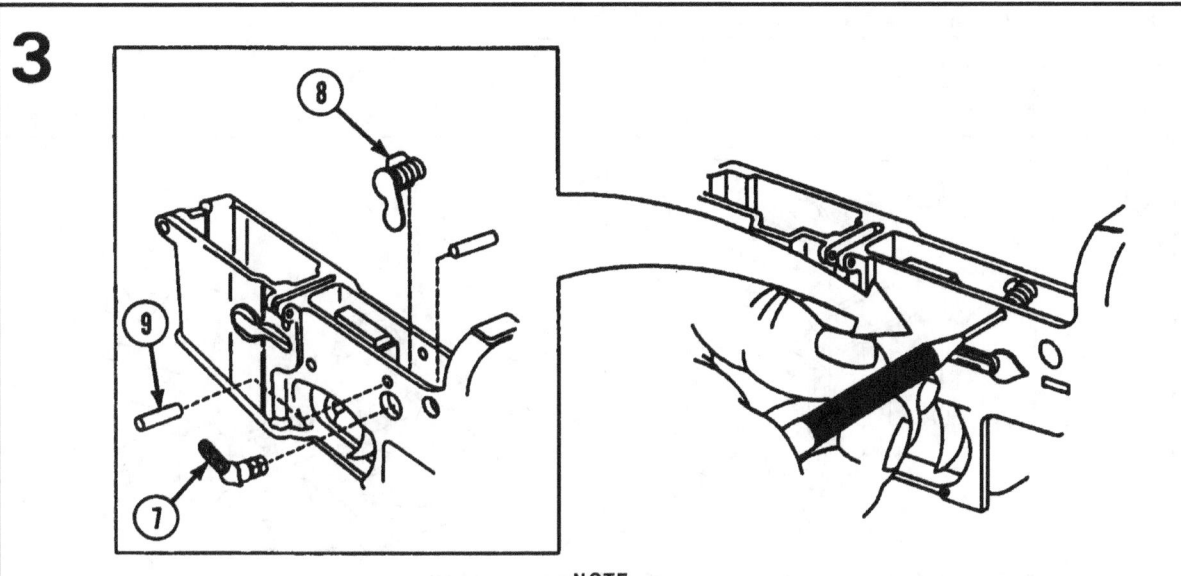

<u>NOTE</u>

Selector lever (7), if installed, must be positioned in automatic. Long leg of automatic sear (8) spring must rest on top of selector lever.

(a) Install selector lever (7) and automatic sear (8).

(b) install automatic sear pin (9) into receiver using drive pin punch. Push in until flush.

4

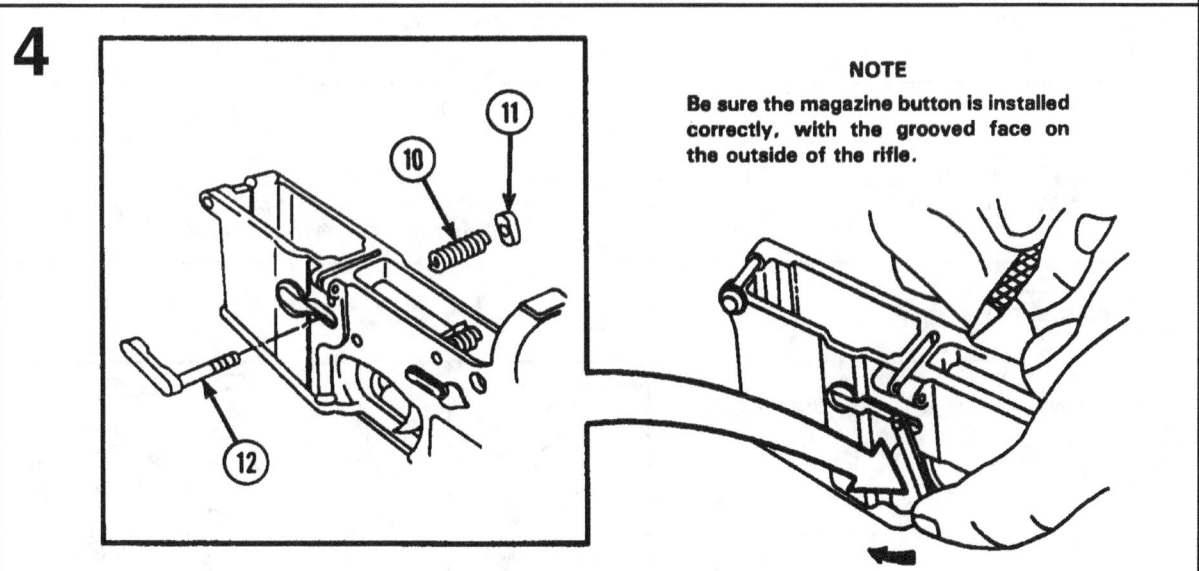

NOTE

Be sure the magazine button is installed correctly, with the grooved face on the outside of the rifle.

(a) Install magazine catch spring (10) and magazine button (11).

(b) Install magazine catch (12). Push in on magazine button (1 1) using a drive pin punch and turn magazine catch (12) clockwise until threaded end of catch is flush with magazine button head.

3-16. LOWER RECEIVER AND EXTENSION ASSEMBLY (CONT).

g. REASSEMBLY (CONT)

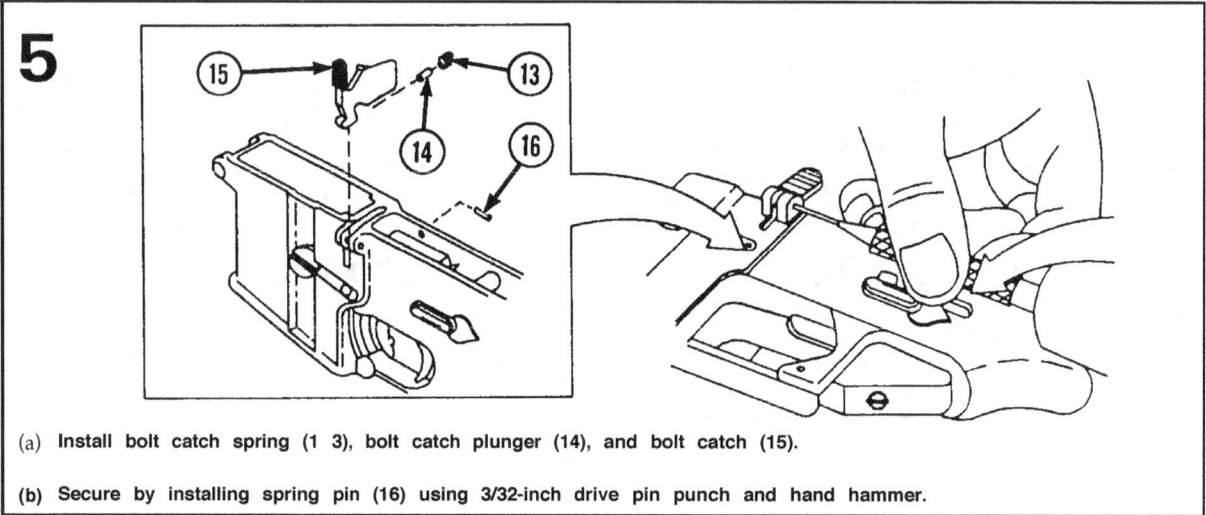

5

(a) Install bolt catch spring (1 3), bolt catch plunger (14), and bolt catch (15).

(b) Secure by installing spring pin (16) using 3/32-inch drive pin punch and hand hammer.

3-17. HAMMER ASSEMBLY.

This task covers:

a. Inspection
b. Repair

c. Reassembly

INITIAL SETUP

Applicable Configuration
   All M16/M16A1 Rifles

Equipment Condition
   Page Condition Description
   3-50 Hammer assembly removed

a. DISASSEMBLY

Remove hammer spring (1) from hammer (2).

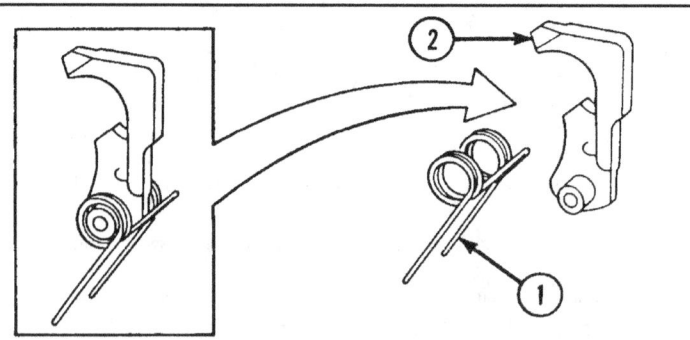

b. inspection/REPAIR

1. Inspect hammer spring for deformities, breaks, and bends. Replace if defective.

2. Inspect hammer for chips and breaks and excessive wear on automatic sear notch, disconnector notch, or sear notch. Replace if defective.

3. Install hammer pin into hole in hammer to check if the spring retains the hammer pin.

c. REASSEMBLY

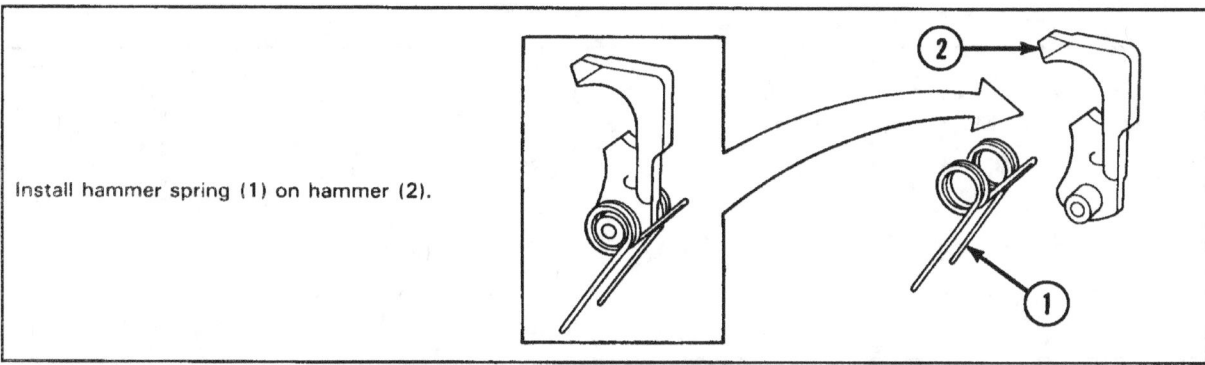

Install hammer spring (1) on hammer (2).

3-18. TRIGGER ASSEMBLY.

This task covers:

a. Disassembly
b. Inspection/Repair

c. Reassembly

INITIAL SETUP

Applicable Configuration
  All M16/M16A1 Rifles

General Safety Instructions
  To avoid injury to your eyes, use care when removing
  and installing spring-loaded parts.

Equipment Condition
  Page   Condition Description
3-50 Trigger assembly removed

a. DISASSEMBLY

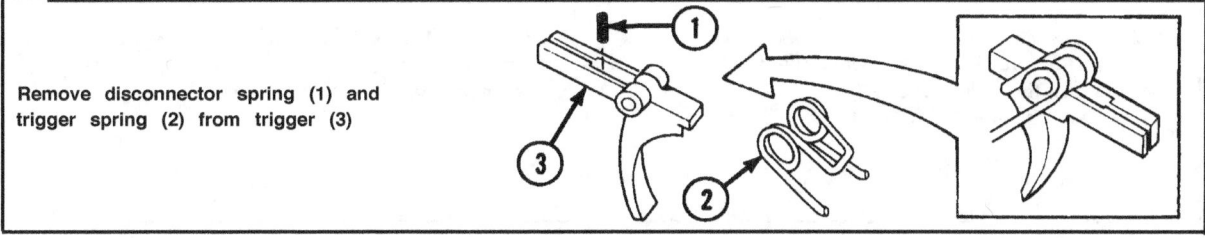

Remove disconnector spring (1) and trigger spring (2) from trigger (3)

3-18. TRIGGER ASSEMBLY (CONT).

b. INSPECTION/REPAIR

1. Inspect trigger spring for kinks, deformities, and weakness. Replace if defective.

2. Inspect disconnector spring for deformities, bends, breaks, and weakness. Replace If defective.

3. Inspect trigger for chips and cracks and excessive wear on trigger nose. Replace if defective.

c. REASSEMBLY

1. Install disconnector spring (1) by inserting large end of spring into trigger (2).

2. Install trigger spring (3) on trigger (2).

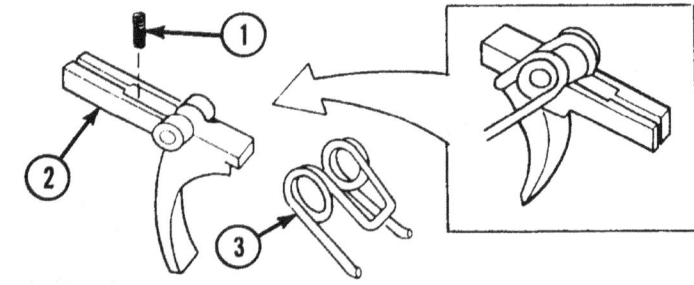

3-19. LOWER RECEIVER AND EXTENSION SUBASSEMBLY.

This task covers:

a. Disassembly
b. Inspection
c. Repair/Modify

d. Test
e. Reassembly

INITIAL SETUP

Applicable Configuration
All M16/M16A1 rifles. The lower receivers have serial numbers and model numbers and will not be replaced by Direct Support Maintenance.

Test Equipment
Tool and Gage Set 8426685 (1 9204)

Tools
Field Maintenance Basic Less Power Small Arms Shop Set SC 4933-95-CL-A11 (19204)
Small Arms Repairman Tool Kit SC 5180-95-CL-A07 (19204)

Materials/Parts
Cloth, abrasive (item 12, app D)
Grease, molybdenum disulfide (item 17, app D)
Lubricant, solid film (item 19, app D)

Equipment Condition
Page Condition Description
3-50 Lower receiver and extension subassembly removed.

General Safety Instructions
To avoid injury to your eyes, use care when removing and installing spring-loaded parts.

a. DISASSEMBLY

1

(a) Remove spring pin (1) from lower receiver and extension subassembly (2) using 1/8-inch drive pin punch and hammer.

(b) Remove trigger guard (3).

2

<u>NOTE</u>

Old type receiver extension requires removal discard of spring pin (4).

(a) If spring pin (4) is installed, remove and discard.

(b) Modify lower receiver extension prior to reassembly. See page 3-65, REPAIR/MODIFY.

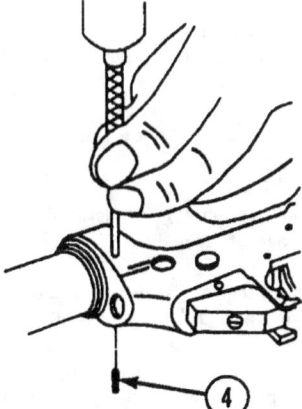

3-19. LOWER RECEIVER AND EXTENSION SUBASSEMBLY (CONT).

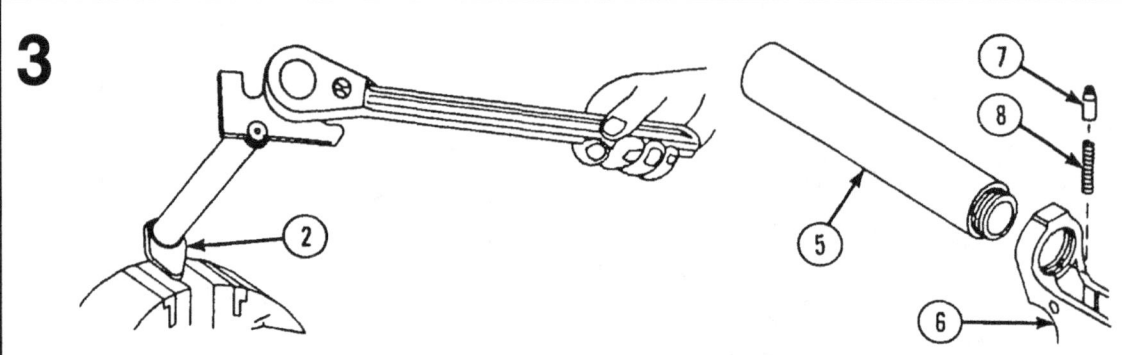

WARNING

To avoid injury to your eyes, use care when removing and installing spring-loaded parts.

NOTE

Grip the solid portion of the lower receiver with wooden or brass vise jaws. Use wooden vise jaws instead of brass vise jaw caps if available.

(a) Clamp lower receiver and extension subassembly (2) in a machinist's vise using vise jaw caps and tighten on solid portion just tight enough to hold,

NOTE

As lower receiver extension is removed, catch buffer retainer and spring. Lower receiver is a serial number controlled item.

(b) Remove lower receiver extension (5) from lower receiver (6) using combination wrench and socket wrench handle. Catch buffer retainer (7) and helical spring (8).

b. INSPECTION

1. Inspect lower receiver extension (1) for corrosion, dents, and wear. Repair or replace if defective. See page 3-55, REPAIR.

2. Inspect buffer retainer (2) for wear and replace if defective.

3. Inspect helical spring (3) for deformities and breaks. Replace if defective,

4. Inspect lower receiver (4) for corrosion, wear, and damage, See page 3-53, INSPECTION.

5. Inspect trigger guard (5) for deformities and check operation of plunger and spring (6). Replace trigger guard if defective.

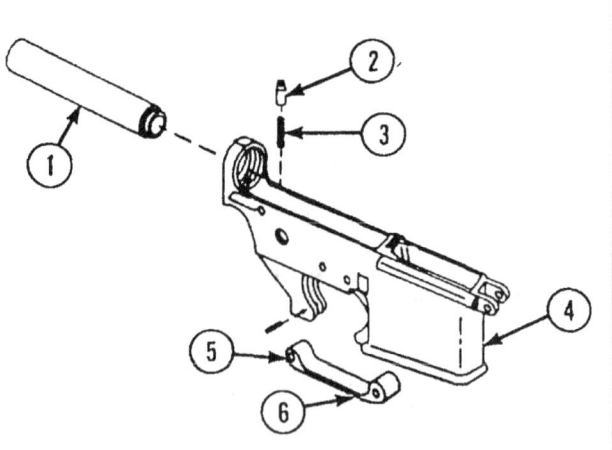

c. REPAIR/MODIFY

1

Repair lower receiver extension (1) by using abrasive cloth to remove light corrosion. Retouch using solid film lubricant,

2

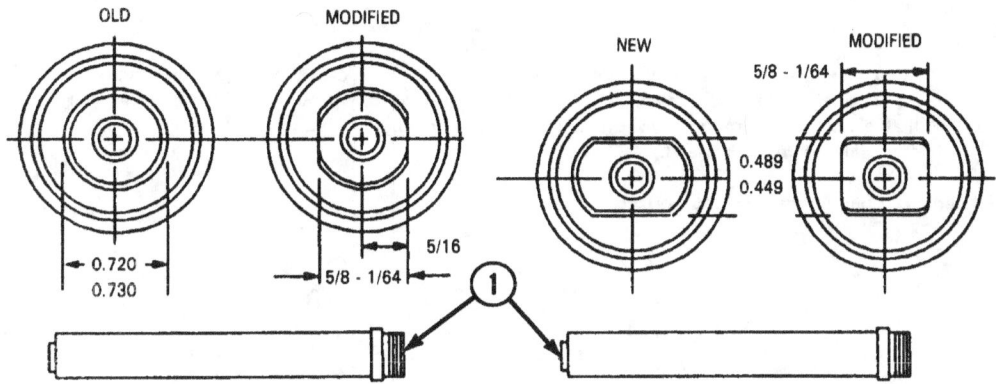

NOTE

Lower receiver extensions are usable after forming of flats.

Modify lower receiver extensions (1) (when required) to above drawing dimensions using file handle, hand file, machinist's vise, and vise jaw caps.

3

(a) Inspect lower receiver (2) for damage. wear. anti corrosion (p 3-53). Repair or replace weapon.

CAUTION

Use extreme care when drilling hole so that you do not penetrate inner wall of spring Cavity .

NOTE

Spring must be removed before drilling.

(b) Modify lower receiver (2), when required, to dimensions depicted using 1/1 6 twist drill and portable electric drill.

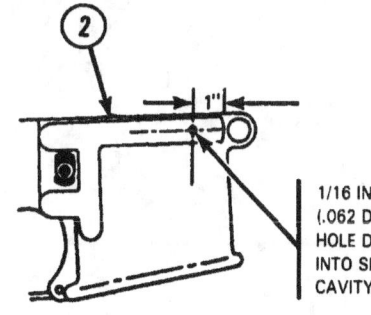

3-19. LOWER RECEIVER AND EXTENSION SUBASSEMBLY (CONT).

4

If serial number is hard to read on weapon, restamp as follows"

(a) Support the receiver in the stamping area to prevent bending and distortion of the receiver.

(b) Exercise extreme care to restamp the same serial number as original

(c) Restamp the serial number the same size as the originalserial number.

NOTE

Most weapon serial numbers are 1/8 inch in height, or close enough that this size is acceptable for such restamping. In the event that a weapon has a serial number that cannot be reproduced by the use of the die sets, local purchase of an appropriate size die set is authorized.

Replace defective components as authorized

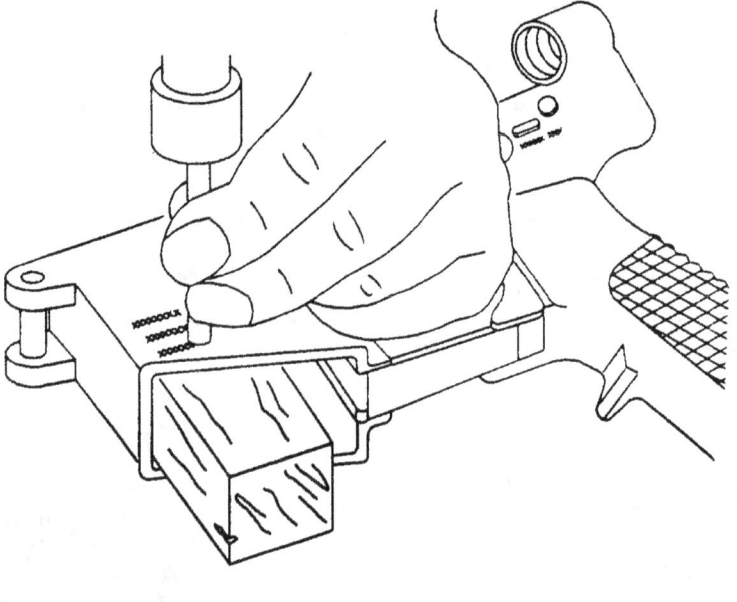

d. TEST

Test lower receiver and extension subassembly trigger pin holes and hammer pin holes. See page 3-56. Test lower receiver lobe area spacing. See page 3-56, TEST.

e. REASSEMBLY

1

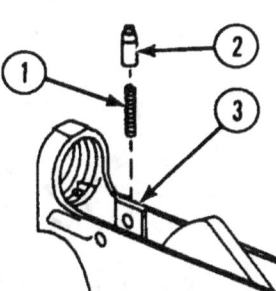

WARNING

To avoid injury to your eyes, use care when removing and installing spring-loaded parts.

Install helical spring (1) and buffer retainer (2) into lower receiver (3).

2

(a) Lubricate threads of lower receiver (3) and lower receiver extension (4) with molybdenum disulfide grease before reassembly.

(b) Install lower receiver extension (4) into lower receiver (3) while depressing buffer retainer (2).

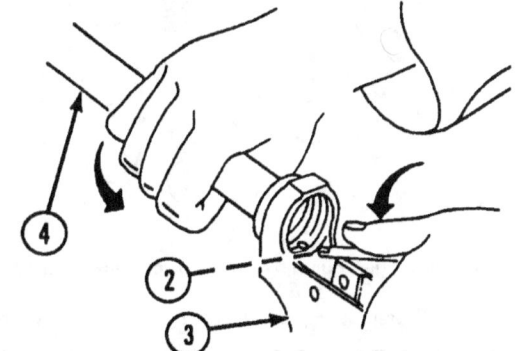

3

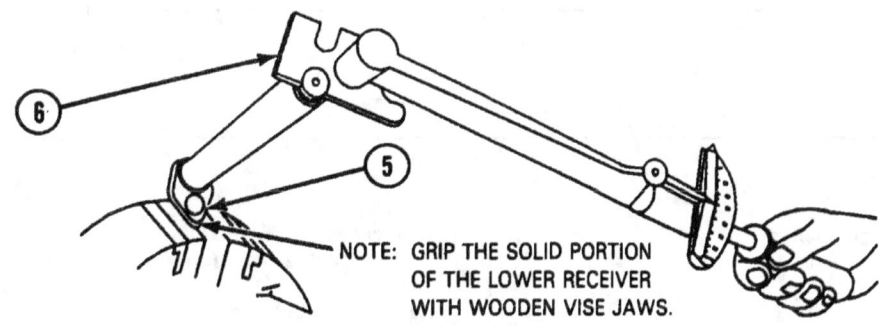

NOTE: GRIP THE SOLID PORTION OF THE LOWER RECEIVER WITH WOODEN VISE JAWS.

NOTE

Use wooden vise jaws in machinist'a vise in place of brass vise jaw caps, if available.

(a) Clamp solid portion of lower receiver and extension assembly (5) in a machinist's vise using wooden vise jaws.

(b) Using combination wrench 11010033 (6) and torque wrench, torque lower receiver extension to 35-39 ft-lb. Torque is read when both wrenches are used together.

3-19. LOWER RECEIVER AND EXTENSION SUBASSEMBLY (CONT).

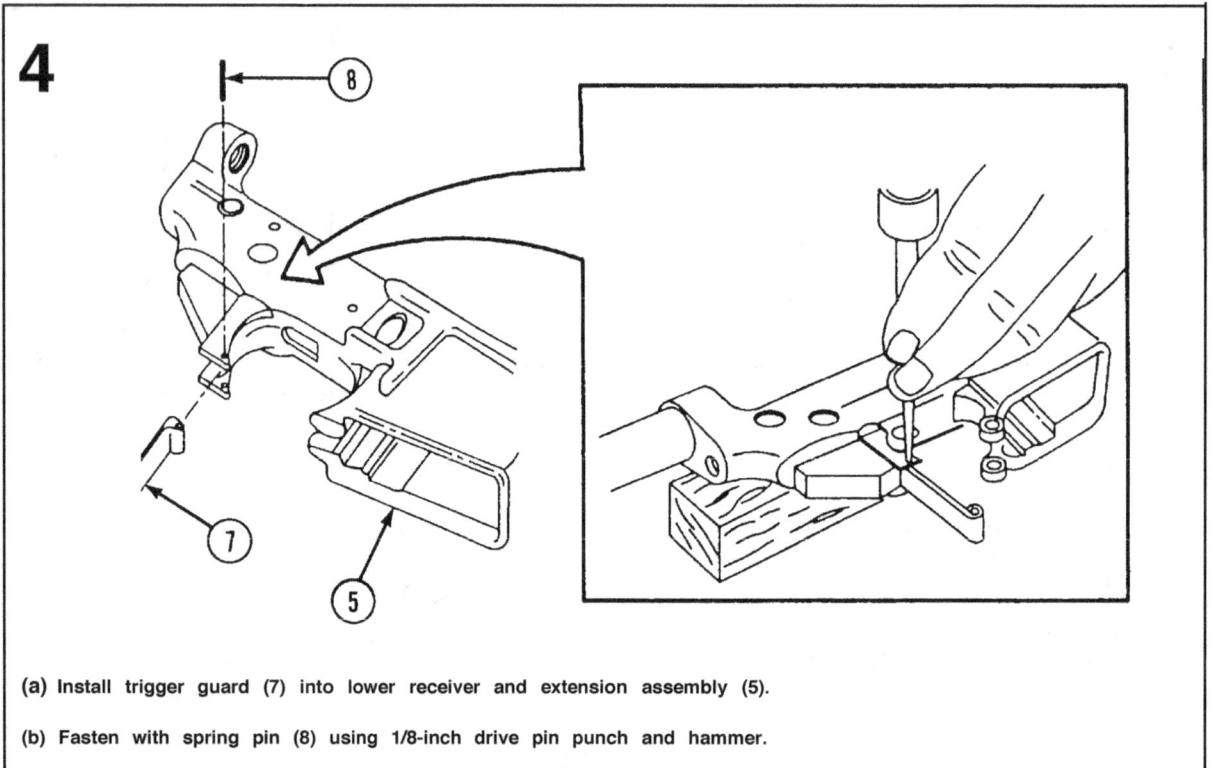

(a) Install trigger guard (7) into lower receiver and extension assembly (5).

(b) Fasten with spring pin (8) using 1/8-inch drive pin punch and hammer.

3-20. MAJOR COMPONENTS OF M16 AND M16A1 RIFLE.

This task covers:

a. Reassembly   b. Test

INITIAL SETUP

Applicable Configuration
  All M16/M16A1 Rifles

Reference
  TM 9-1005-249-10 (operator's manual)

Test Equipment
  Tool and Gage Set 846685 (1 9204

Equipment Condition
  Weapon disassembled

Tools
  Small Arms Repairman Tool Kit
    SC 5180-95-CL-A07 (19204)

General Safety Instructions
  To avoid injury to your eyes, use care when removing
    and installing spring-loaded parts.
  Live ammunition must not be near the work area.

a. REASSEMBLY

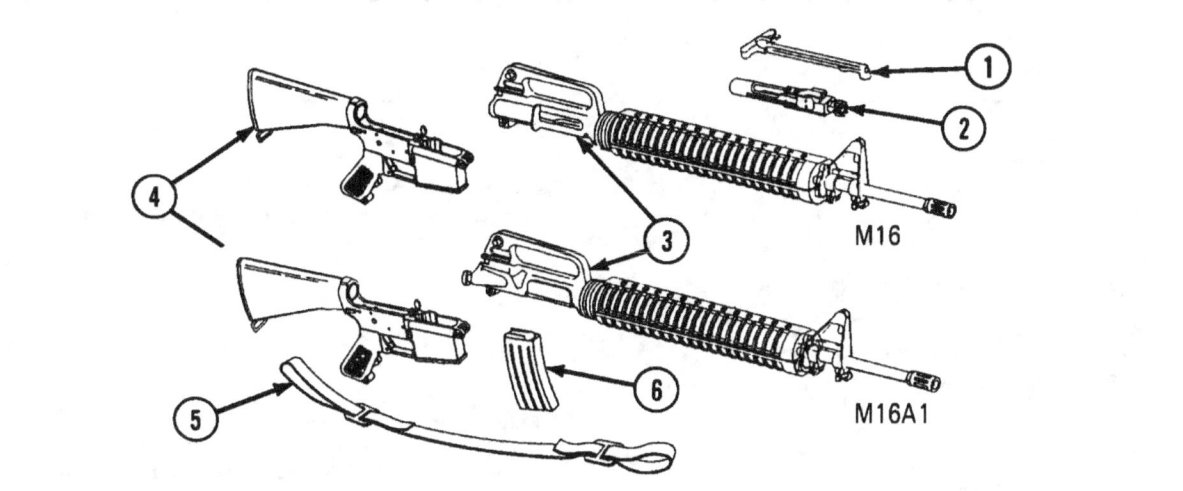

M16

M16A1

1. Refer to operator's manual.

2. Install charging handle (1) and bolt carrier assembly (2) into upper receiver assembly (3). Join upper receiver assembly (3) and lower receiver assembly (4).

3. Snap on small arms sling (5) and install cartridge magazine (6).

b. TEST

1. Place test fixture rod (1) on bench and add test weights (2) until minimum load of 5.5 lbs is reached.

2. Charge the rifle. Place the selector lever in the semi position.

3. Hold the rifle (3) in a vertical position. Place the end of the test fixture (1) over the trigger (4). Slowly raise the rifle in a line parallel to the barrel until the fixture and weights are suspended.

4. The hammer must not fall. If the hammer falls, the trigger pull is too light and the trigger and/or hammer must be replaced. Replace the trigger and/or hammer in accordance with the maintenance procedures provided on pages 3-60 and 3-61. If replacement of hammer and/or trigger fails to correct light trigger pull, replace hammer spring (pg 3-60 and 3-61).

5. Add weights until maximum load of 8.5 lbs is reached. Repeat the above procedures. The hammer must fall. If the hammer does not fall, replace the trigger and/or hammer (see pg 3-60 and 3-61).

<u>NOTE</u>

Hammer must not trip until 5.5 pounds have been applied, and it must trip on applying 8.5 pounds.

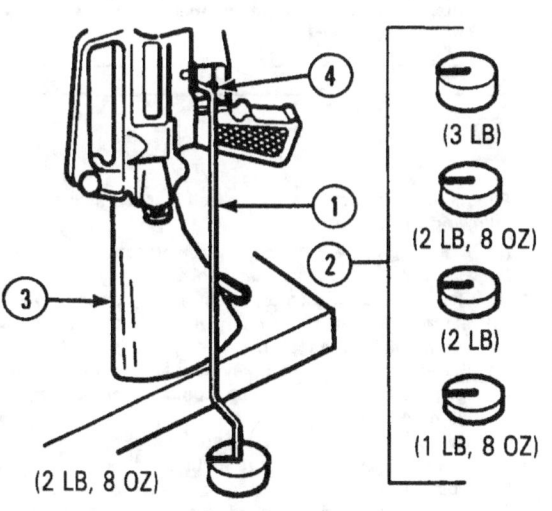

(3 LB)

(2 LB, 8 OZ)

(2 LB)

(1 LB, 8 OZ)

(2 LB, 8 OZ)

3-21. MI 6 AND M16A1 RIFLE FINAL INSPECTION.

This task covers:

    a. Inspection   b. Test

INITIAL SETUP

Applicable Configuration
    All M16/M16A1 Rifles

Test Equipment
    Tool and Gage Set 8426685 (1 9204

Tools
    Small Arms Repairman Tool Kit
      SC 5180-95-CL-A07 (19204)

Reference
    TM 9-1005-249-10 (operator's manual)

Equipment Condition
    Weapon assembled

General Safety Instructions
    Live ammunition must not be near the work area.

Before starting an inspection on a weapon equipped with a low light level sight, check for damage to the low light level sight. See procedures listed on page 2-19.

a. INSPECTION

1

(a) Visually inspect general appearance of weapon. Weapon should look almost new. All metal surfaces are to have a dull, rust-or corrosion-resistant finish with no burrs or deep scratches. Solid film lubricant (item 19, app D) is the only authorized touch up for this weapon.

(b) Visually inspect barrel for serviceability. Barrels must be straight, clean, free of rust, powder fouling, and free of bulges and rings. Fine pitting is allowable.

(c) Visually inspect weapon for missing parts and serial numbers. All parts must be attached and all modifications must be applied. Serial numbers must be legible and steel parts must be rust free. Spring pins must be secure and screws must be tight.

2

Functionally inspect key and bolt carrier assembly and gas tube alignment. Refer to operator's manual and use the following procedures:

(a) Disengage the takedown pin and open the receiver.

(b) Remove bolt carrier assembly.

(c) Remove bolt assembly from bolt carrier assembly.

(d) Insert bolt carrier and key into upper receiver and barrel assembly. The bolt assembly must not be installed while performing test.

(e) Slide bolt carrier and key forward to detect binding between key and bolt carrier assembly and gas tube by feel. Badly bent gas tube could cause damage to both the key and bolt carrier assembly and the gas tube. A slightly bent gas tube will cause unnecessary wear of the carrier and key assembly and gas tube.

(f) Correct slight binding by removing hand guards and slightly bending gas tube in the handguard area while repeating step (e) above until no binding is detected. Badly bent gas tubes will be replaced and realigned.

(g) Remove key and bolt carrier assembly from upper receiver and barrel assembly.

(h) Reassemble bolt assembly into key and bolt carrier assembly.

(i) Reinstall bolt carrier assembly into upper receiver and barrel assembly.

3-21. M16 AND M16A1 RIFLE FINAL INSPECTION (CONT).

a. INSPECTION (CONT)

3

(a) Make the following functional checks on assembled rifle with selector lever in SAFE, SEMI, and AUTO position. The test sequence is used for a rapid complete check. Any portion may be used alone to determine the operational condition of any special firing' position selected:

(1) Remove magazine, if installed.

(2) Pull charging handle assembly to rear. Check that chamber is clear. Let bolt and bolt carrier close. Leave hammer in cocked position. Do not pull trigger.

WARNING

If weapon fails any of the following tests, continued use of the weapon could result in injury to, or death of, personnel.

(3) Place selector lever in SAFE position and pull trigger. Hammer should not fall.

(4) Place selector lever in SEMI position.

(5) Pull trigger. Hammer should fall.

NOTE

For the purpose of the following test "SLOW" is defined as 1/4 to 1/2 the normal rate of trigger release.

(6) Hold trigger to the rear, charge weapon and release the trigger with a slow, smooth motion without hesitations or stops, until the trigger is fully forward (an audible click should be heard). Hammer should not fall.

(7) Repeat the above selector lever SEMI position test five times. The weapon must not malfunction during any of these five tests. If the weapon malfunctions during any of these five tests, see repair of lower receiver and extension assembly (p 3-55).

(8) Place selector lever in AUTO position. Charge weapon and pull trigger. Hammer should fall.

(9) Hold trigger to the rear, charge weapon, and release trigger. Pull trigger. Hammer should not fall. Automatic assembly sear should have released the hammer as the bolt closed.

(10) With the hammer in the forward position and using finger/thumb pressure, attempt to place the selector lever in SAFE position. The selector lever must not move into SAFE position.

(b) Perform the following additional functional checks and adjustment on assembled rifle:

(1) Press magazine catch button. Make sure it functions properly.

(2) Press bolt catch. Make certain it operates smoothly and holds bolt in open position.

(3) Adjust front sight and rear sight. Make certain they can be adjusted properly. Refer to operator's manual.

(4) Actuate forward assist assembly (M16A1 rifles only). It must work freely.

b. TEST

1. Check headspace using headspace gage PN 7799734. See page 3-38, TEST.
2. Check firing pin protrusion using firing pin protrusion gage PN 7799735. See page 3-13, TEST.
3. Check extent of barrel erosion using barrel erosion gage PN 8448496 or PN 7799792. See pages 3-35 and 3-37, TEST.
4. Check muzzle erosion using muzzle erosion gage PN 8448677 (non-chrome barrels only) (p 3-35).
5. Check barrel straightness using barrel straightness gage PN 8448202 (p 3-37).
6. Check firing pin hole using firing pin hole gage PN 12620101 (p 3-1 8).
7. Refer to trigger pull test (p 3-69).

3-22. M16 AND M16A1 RIFLE ANNUAL INSPECTION AND GAGE REQUIREMENTS.

This task covers:

a. Inspection

b. Gaging

INITIAL SETUP

Applicable Configuration
All M16/M16A1 Rifles

Test Equipment
Tool and Gage Set 8426685

Tools
DA Form 2407
Small Arms Repair Tool Kit
SC 5180-95-CL-A07 (19204)
Field Maintenance Basic Less Power Small Arms
Shop Equipment SC 4933-95-CL-A11 (19204)

Reference
TM 9-1005-249-10 (operator's manual)
AFR 50-36. Volume 1

Equipment Condition
Weapon assembled.

General Safety Instructions
To avoid injury to your eyes, use care when
removing and installing spring-loaded parts.
Before starting an inspection on a weapon
equipped with a low light level sight, check for
damage to the sight and decontaminate if required. See procedures in Chapter 2, Section V.

All rifles used at training centers (Army only) should
be inspected and gaged at the end of each training
cycle. This gaging/inspection will be conducted at
the discretion of the unit commander. However, the
time between inspection shall not exceed one year.
All Active Army M16/M16A1 rifles must be inspected
and gaged at least once annually for safety.
All Army Reserve and Army National Guard
M16/M16A1 rifles must be inspected and gaged at
least once every two years, after the initial inspec-
tion/gaging procedures have been accomplished.
This two year interval may be maintained unless
preventive maintenance checks and services
(PMCS), or other physical evidence indicates that
an individual unit's M16/M16A1 rifles require inspection at a more frequent interval. If it is determined that a yearly inspection is necessary for an
individual unit, only that unit will be affected. This
will not affect other units in regard to the interval
of inspection.
Air Force M16 rifle will be inspected in accordance
with AFR 50-36, Volume 1, Chapter 5.

a. INSPECTION

1. Visually inspect general appearance of rifle. Overall appearance will be approximately that of a new weapon. For
inspection criteria refer to final inspection, page 3-73. All visual and functional inspection requirements must be
met.

NOTE

To perform the following tests, disassemble weapon only as far as allowed in
chapter 2 (Unit Maintenance Instructions), unless a deficiency is uncovered.

2. Perform a general inspection of rifle per chapter 3 (Direct Support Maintenance Instructions) section V. Repair
as required and authorized.

3-22. M16 AND M16A1 RIFLE ANNUAL INSPECTION AND GAGE REQUIREMENTS (CONT).

b. GAGING

1. Gage bolt assembly for firing pin protrusion using firing pin protrusion gage PN 7799735. See page 3-13, TEST.

2. Gage bolt assembly for firing pin hole wear using not-go plug gage PN 12620101. See page 3-13, TEST.

3. Inspect chamber in upper receiver and barrel assembly using chamber reflector tool PN 8448201. See page 3-26, inspection/CLEANING.

4. Gage barrel in upper receiver and barrel assembly using barrel erosion gage PN 7799792 or PN 8448496 as applicable. Use muzzle erosion gage PN 8448677 on nonchromed barrels only. Use bore straightness gage PN 8448202 on all barrels. See pages 3-35 through 3-39, TEST.

5. Check headspace in upper receiver and barrel assembly by inserting headspace gage PN 7799734 in chamber. See page 3-38, TEST.

6. Gage hammer and trigger pin holes in lower receiver assembly using not-go plug gage PN 12006472. See page 3-56, TEST.

7. Gage trigger pull using trigger pull measuring fixture PN 7274758. See page 3-69, TEST.

8. Document inspection with DA Form 2407 and DD Form 314 when completed. Air Force users refer to AFTO Form 105.

Section VI. PREEMBARKATION INSPECTION OF MATERIEL IN UNITS ALERTED FOR OVERSEAS MOVEMENT

3-23. GENERAL. Refer to TB 9-1000-247-34.

CHAPTER 4

MAINTENANCE OF AUXILIARY EQUIPMENT

CHAPTER OVERVIEW

This chapter contains information and instructions to keep auxiliary equipment used with your weapon in good repair.

Section I. UNIT AUXILIARY EQUIPMENT

4-1. **GENERAL. This chapter covers Unit and Direct** Support Maintenance of Auxiliary Equipment.

a. The following materiel is used in conjunction with the M16/M16A1 rifle:

(1) Bayonet-knife M7, NSN 1005-00-073-9238.

(2) Bayonet-knife scabbard M10, NSN 1095-00-223-7164.

(3) 40-mm Grenade Launcher M203, NSN 1010-00-179-6447.

(4) Low Light Level Sight (front), NSN 1005-00-234-1568, Low Light Level Sight (rear), NSN 1005-00-071-8015.

NOTE

The Low Light Level Sights (front and rear) are no longer being manufactured and are obsolete items.

(5) Lock Plate, NSN 1005-00-233-9031.

(6) Top Sling Adapter, NSN 1005-00-406-1570

(7) Rifle Bipod M3, NSN 1005-00-992-6676.

(8) Bipod Carrying Case, NSN 1005-00-283-9439.

(9) Blank Firing Attachment M15A2, NSN 1005-00-118-6192.

b. Refer to TM 9-1010-221-24&P for unit maintenance for the Grenade Launcher M203.

c. Refer to TM 9-1005-237-23&P for repair instructions and repair parts for Bayonet-Knife M7 and Bayonet-Knife Scabbard M10.

d. Refer to TM 9-6920-363-12&P for unit maintenance of the M261 Conversion Kit (caliber .22 rimfire adapter).

e. Coast Guard (ONLY) NAVSEA OP 4445 M87 MOD 1 Line Throwing Rifle Adapter Kit.

4-2. **LOW LIGHT LEVEL FRONT SIGHT.**

This task covers:

a. Disassembly   c. Reassembly
b. Inspection   d. Wrapping and Packaging

INITIAL SETUP

Applicable Configuration
  All M16/M16A1 Rifles

Tools
  Front sight post and low light level front sight post
  removal/installation tool (fig E 1, app E)

Reference
  Warning page radiation hazard.

General Safety Instructions
  Low light level sights will be removed from weapons
  that are being transferred or unserviceable or are
  being disposed.

Low light level front sight contains radioactive
  material.
Do not insert metal objects into the post slot or other
  wise treat sight roughly to cause breakage of the
  radioactive element.
Do not eat, drink, or smoke while working on the low
  light level sights.

---

a. DISASSEMBLY

1. Remove low light level front sight (1) using front sight post and low light level front sight post removing and installation tool (2).

2. Catch front sight detent (3) and helical spring (4) to prevent loss.

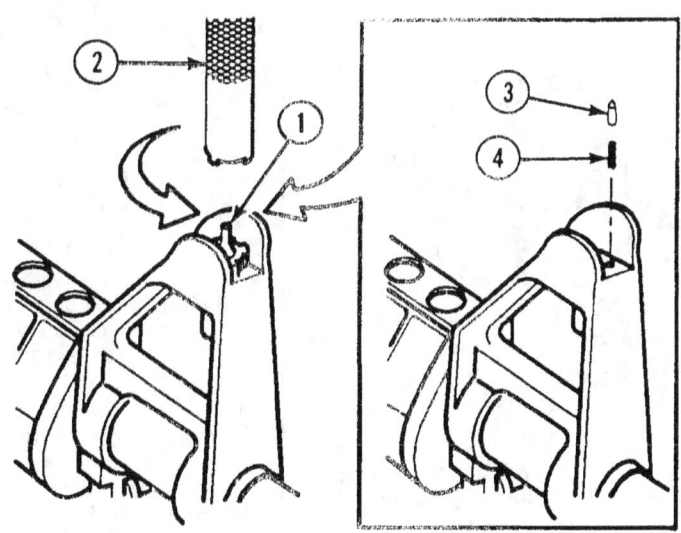

b. INSPECTION

Visually inspect low light level front sight for broken/or damaged radioactive element. Inspect manufacturer's data. Replace sight if more than 144 months have elapsed. Ensure that the rear sight is the rear low light level sight (1). If not, you must have direct support maintenance replace the standard rear sight with the rear low light level sight as the sights must mate. Ensure the sight is marked with luminous material H3. Sights with any other luminous material must be replaced with the appropriate sight.

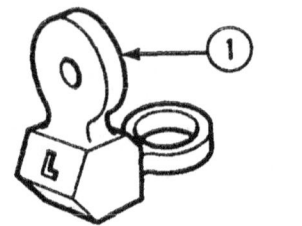

c. REASSEMBLY

1. Install helical spring (1), front sight detent (2) and hold in position.

2. Install low light level front sight (3) using front sight post and low light level front sight post removing and installation tool (4).

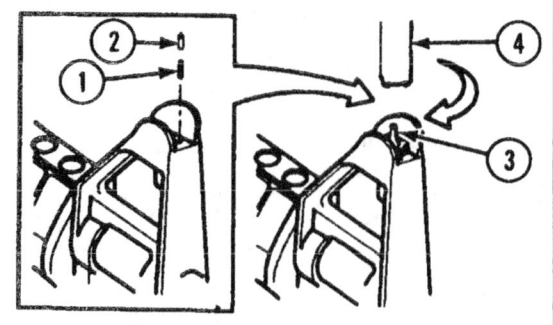

d. WRAPPING AND PACKAGING

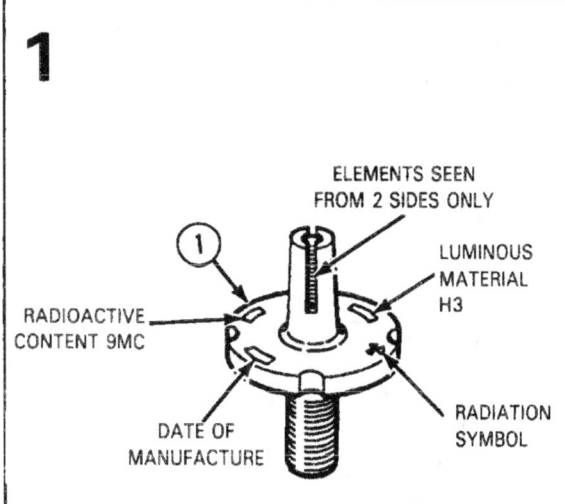

1

RADIOACTIVE CONTENT 9MC

ELEMENTS SEEN FROM 2 SIDES ONLY

LUMINOUS MATERIAL H3

DATE OF MANUFACTURE

RADIATION SYMBOL

Broken low light level sight post (1) will be removed and placed in a plastic bag. All defective and/or outdated components will be returned to the storage activity for disposal in accordance with AR 385-11.

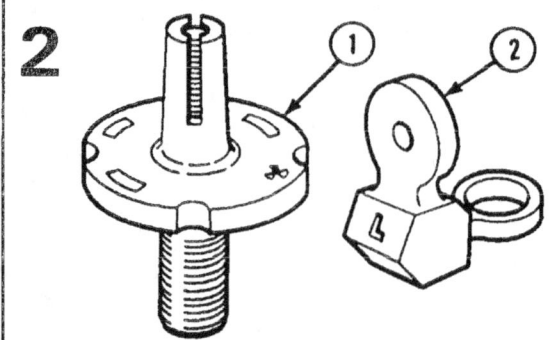

2

(a) Low light level systems that have been removed from rifles will be protected by applying a protective, chemically-neutral paper conforming to MIL-P-17667 (SB 38-100) and placed in a plastic bag.

(b) Final packaging of rear (2) and front (1) low light level sights will be in accordance with instructions provided in MIL-STD-1169, pending possible reuse or disposal. These packaging criteria are furnished since a terminal test for radiation and luminosity will be required.

4-3. LOCK PLATE.

This task covers:

a. Installation
b. Removal

c. Inspection

INITIAL SETUP

Applicable Configuration
  All M16/M16A1 Rifles

Tools
  Small Arms Repairman Tool Kit
    SC 5180-95-CL-A07 (19204)

WARNING

The lock plate prevents the selector from being placed in AUTO and will be installed at the discretion of the unit commander. It is mandatory for use in civil disturbance (riot control).

a. INSTALLATION

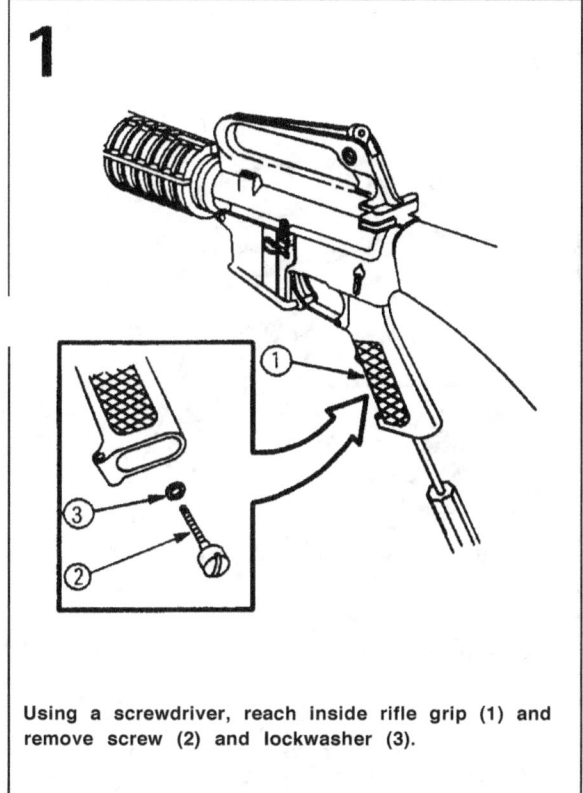

1

Using a screwdriver, reach inside rifle grip (1) and remove screw (2) and lockwasher (3).

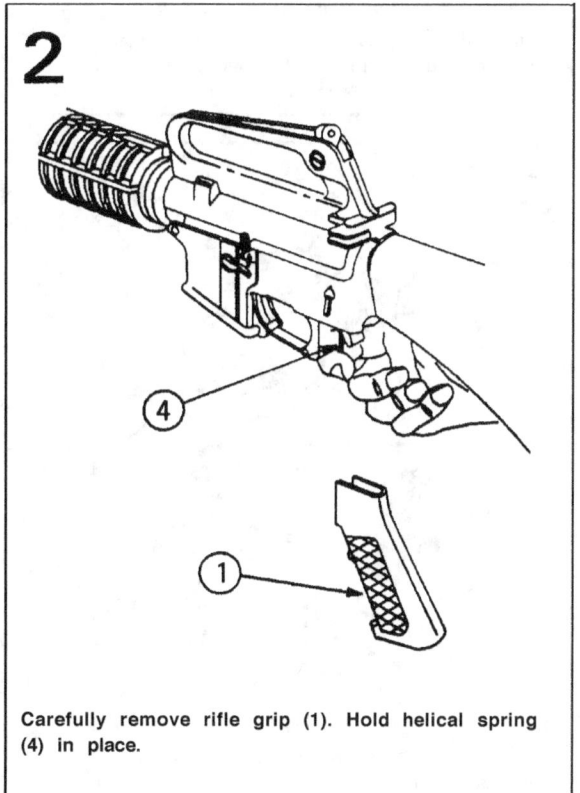

2

Carefully remove rifle grip (1). Hold helical spring (4) in place.

3

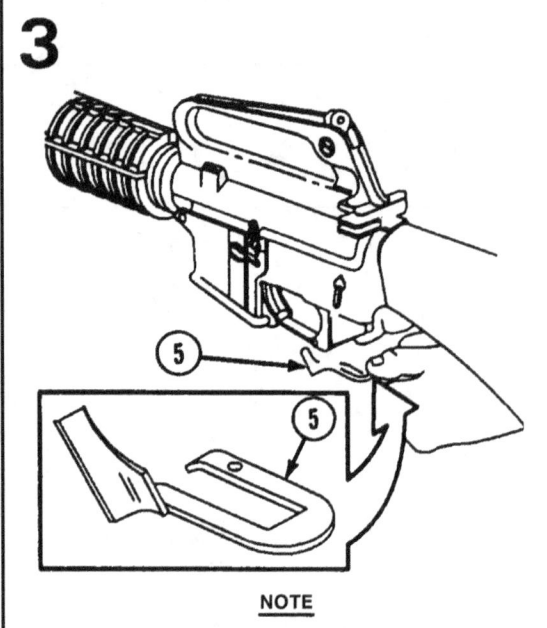

NOTE

Selector lever must be in SAFE or SEMI position.

Install lock plate (5) with the detect helical spring passing through the hole in the right side of the lockplate, and the arm on the outside of the receiver pointing to the SAFE position.

5

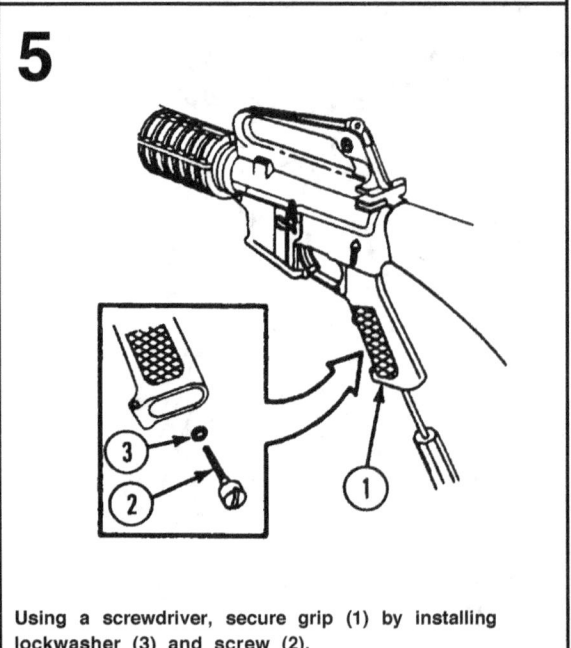

Using a screwdriver, secure grip (1) by installing lockwasher (3) and screw (2).

4

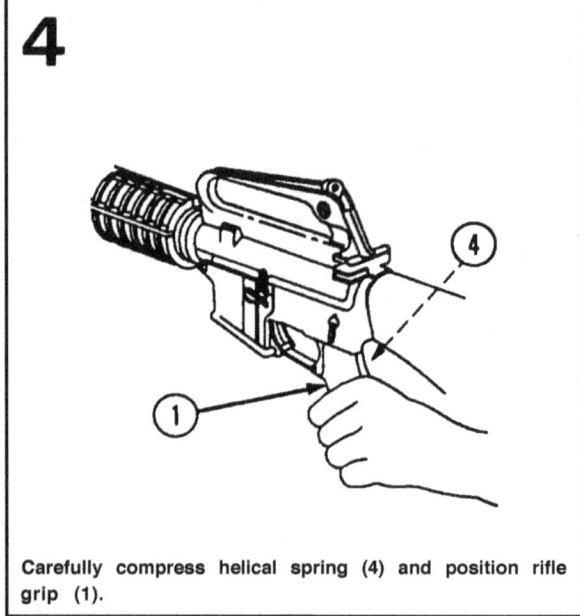

Carefully compress helical spring (4) and position rifle grip (1).

b. REMOVAL

1

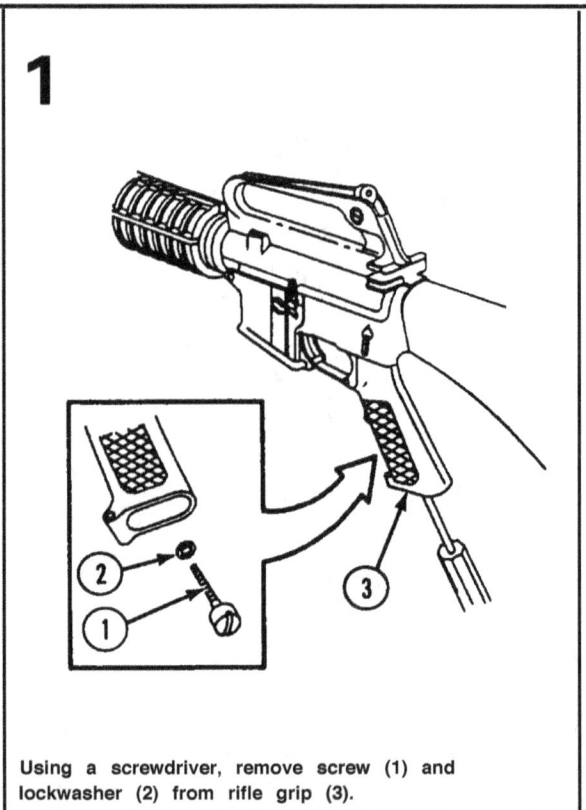

Using a screwdriver, remove screw (1) and lockwasher (2) from rifle grip (3).

4-3. LOCK PLATE (CONT).

b. REMOVAL (CONT)

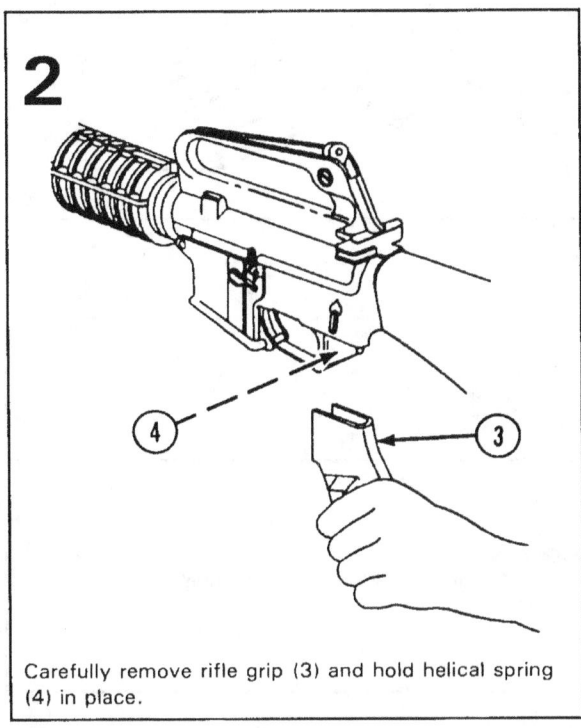

Carefully remove rifle grip (3) and hold helical spring (4) in place.

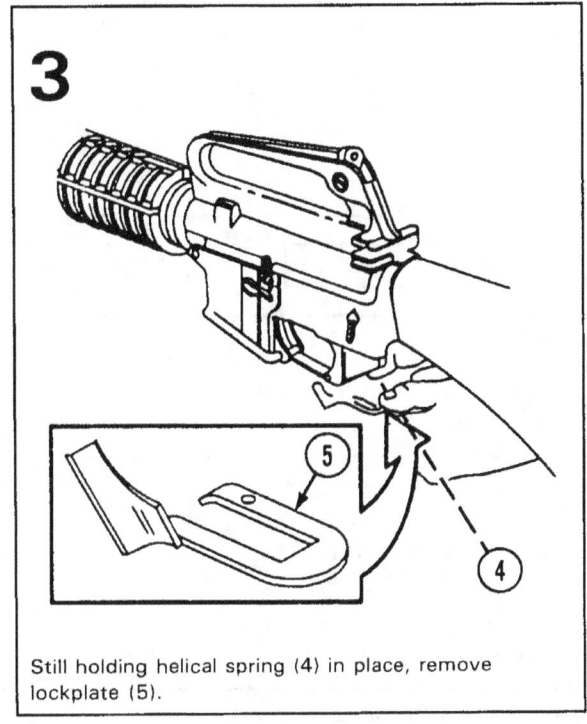

Still holding helical spring (4) in place, remove lockplate (5).

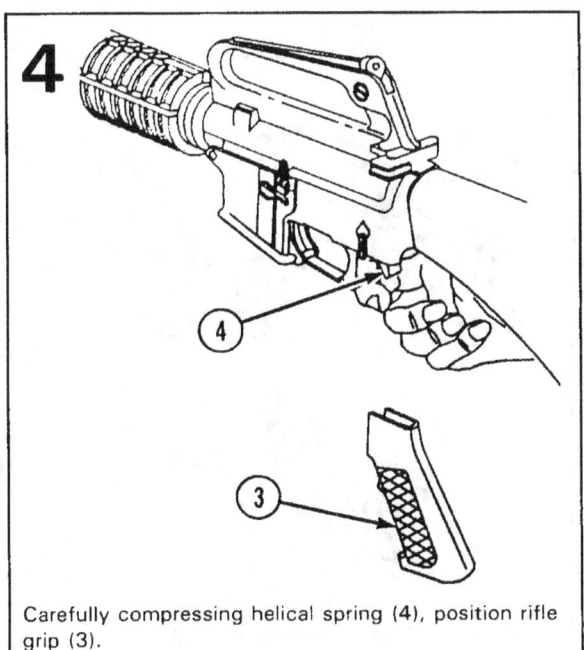

Carefully compressing helical spring (4), position rifle grip (3).

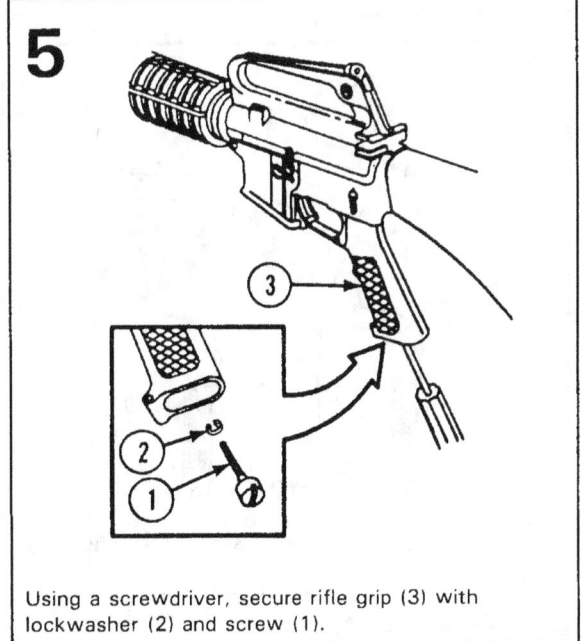

Using a screwdriver, secure rifle grip (3) with lockwasher (2) and screw (1).

c. INSPECTION

Inspect lock plate (1) for bends affecting serviceability or for missing tang (2). Replace if unserviceable or if tang (2) is broken off.

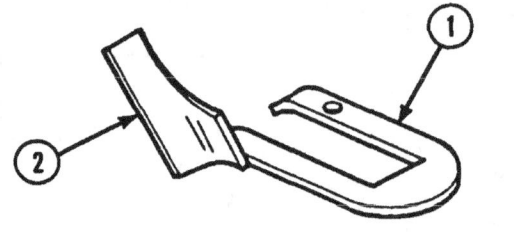

4-4. TOP SLING ADAPTER.

This task covers:

a. Installation

c. Inspection

b. Removal

INITIAL SETUP

Applicable Configuration
All M16/M16A1 Rifles

Reference
TM 9-1005-249-10 (operator's manual)

Materials/Parts
Top sling adapter kit PN 8448471

a. INSTALLATION

1

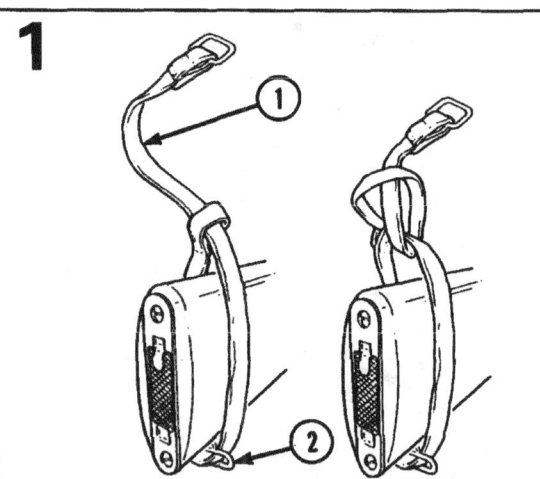

(a) Refer to operator's manual and remove rifle sling.

(b) Install top sling adapter strap (1) through sling swivel (2) and tie.

2

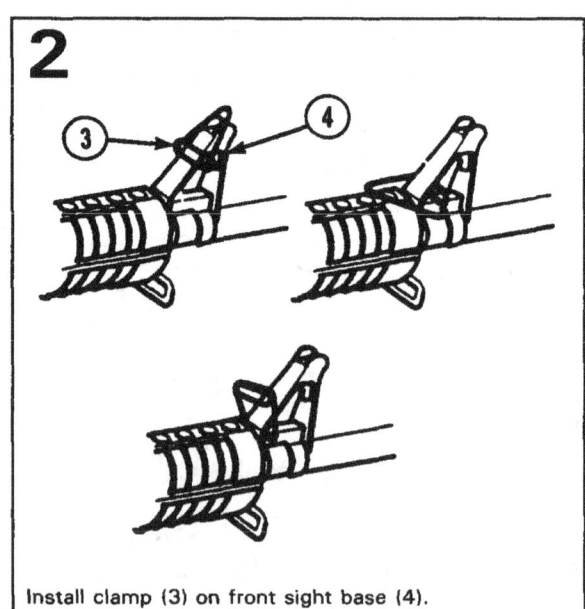

Install clamp (3) on front sight base (4).

4-4. TOP SLING ADAPTER (CONT).

a. INSTALLATION (CONT)

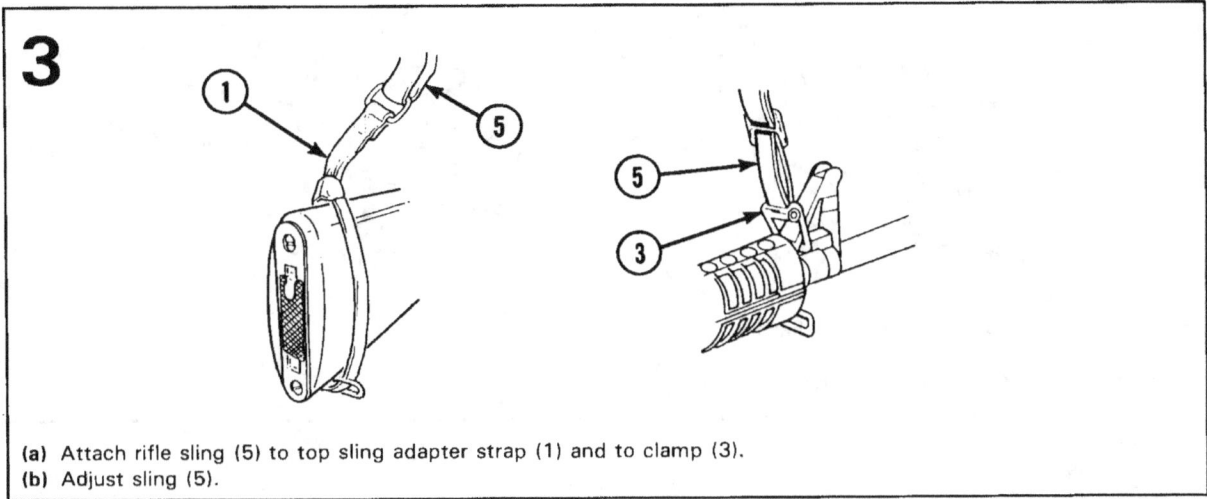

3

(a) Attach rifle sling (5) to top sling adapter strap (1) and to clamp (3).
(b) Adjust sling (5).

b. REMOVAL

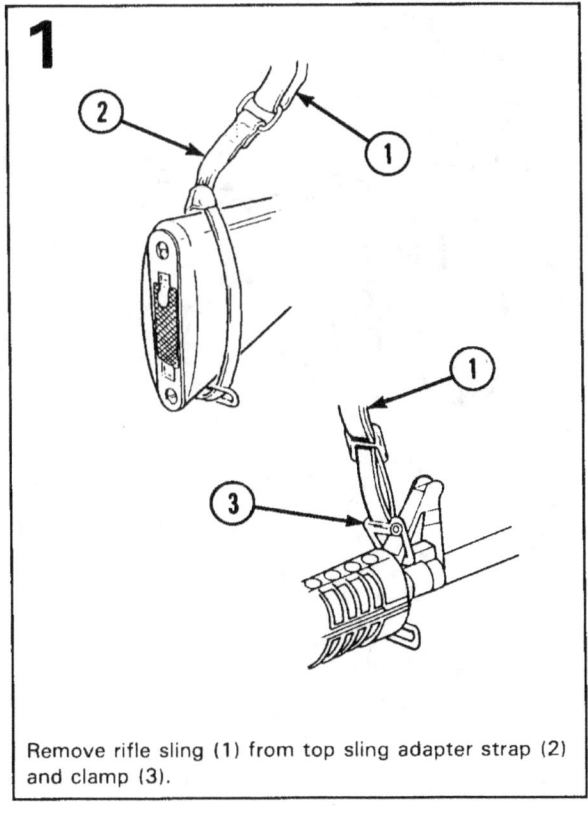

1

Remove rifle sling (1) from top sling adapter strap (2) and clamp (3).

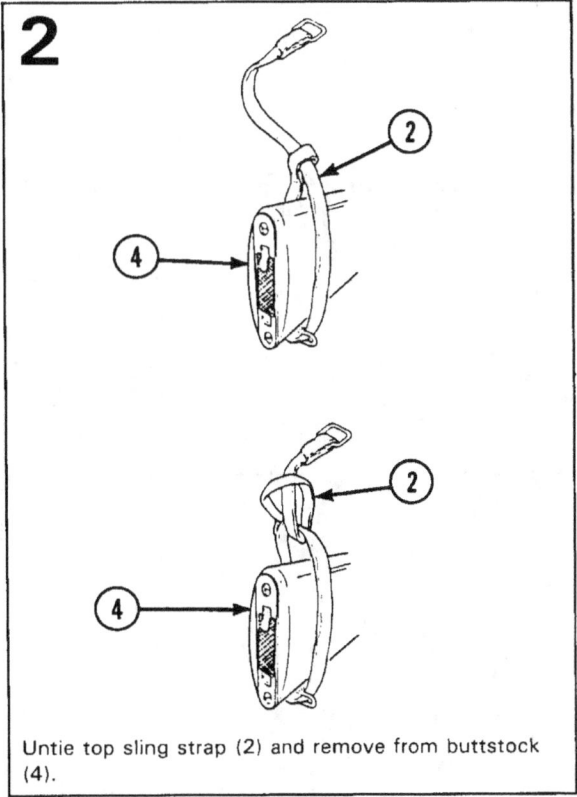

2

Untie top sling strap (2) and remove from buttstock (4).

3

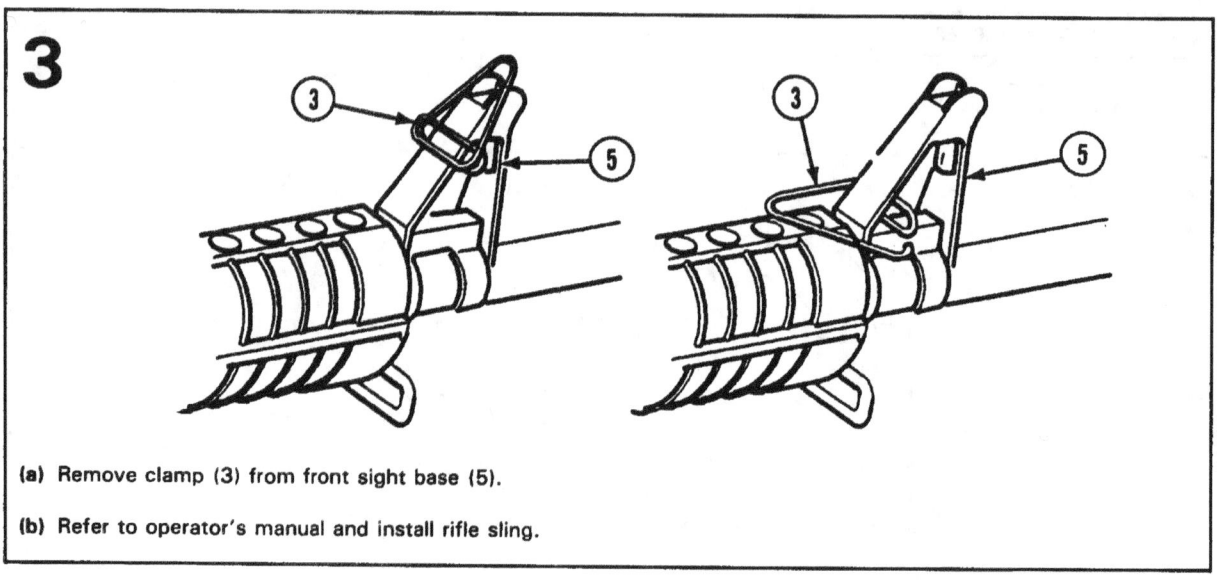

(a) Remove clamp (3) from front sight base (5).

(b) Refer to operator's manual and install rifle sling.

c. INSPECTION

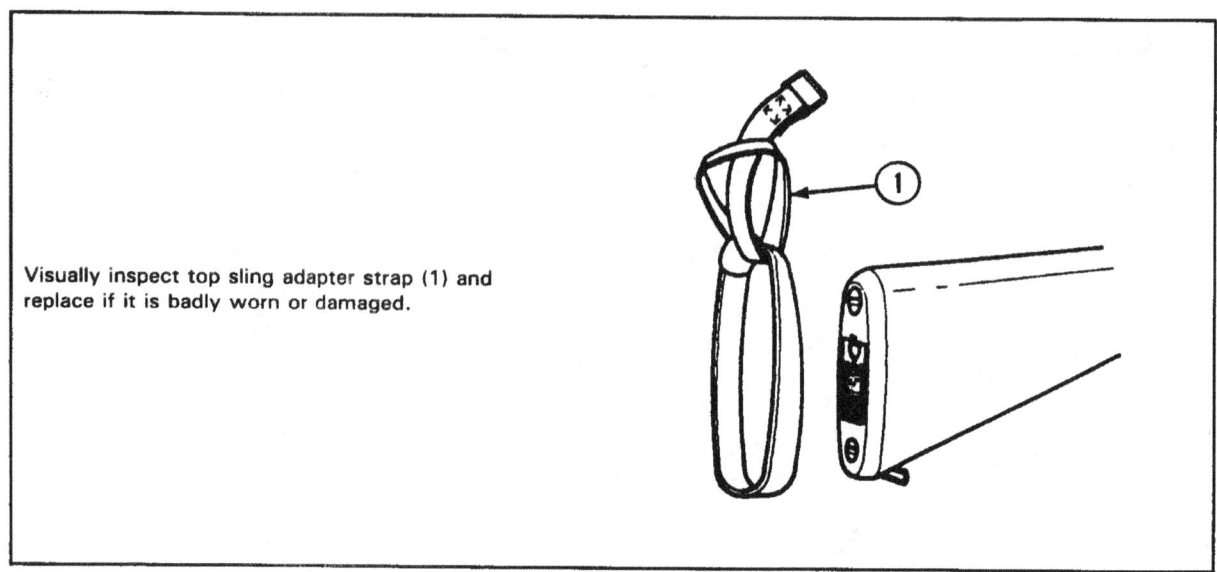

Visually inspect top sling adapter strap (1) and replace if it is badly worn or damaged.

4-5. RIFLE BIPOD M3.

This task covers:

a. Installation
b. Removal

c. Inspection

INITIAL SETUP

Applicable Configuration
    All M16/M16A1 Rifles

Materials/Parts
    Carrying case NSN 1005-00-283-9439
    Rifle biped M3 NSN 1005-00-992-6676

a. INSTALLATION

1

Remove rifle biped M3 (1) from case (2).

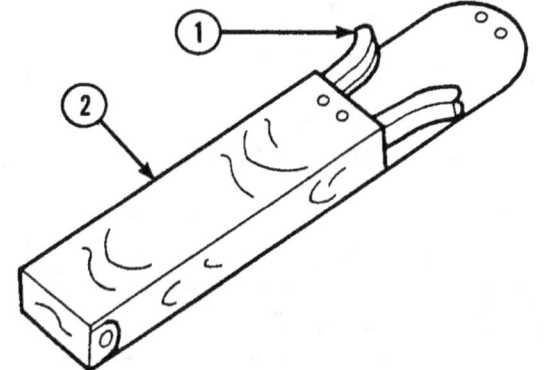

2

To install rifle biped M3 (1), squeeze biped legs together, snap on rifle barrel (3), and release biped legs.

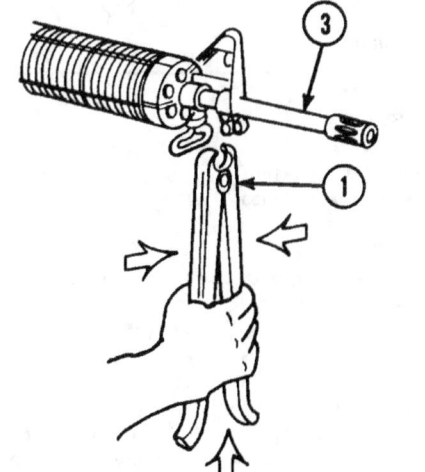

b. REMOVAL

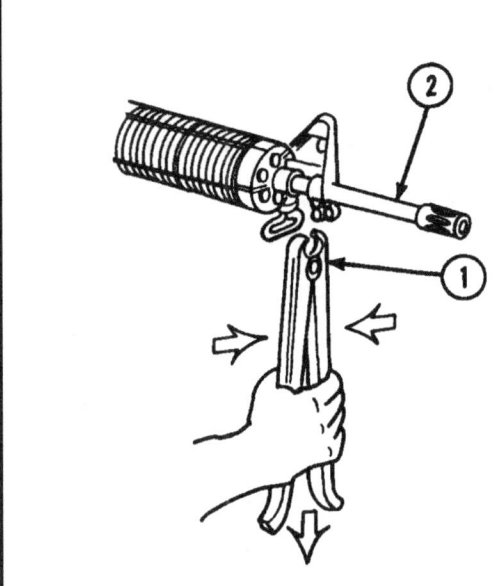

1. Squeeze bipod legs (1) together and remove from rifle barrel (2).
2. Install bipod in case.

c. INSPECTION

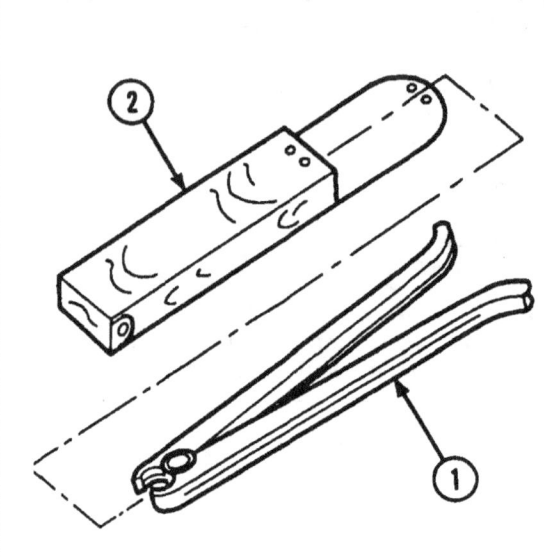

1. Visually inspect bipod (1) for bent or broken parts. Damaged, broken, or bent bipods should be replaced. Bipod must have a good finish.
2. Inspect bipod case (2) for wear. Badly worn cases should be replaced.

4-6. BLANK FIRING ATTACHMENT M15A2.

This task covers:

a. Installation
b. Removal
c. Cleaning

d. Inspection
e. Repainting
f. Replacement

INITIAL SETUP

Applicable Configuration
All M16/M16A1 Rifles

Materials/Parts
Cleaner, lubricant and preservative (CLP) (item 9, app D)
Cleaning compound, rifle bore (RBC) (item 11, app D)
Coating compound, fluorescent (item 13, app D)
Lubricating Oil, Weapons (LAW) (item 20, app D)
Lubricating Oil, Weapons (LSA) (item 21, app D)

General Safety Instructions
Do not keep live ammunition near the work area. Only blank cartridge M200 is to be used when the blank firing attachment is attached to the rifle.

4-6. BLANK FIRING ATTACHMENT M15A2 (CONT).

a. INSTALLATION

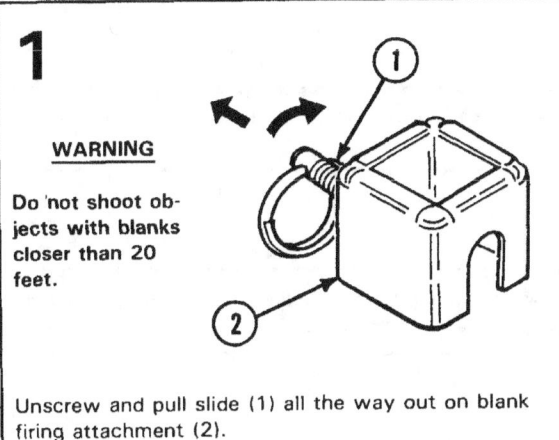

1

WARNING

Do not shoot objects with blanks closer than 20 feet.

Unscrew and pull slide (1) all the way out on blank firing attachment (2).

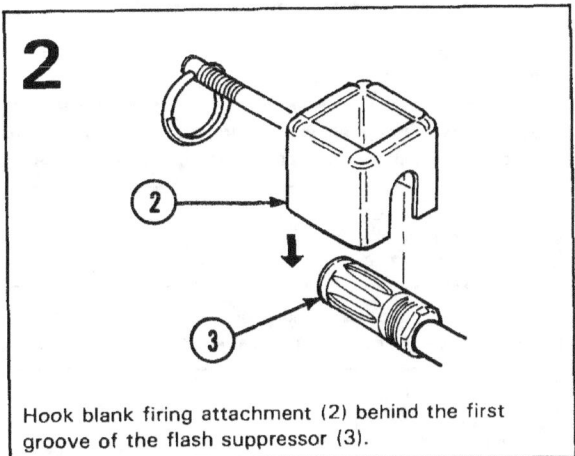

2

Hook blank firing attachment (2) behind the first groove of the flash suppressor (3).

b. REMOVAL

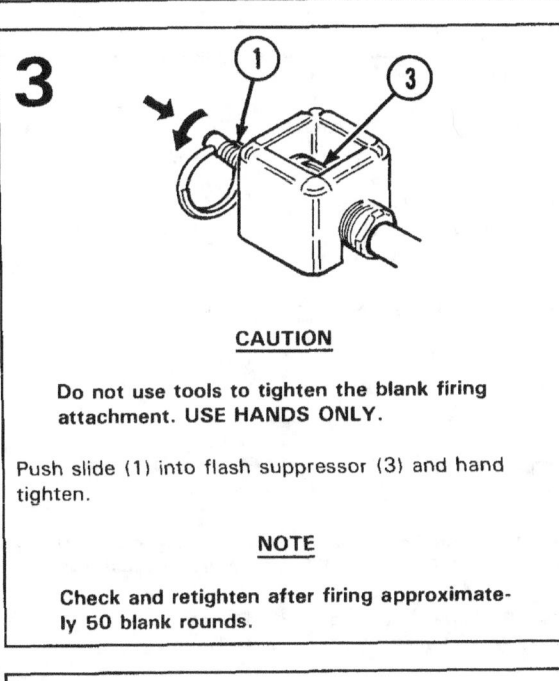

3

CAUTION

Do not use tools to tighten the blank firing attachment. USE HANDS ONLY.

Push slide (1) into flash suppressor (3) and hand tighten.

NOTE

Check and retighten after firing approximately 50 blank rounds.

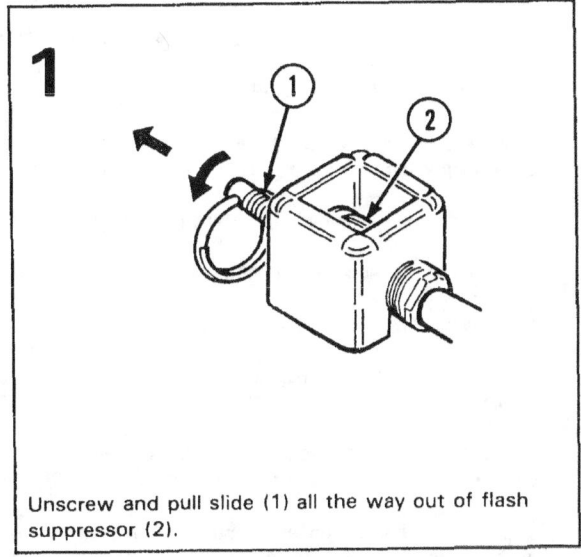

1

Unscrew and pull slide (1) all the way out of flash suppressor (2).

2

Lift blank firing attachment (3) up off of flash suppressor (2).

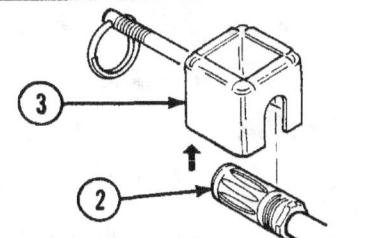

c. CLEANING

Clean blank firing attachment with CLP or RBC, wipe dry, and lubricate with CLP, LSA, or LAW (p 2-22).

d. INSPECTION

Inspect blank firing attachment for cracks or distortion. Be sure the parts in the slide are clear and clean. If blank firing attachment is cracked or distorted, it is unserviceable.

e. REPAINTING

Blank firing attachment must be clean and all lubricant must be removed prior to painting. Repaint blank firing attachment using fluorescent coating compound. Painting is the only repair authorized.

f. REPLACEMENT

Replace blank firing attachment if unserviceable.

Section II. PREPARATION FOR STORAGE OR SHIPMENT

4-7. PREPARATION FOR SHIPMENT.

a. Rifles, bipod assemblies, or grenade launchers removed from storage for shipment need not be reprocessed unless inspection reveals them to be inadequately preserved,

b. Packaging, if required, for shipping/storage which will not exceed 90 days shall be as follows:

(1) Clean in accordance with TM.

(2) Wrap with MIL-B-121 waterproof material.

(3) Place in barrier bag MIL-B-117, Type I, Class C, or wrap with MIL-B-121, Type 1, Grade A, and seal with tape, PPP-T-76.

(4) Place One Or more Of item in minimum size container. Block and brace in accordance with MIL-STD-1186. Cushion the M16 and similar weight items with PPP-C-843, and use PPP-F-320 as filler, to create a tight pack.

(a) Fiberboard containers shall be in accordance with PPP-B-636 and may be Class Domestic. Gross weight and size of material shall determine grade of fiberboard container. PPP-B-640 may also be used.

(b) Wood containers shall be in accordance with PPP-B-601 or PPP-B-621.

(5) Equivalent materials may be used.

(6) Mark IAW MIL-STD-129.

4-8. SHIPMENT OF RIFLES TO DEPOT THAT ARE IN EXCESS TO USER. All rifles that are being returned to depot that are in excess to user will be returned in serviceable condition, condition code A, if local CATM has the ability to repair. (Rifles will be returned with magazine and sling.)

APPENDIX A

REFERENCES

A-1. TECHNICAL BULLETINS.

TB 9-1000-247 -34 . . . . Standards for Overseas Shipment or Domestic Issue of Small Arms, Aircraft Armament, Towed Howitzers, Mortars, Recoilless Rifles, Rocket Launchers and Associated Fire Control Equipment

TB 43-0002-73 . . . . Maintenance Expenditures Limits for FSC Group 10; FSC Classes 1005, 1010, 1015, 1030, 1055, 1090, and 1095

TB 43-0196 . . . . Inspection and Certification of Gages - Small Arms

A-2. TECHNICAL MANUAL/TECHNICAL ORDERS.

TM 9-1005-237 -23&P . . . . Unit and Direct Support Maintenance Manual (Including Repair Parts and Special Tools List) for Bayonet-Knife M6 and M7, with Bayonet Knife Scabbard M10

TM 9-1005-249 -10 . . . . Operator's Manual for Rifle, 5.56MM, M16 and M16A1

TM 9-1010-221 -24&P . . . . Organizational, Direct Support and General Support Maintenance Manual Including Repair Parts and Special Tools List for Launcher, Grenade: 40-mm M203 W/E (NSN 1010-00-1 79-6447)

TM 9-6920 -363 -12& P . . . . M261 Conversion Kit

TM 11-1090-268-13 . . . . Operator's, Organizational, and Direct Support Maintenance Manual: Night Vision Sight, Individual Served Weapon AN/PVS-1

TM 750-244-7 . . . . Procedures for Destruction of Equipment in Federal Supply Classifications 1000, 1005, 1010, 1015, 1020, 1025, 1030, 1055, 1090, and 1095 to Prevent Enemy Use

TO 00-35D-54 . . . . Technical Order, Materiel Deficiency Reporting and Investigating System

TO 11W-1-10 . . . . Recording of Inspection, Maintenance, and Firing Date for Ground Weapons

TO11W3-5-5-1 . . . . Operator's Manual for Rifle, 5.56 MM, MI 6 and M16A1

TO 33K-1-100 . . . . Technical Manual (TMDE) Interval Calibration and Repair TO Reference Guide and Work Unit Code Manual

TO 11 A 13-10 -7 . . . . Storage and Maintenance Procedures for Small Arms Ammunition

A-3. ARMY/AIR FORCE REGULATIONS

AR 385-11 . . . . Ionizing Radiation Protection (Licensing, Control, Transportation, Disposal, and Radiation Safety)

AR 700-64 . . . . Radioactive Commodities in the DOD Supply System (NAVSUPPUB 5012/AFM 67-8/MCO P4400. 105/DSAM 41 45.8)

AFR 50-36 Volume 1 . . . . Combat Arms Training and Maintenance Program Management

A-4. FIELD MANUALS

FM 21-11 . . . .   **First Aid for Soldiers**

FM 23-9 . . . .   **M16A1 Rifle and Rifle Marksmanship**

A-5. PAMPHLETS

DA PAM 25-30, ...   **Consolidated Index Army Publications and Forms**

DA PAM 738-750, ...   **The Army Maintenance Management System (TAMMS)**

A-6. RELATED PUBLICATIONS

COMDTINST M4855.1 .,   **Comptroller Manual Volume 10 Quality Assurance**

CTA 8-100 . . . .   **Army Medical Department Expendable/Durable Items**

CTA 50-970 . . . .   **Expendable/Durable Items (Except: Medical, Class V, Repair Parts and Heraldic Items)**

MIL-STD-1169 . . . .   **Packaging, Packing and Marking for Shipment to Inert Ammunition Components**

MIL-B-121 . . . .   **Barrier Material, Greaseproofed, Waterproofed, Flexible (NSN 8135-00-753-4661)**

MIL-B-117 . . . .   **Bag, Sleeve and Tubing-interior Packaging (NSN 8135-00-543-6574)**

PPP-B-636 . . . .   **Boxes, Shipping, Fiberboard**

PPP-B-601 . . . .   **Boxes, Wood, Cleated Plywood**

MIL-STD-129 . . . .   **Marking for Shipment and Storage**

PPP-T-76 . . . .   **Tape, Packaging, Paper**

MIL-STD-1186 . ., ., ...   **Cushioning, Anchoring, Bracing, Blocking and Waterproofing; with appropriated test methods**

PPP-C-843 . . . .   **Cushioning Material, Cellulosic**

PPP-F-320 . . . .   **Fiberboard, Corrugated and Solid Sheet Stock (Container Grade), and Cut Shapes**

PPP-B-640 . . . .   **Boxes, Fiberboard, Corrugated, Triple-Wall**

PPP-B-621 . . . .   **Boxes, Wood, Nailed and Locked-Corner**

SPI 00-856-6885 . . . .   **Special Packaging Instructions**

A-7. SUPPLY CATALOGS.

SC 5180-95-CL-A07 . . . .   **Small Arms Repairman Tool Kit**

SC 4933-95-CL-A11 . . . .   **Field Maintenance Basic Less Power Small Arms Shop Set**

APPENDIX B

MAINTENANCE ALLOCATION CHART

Section 1. INTRODUCTION

B-1 . GENERAL.

   a. This section provides a general explanation of all maintenance and repair functions authorized at various maintenance categories.

   b. The Maintenance Allocation Chart (MAC) in section II designates overall authority and responsibility for the performance of maintenance functions on the identified end item or component. The application of the maintenance functions to the end item or component will be consistent with the capacities and capabilities of the designated maintenance categories.

   c. Section III lists the tools and test equipment (both special tools and common tool sets) required for each maintenance function as referenced from section II.

   d. Section IV contains supplemental instructions and explanatory notes for a particular maintenance function.

B-2. MAINTENANCE FUNCTIONS. Maintenance functions will be limited to and defined as follows: (except for ammunition MAC').

   a. Inspect. To determine the serviceability of any item by comparing its physical, mechanical, and/or electrical characteristics with established standards through examination (e.g., by sight, sound, or feel).

   b. Test. To verify serviceability by measuring the mechanical, pneumatic, hydraulic, or electrical characteristics of an item and comparing those characteristics with prescribed standards.

   c. Service. Operations required periodically to keep an item in proper operating condition, i.e., to clean (includes decontaminate, when required), to preserve, to drain, to paint, or to replenish fuel, lubricants, chemical fluids, or gases.

   d. Adjust. To maintain or regulate, within prescribed limits, by bringing into proper or exact position, or by setting the operating characteristics to specified parameters.

   e. Align. To adjust specified variable elements of an item to bring about optimum or desired performance.

   f. Calibrate. To determine and cause corrections to be made or to be adjusted on instruments or test, measuring and diagnostic equipments used in precision measurement. Consists of comparison of two instruments, one of which is a certified standard of known accuracy, to detect and adjust any discrepancy in the accuracy of the instrument being compared.

NOTE

Air Force Precision Measurement Equipment Laboratory (PMEL) person will calibrate
small arms inspection gages in accordance with TO 33K-1 -100.

   g. Remove/Install. To remove and install the same item when required to perform service or other maintenance functions. Install may be the act of emplacing, seating, or fixing into position a spare, repair part, or module (component or assembly) in a manner to allow the proper functioning of an equipment or system.

   h. Replace. To remove an unserviceable item and install a serviceable counterpart in its place. "Replace" is authorized by the MAC and is shown as the 3d position code of the SMR code.

   'Exception is authorized for ammunition MAC to permit the redesignation/redefinition of maintenance function headings to more adequately identify ammunition maintenance functions. The, heading designations and definitions will be included in the appropriate technical manual for each category of ammunition.

i. Repair. The application of maintenance services[2], including fault location/troubleshooting[3], removal/installation, and disassembly/assembly[4] procedures, and maintenance actions[5] to identify troubles and restore serviceability to an item by correcting specific damage, fault, malfunction, or failure in a part, subassembly, module (component or assembly), end item, or system.

j. Overhaul. That maintenance effort (service/action) prescribed to restore an item to a completely serviceable/operational condition as required by maintenance standards in appropriate technical publications (i. e., DMWR). Overhaul is normally the highest degree of maintenance performed by the Army. Overhaul does not normally return an item to like new condition.

k. Rebuild. Consists of those services/actions necessary for the restoration of unserviceable equipment to a like new condition in accordance with original manufacturing standards. Rebuild is the highest degree of materiel maintenance applied to Army equipment. The rebuild operation includes the act of returning to zero those age measurements (hours/miles, etc.) considered in classifying Army equipment/components.

B-3. EXPLANATION OF COLUMNS IN THE MAC, SECTION II.

a. Column 1, Group Number. Column 1 lists functional group code numbers, the purpose of which is to identify maintenance significant components, assemblies, subassemblies, and modules with the next higher assembly. End item group number shall be "00. "

b. Column 2, Component/Assembly. Column 2 contains the names of components, assemblies, subassemblies, and modules for which maintenance is authorized.

c. Column 3, Maintenance Function. Column 3 lists the functions to be performed on the item listed in column 2. (For detailed explanation of these functions, see paragraph B-2.)

d. Column 4, Maintenance Level. Column 4 specifies, by the listing of a work time figure in the appropriate sub-column(s), the level of maintenance authorized to perform the function listed in column 3. This figure represents the active time required to perform that maintenance function at the indicated level of maintenance. If the number or complexity of the tasks within the listed maintenance function vary at different maintenance levels, appropriate work time figures will be shown for each level. The work time figure represents the average time required to restore an item (assembly, subassembly, component, module, end item, or system) to a serviceable condition under typical field operating conditions. This time includes preparation time (including any necessary disassembly/assembly time), troubleshooting/fault location time, and quality assurance/quality control time in addition to the time required to perform the specific tasks identified for the maintenance functions authorized in the maintenance allocation chart. The symbol designations for the various maintenance levels are as follows:

C . . . Operator or Crew   H . General Support Maintenance
O . . . . Unit Maintenance   L... . . . . Specialized Repair Activity (SRA)[6]
F... . . . . Direct Support Maintenance   D . Depot Maintenance

---

[2] Services—inspect, test, service, adjust, align, calibrate, and/or replace.

[3] Fault locate/troubleshoot—The process of investigating and detecting the cause of equipment malfunctioning; the act of isolating a fault within a system or unit under test (UUT).

[4] Disassemble/assembly—encompasses the step-by-step taking apart (or breakdown) of a spare/functional group coded item to the level of its least componency identified as maintenance significant (i. e., assigned as SMR code) for the category of maintenance under consideration.

[5] Actions—welding, grinding, riveting, straightening, facing, remachining, and/or resurfacing.

[6] This maintenance level is not included in Section 11, column (4) of the Maintenance Allocation Chart. To identify functions to this level of maintenance, enter a work time figure in the "H" column of Section 11, column (4), and use an associated reference code in the Remarks column (6). Key the code to Section IV, Remarks, and explain the SRA complete repair application there. The explanatory remark(s) shall reference the specific Repair Parts and Special Tools List (RPSTL) TM which contains additional SRA criteria and the authorized spare/repair parts.

e. Column 5, Tools and Equipment. Column 5 specifies, by code, those common tool sets (not individual tools) and special tools, TMDE, and support equipment required to perform the designated function.

f. Column 6, Remarks. This column shall, when applicable, contain a letter code, in alphabetic order, which shall be keyed to the remarks contained in Section IV.

B-4. EXPLANATION OF COLUMNS IN TOOL AND TEST EQUIPMENT REQUIREMENTS, SECTION III.

a. Column 1, Reference Code. The tool and test equipment reference code correlates with a code used in the MAC, section II, column 5.

b. Column 2, Maintenance Level. The lowest level of maintenance authorized to use the tool or test equipment.

c. Column 3, Nomenclature. Name or identification of the tool or test equipment.

d. Column 4, National Stock Number. The National stock number oft he tool or test equipment

e. Column 5, Tool Number. The manufacturer's part number,

B-5. EXPLANATION OF COLUMNS IN REMARKS, SECTION IV.

a. Column 1, Reference Code The code recorded in column 6, Section II.

b. Column 2. Remarks. This column lists information pertinent to the maintenance function being performed as indicated in the MAC, section II.

Section II. MAINTENANCE ALLOCATION CHART
FOR
M16/M16A1 RIFLE

(1)	(2)	(3)	(4) Maintenance Level					(5)	(6)
			Unit		Direct Support	General Support	Depot	Tools and EQPT	
Group Number	Component/ Assembly	Maintenance Function	C	O	F	H	D		Remarks
00	M16/M16A1 RIFLE	Inspect	0.1	0.2	0.3				
		Test			0.3			3	
		Service	0.2	0.3					
		Replace		0.1					
		*Overhaul							
01	BOLT CARRIER ASSEMBLY	Inspect	0.1	0.1	0.1				
		Test			0.1			3	
		Service	0.1	0.1					
		Remove/ Install	0.1						
		Replace			0.1				
		Repair		0.1	0.2			2	
0101	Bolt Assembly	Inspect	0.1	0.1	0.1				
		Test			0.1			3	
		Service	0.1	0.1					
		Remove/ Install	0.1						
		Replace			0.1				
		Repair		0.2	0.2			2	
0102	Key and Bolt Carrier Assembly	Inspect	0.1	0.1	0.1				
		Service	0.1						
		Replace			0.2			1,2	
		Repair		0.1	0.2			1,3	A
02	CHARGING HANDLE ASSEMBLY	Inspect	0.1	0.1					
		Service	0.1	0.1					
		Remove/ Install	0.1						
		Replace		0.1					
		Repair		0.1				2	

*Work items тor Depot Overhaul are not included

Section II. MAINTENANCE ALLOCATION CHART
FOR
M16/M16A1   RIFLE (Continued)

(1) Group Number	(2) Component/ Assembly	(3) Maintenance Function	(4) Maintenance Level					(5) Tools and EQPT	(6) Remarks
			Unit		Direct Support	General Support	Depot		
			C	O	F	H	D		
03	UPPER RECEIVER AND BARREL ASSEMBLY	Inspect	0.1	0.2	0.1				
		Test			0.2			2	
		Service	0.2	0.2					
		Remove/ Install	0.1						
		Replace			1.2			1,2,3,4	
		Repair		0.5	0.5			1,2,3	B
0301	Rifle Barrel Assembly	Replace			0.5				
		Remove/ Install			0.2			2,3,4	
0302	Upper Receiver Assembly	Inspect			0.1				
		Replace			0.5			2,3,4	
		Repair			0.3			3,4	
030201	Forward Assist Assembly	Inspect			0.1				
		Remove/ Install			0.2			3	
		Replace			0.2			3	
		Repair			0.2			3	
		Service			0.1			3	
04	LOWER RECEIVER AND EXTENSION ASSEM-BLY	Inspect	0.1	0.2	0.2				
		Test			0.1			3	E
		Service	0.2	0.2					
		Repair		0.3	0.3			2,3,6	C
0401	Buttstock Assembly	Inspect		0.1					
		Remove/ Install		0.1				3	
		Replace			0.1			3	
		Repair		0.1				3	
		Service		0.1					
0402	Hammer Assembly	Inspect			0.1				
		Remove/ Install			0.1			3	
		Replace			0.1			3	
					0.1			3	

Section II. MAINTENANCE ALLOCATION CHART
FOR
M16/M16A1 RIFLE (Continued)

(1) Group Number	(2) Component/ Assembly	(3) Maintenance Function	(4) Maintenance Level					(5) Tools and EQPT	(6) Remarks
			Unit		Direct Support	General Support	Depot		
			C	O	F	H	D		
0403	Trigger Assembly	Inspect			0.1			3	
		Remove/ Install			0.1				
		Replace			0.1			3	
		Repair			0.1			3	
0404	Lower Receiver and Extension Subassembly	Inspect			0.1				
		Test			0.1			3,6	
		Repair			0.3	0.1		3	D

Section III. TOOL AND TEST EQUIPMENT REQUIREMENTS
FOR
M16/M16A1 RIFLE

(1) Tool/Test Equipment Ref. Code	(2) Maintenance Level	(3) Nomenclature	(4) National/NATO Stock Number	(5) Tool Number
1	F	Shop Set, Small Arms; Field Maintenance, Basic Less Power	4933-00-754-0664	SC 4933-95-CL-A11
2	F	Tool and Gage Set DS/GS Maintenance for 5.56mm Rifle, M16 Series	4933-00-056-7106	8426685
3	O,F	Tool Kit, Small Arms Repairman	5180-00-357-7770	SC 5180-95-CL-A07
4	F	Torque Wrench ft. lb	5120-00-640-6365	Part of Army Tool Set
5	F	Torque Wrench in. lb.	5120-00-230-6380	Part of Army Tool Set
6	F	Trigger Weights	4933-00-647-3696	Part of Army Tool Set

Section IV. REMARKS

REFERENCE CODE	REMARKS
A	Tool, Key
B	Tool, Sight Remover
C	Tool, Pivot Pin Removing
D	Only direct support level maintenance is authorized to restamp serial numbers
E	Lower Receiver Go-No Go Gage

APPENDIX C

**UNIT AND DIRECT SUPPORT MAINTENANCE
REPAIR PARTS AND SPECIAL TOOLS LIST
(INCLUDING DEPOT MAINTENANCE REPAIR PARTS)**

---

section I. INTRODUCTION

C-1. SCOPE. This RPSTL lists and authorizes spares and repair parts; special tools; special test, measurement, and diagnostic equipment (TMDE); and other special support equipment required for performance of unit and direct support maintenance of the rifle. It authorizes the requisitioning, issue, and disposition of spares, repair parts, and special tools indicated by the Source, Maintenance, and Recoverability (SMR) codes.

C-2. GENERAL. In addition to Section I, Introduction, this Repair Parts and Special Tools List is divided into the following sections:

a. **Section II. Repair Parts List.** A list of spares and repair parts authorized by this RPSTL for use in the performance of maintenance. The list also includes parts which must be removed for replacement of the authorized parts. Parts lists are composed of functional groups in ascending alphanumeric sequence, with the parts in each group listed in ascending figure and item number sequence. Bulk materials are listed by item name in FIG. BULK at the end of the section. Repair parts kits are listed separately in their own functional group within section II. Repair parts for repairable special tools are also listed in this section. Items listed are shown on the associated illustration(s)/figure(s).

b. Section III. **Special Tools List.** A list of special tools, special TMDE, and other special support, equipment authorized by this RPSTL (as indicated by Basis of Issue (BOI) information in DESCRIPTION AND USABLE ON CODE column) for the performance of maintenance.

c. Section **IV. Cross-Reference Index.** A list, in National item identification number (NIIN) sequence, of all National stock numbered items appearing in the listing, followed by a list in alphanumeric sequence of all part numbers appearing in the listings. National stock numbers and part numbers are cross-referenced to each illustration figure and item number appearance. The figure and item number index lists figure and item numbers in alphanumeric sequence and cross-references NSN, FSCM and part numbers.

C-3. EXPLANTION OF COLUMNS (SECTIONS II AND III).

a. **ITEM NO. (Column (1)).** Indicates the number used to identify items called out in the illustration.

b. **SMR Code (Column (2)).** The Source, Maintenance, and Recoverability (SMR) code is a 5-position code containing supply/requisitioning information, maintenance level authorization criteria, and disposition instructions, as shown in the following breakout.

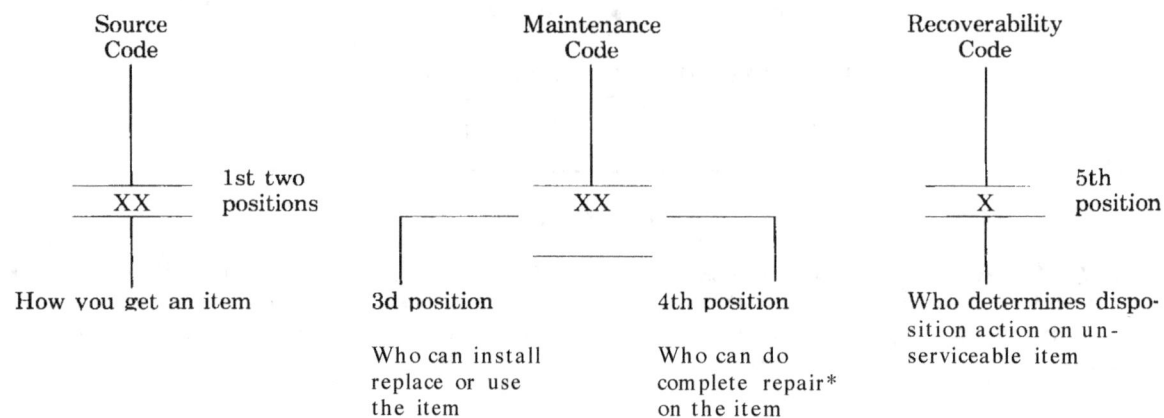

*Complete Repair: Maintenance capacity, capability, and authority to perform all corrective maintenance tasks of the "Repair" function in a use/user environment in order to restore serviceability to a failed item.

    (1) <u>Source Code</u>. The source code tells you how to get an item needed for maintenance, repair, or overhaul of an end item/equipment. Explanations of source codes follows:

Code	Explanation
PA PB PC** PD PE PF PG	Stocked items; use the applicable NSN to request/requisition items with these source codes. They are authorized to the level indicated by the code entered in the 3d position of the SMR code. **NOTE.Items coded PC are subject to deterioration.
KD KF KB	Items with these codes are not to be requested /requisitioned individually. They are part of a kit which is authorized to the maintenance level indicated in the 3d position of the SMR code. The complete kit must be requisitioned and applied.
MO - (Made at Unit AVUM Level) MF - (Made at DS/AVIM Level) MH - (Made at GS Level) ML - (Made at Specialized Repair Act (SRA) MD - (Made at Depot)	Items with these codes are not to be requested/requisitioned individually. They must be made from bulk material which is identified by the part number in the DESCRIPTION AND USABLE ON CODE (UOC) column and listed in the bulk material group of the repair parts list in this RPSTL. If the item is authorized to you by the 3d position code of the SMR code, but the source code indicates it is made at a higher level, order the item from the higher level of maintenance.

Code	Explanation

Code   **Explanation**

AO - (Assembled by unit/ AVUM Level)
AF - (Assembled by DS/AVIM Level)
AH - (Assembled by GS Level)
AL - (Assembled by SRA)
AD - (Assembled by Depot)

Items with these codes are not to be requested/requisitioned individually. The parts that make up the assembled item must be requisitiond or fabricated and assembled at the level of maintenance indicated by the source code. If the 3d position code of the SMR code authorizes you to replace the item, but the source code indicates the item is assembled at a higher level, order the item from the higher level of maintenance.

XA - Do not requisition an "XA"-coded item. Order its next higher assembly. (Also, refer to the NOTE below.)

XB - If an "XB" item is not available from salvage, order it using the FSCM and part number given.

XC - Installation drawing, diagram, instruction sheet, field service drawing, that is identified by manufacturer's part number.

XD - Item is not stocked. Order am "XD"-coded item through normal supply channels using the FSCM and part number given, if no NSN is available.

NOTE: Cannibalization or controlled exchange, when authorized, may be used as a source of supply for items with the above source codes, except for those source coded "XA" or those aircraft support items restricted **by** requirements of AR 700-42.

(2) <u>Maintenance Code</u>. Maintenance codes tell you the level(s) of maintenance authorized to USE and REPAIR support items. The maintenance codes are entered in the third and fourth positions of the SMR code as follows

(a) The maintenance code entered in the third position tells you the lowest maintenance level authorized to remove, replace, and use an item. The maintenance code entered in the third position will indicate authorization to one of the following levels of maintenance.

Code	Application/Explanation
C	Crew or operator maintenance done within unit or aviation unit maintenance.
O	Unit or aviation unit level can remove, replace, and use the item.
F	Direct support or aviation level can remove, replace and use the item.
H	General support level can remove, replace, and use the item.
L	Specialized repair activity can remove, replace, and use the item.
D	Depot level can remove, replace, and use the item.

(b) The maintenance code entered in the fourth position tells whether or not the item is to be repaired and identifies the lowest maintenance level with the capability to do complete repair (i.e., perform all authorized repair functions). (NOTE: Some limited repair may be done on the item at a lower level of maintenance, if authorized by the Maintenance Allocation Chart (MAC) and SMR codes.) This position will contain one of the following maintenance codes.

Code	Application/Explanation
O	Unit or aviation unit is the lowest level that can do complete repair of the item.
F	Direct support or aviation is the lowest level that can do complete repair of the item.
H	General support is the lowest level that can do complete repair of the item.
L	Specialized repair activity (designate the specialized repair activity) is the lowest level that can do complete repair of the item.
D	Depot is the lowest level that can do complete repair of the item.
Z	Nonreparable. No repair is authorized.
B	No repair is authorized. No parts or special tools are authorized for the maintenance of a "B" coded item. However, the item may be reconditioned by adjusting, lubricating, etc., at the user level.

(3) Recoverability Code. Recoverability codes are assigned to items to indicate the disposition action on unserviceable items. The recoverability code is entered in the fifth position of the SMR Code as follows:

Recoverability Code	Application/Explanation
Z	Nonreparable item. When unserviceable, condemn and dispose of the item at the level of maintenance shown in 3d position of SMR Code.
O	Reparable item. When uneconomically reparable, condemn and dispose of the item at unit or aviation unit level.
F	Reparable item. When uneconomically reparable, condemn and dispose of the item at the direct support or aviation level.
H	Reparable item. When uneconomically reparable, condemn and dispose of the item at the general support.
D	Reparable item. When beyond lower level repair capability, return to depot. Condemnation and disposal of item not authorized below depot level.
L	Reparable item. Condemnation and disposal not authorized below specialized repair activity (SRA).
A	Item requires special handling or condemnation procedures because of specific reasons (e.g., precious metal content, high dollar value, critical material, or hazardous material). Refer to appropriate manuals/directives for specific instructions.

c. FSCM (Column (3)). The Federal Supply Code for Manufacturer (FSCM) is a **5-digit** numeric code which is used to identify the manufacturer, distributor, or Government agency, etc., that supplies the item.

d. PART NUMBER (Column (4)). Indicates the primary number used by the manufacturer (individual, company, firm, corporation, or Government activity), which controls the design and characteristics of the item by means of its engineering drawings, specifications standards, and inspection requirements to identify an item or range of items.

NOTE: When you use a NSN to requisition an item, the item you receive may have a different part number from the part ordered.

e. DESCRIPTION AND USABLE ON CODE (UOC) (Column (5)). This column includes the following information:

(1) The Federal item name and, when required, a minimum description to identify the item.

(2) Spare/repair parts that make up an assembled item are listed immediately following the assembled item line entry.

(3) NSNs for bulk materials are referenced in this column in the line item entry for the item to be manufactured/fabricated.

(4) When the item is not used with all serial numbers of the same model, the effective serial numbers are shown on the last lines of the description (before UOC).

(5) The usable on code, when applicable (see paragraph C-5, special information).

(6) In the Special Tools List section, the basis of issue (BOI) appears as the last line(s) in the entry for each special tool, special TMDE, and other special support equipment. When density of equipments supported exceeds density spread indicated in the basis of issue, the total authorization is increased proportionately.

(7) The statement "END OF FIGURE" appears just below the last item description in column 5 for a given figure in both section II and section III

f. QTY (Column (6)). The QTY (quantity per figure column) indicates the quantity of the item used in the breakout shown on the illustration figure, which is prepared for a functional group, subfunctional group, or an assembly. A "V" appearing in this column in lieu of a quantity indicates that the quantity is variable and the quantity may vary from application to application.

C-4. EXPLANATION OF COLUMNS (SECTION IV).

a. National Stock Number (NSN) Index.

(1) <u>STOCK NUMBER column</u>. This column lists the NSN by National item identification number (NIIN) sequence. The NIIN consists of the last nine digits of the NSN

$$\underline{\text{NSN}}$$

(i.e., 5385-<u>01-574-1476</u>). When using this column to locate an item, ignore the first 4 digits of the

NIIN

NSN. However, the complete NSN should be used when ordering items by stock number.

(2) <u>FIG. column</u>. This column lists the number of the figure where the item is identified/located. The figures are in numerical order in section II and section III.

(3) <u>ITEM column</u>. The **item** number identifies the item associated with the figure listed in the adjacent FIG. column. This item is also identified by the NSN listed on the same line.

b. <u>PART NUMBER INDEX.</u> Part numbers in this index are listed by part number in ascending alphanumeric sequence (i.e., vertical arrangement of letter and number combination which places the first letter or digit of each group in order A through Z, followed by the numbers O through 9 and each following letter or digit in like order).

(1) <u>FSCM column</u>. The Federal Supply Code for Manufacturer (FSCM) is a 5-digit numeric code used to identify the manufacturer, distributor, or Government agency, etc., that supplies the item.

(2) <u>PART NUMBER column</u>. Indicates the primary number used by the manufacturer (individual, firm, corporation, or Government activity), which controls the design and characteristics of the item by means of its engineering drawings, specifications standards, and inspection requirements to identity an item or range of items.

(3) <u>STOCK NUMBER column</u>. This column lists the NSN for the associated part number and manufacturer identified in the PART NUMBER and FSCM columns to the left.

(4) <u>FIG. column</u>. This column lists the number of the figure where the item is identified/located in sections II and III.

(5) <u>ITEM column</u>. The item number is that number assigned to the item as it appears in the figure referenced in the adjacent figure number column.

c. Figure and Item Number Index.

(1) <u>FIG. column</u>. This column lists the number of the figure where the item is identified/located in section II and III.

(2) <u>ITEM column</u>. The item number is that number assigned to the item as it appears in the figure referenced in the adjacent figure number column.

(3) <u>STOCK NUMBER column</u>. This column lists the NSN for the item.

(4) FSCM column. The Federal Supply Code for Manufacturer (FSCM) is a 5-digit numeric code used to identify the manufacturer, distributor, or Government agency, etc., that supplies the item.

(5) PART NUMBER column. Indicates the primary number used by the manufacturer (individual, firm, corporation, or Government activity), which controls the design and characteristics of the item by means of its engineering drawings, specifications standards, and inspection requirements to identify item or range of items.

C-5. SPECIAL INFORMATION.

a. Usable on Code. The usable on code appears in the lower left comer of the DESCRIPTION column heading. Usable on codes are shown as "UOC..." in DESCRIPTION column (justified left) on the first line applicable item description/nomenclature. Uncoded items are applicable to all models. Identification of the usable on codes used in the RPSTL are:

Code	Used On
755	M16
194	M16A1

b. Assembly Instructions. Detailed assembly instructions for items source coded to be assembled from component spare/repair parts are found in chapter 3. Items that make up the assembly are listed immediately following the assembly item entry or reference is made to an applicable figure.

c. Index Numbers. Items which have the word BULK in the figure column will have an index number shown in the item number column. This index number is a cross-reference between the National Stock Number/Part Number index and the bulk material list in section II.

C-6. HOW TO LOCATE REPAIR PARTS.

a. When National Stock Number or Part Number is Not Known.

(1) First. Using the table of contents, determine the assembly group or subassembly group to which the item belongs. This is necessary since figures are prepared for assembly groups and subassembly groups, and listings are divided into the same groups.

(2) Second. Find the figure covering the assembly group or subassembly group to which the item belongs.

(3) Third. Identify the item on the figure and note the item number.

(4) Fourth. Refer to the Repair Parts List for the figure to find the part number for the item number noted on the figure.

(5) Fifth. Refer to the Part Number Index to find the NSN, if assigned.

b. When National Stock Number or Part Number is Known.

(1) First. Using the index of National stock numbers and part numbers, find the pertinent National stock number or part number. The NSN index is in National Item Identification Number (N I IN) sequence (see C-4a(l)). The part numbers in the PART NUMBER INDEX are listed in ascending alphanumeric sequence (see C-4b). Both indexes cross-reference you to the illustration/figure and item number of the item you are looking for.

(2) Second. Turn to the figure and item number, verify that the item is the one you're looking for, then locate the item number in the repair parts list for the figure.

C-7. **ABBREVIATIONS.** Not applicable.

Section II. REPAIR PARTS LIST

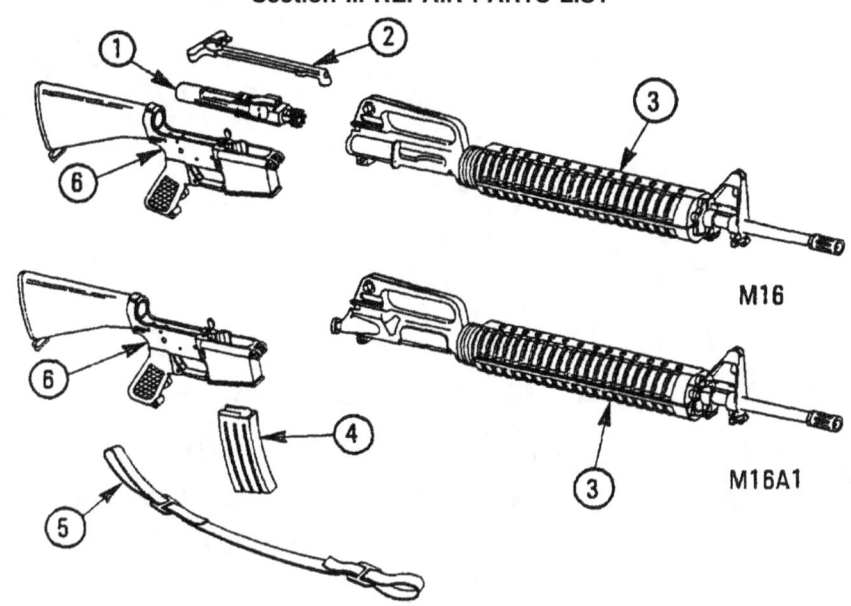

Figure C-1. 5. 5 6MM Rifle M16. 8448600 and M16A1. 8448500.

(1) ITEM NO	(2) SMR CODE	(3) CAGEC	(4) PART Number	(5) DESCRIPTION AND USABLE ON CODES(UOC)	(6) QTY
				GROUP 00 FIG C-1 5.56MM RIFLE M16 (8448600) AND M16A1 (8448500)	
1	AFFFF	19204	8448501	BOLT CARRIER ASSEMBLY (SEE FIG.C-2 FOR BREAKDOWN)	1
2	PAOOO	19204	8448517	HANDLE ASSEMBLY, CHARGING (SEE FIG **C-5 FOR BREAKDOWN**).................	1
3	AFFFF	19204	8448601	UPPER RECEIVER AND BARREL ASSEMBLY, M16, (SEE FIG.C-6 FOR BREAKDOWN) UOC:755	1
3	AFFFF	19204	8448522	UPPER RECEIVER AND BARREL ASSEMBLY, M16A1 (SEE FIG.C-6 FOR BREAKDOWN) ... UOC:194	1
4	PACZZ	19200	8448670	MAGAZINE,CARTRIDGE	1
5	PACZZ	19204	12624561	SLING,SMALL ARMS	1
6	XAFFA	19204	8448604	LOWER RECEIVER AND EXTENSION ASSY, M16 (SEE FIG C-10 FOR BREAKDOWN) UOC:755	1
6	XAFFA	19204	8448578	LOWER RECEIVER AND EXTENSION ASSY, M16A1 (SEE FIG C-10 FOR BREAKDOWN).. UOC:194	1

END OF FIGURE

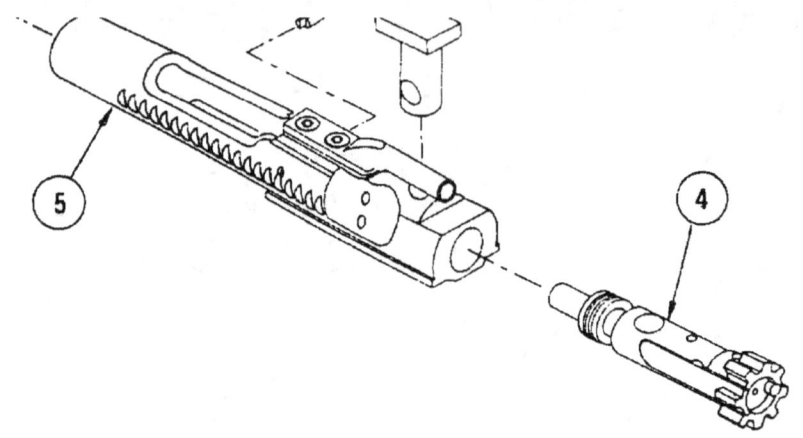

Figure C-2. Bolt Carrier Assembly 8448501.

(1) ITEM NO	(2) SMR CODE	(3) CAGEC	(4) PART NUMBER	(5) DESCRIPTION AND USABLE ON CODES(UOC)	(6) QTY
				GROUP 01 FIG C-2 BOLT CARRIER ASSEMBLY 8448501	
1	PAFZZ	19204	8448503	PIN,FIRING	1
2	PAOZZ	19204	8448504	PIN,FIRING PIN RETAINING	1
3	PAOZZ	19204	8448502	PIN,GROOVED,HEADED	1
4	PAFFF	19200	8448509	BOLT ASSEMBLY (SEE FIG C-3 FOR BREAKDOWN)	1
5	AFFFF	19204	8448505	KEY AND BOLT CARRIER ASSEMBLY (SEE FIG. C-4 FOR BREAKDOWN)	1

END OF FIGURE

C-2-1

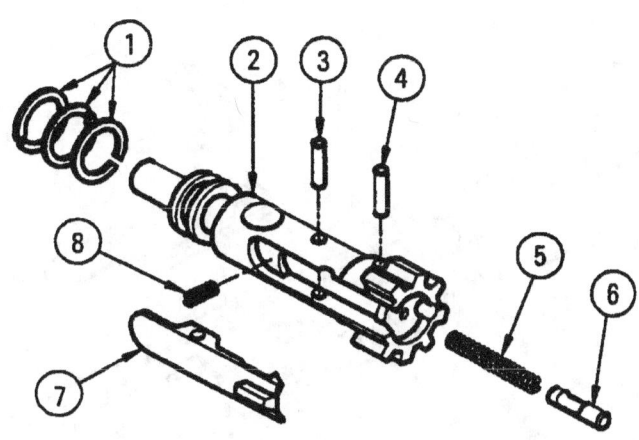

Figure **C-3**. *Bolt Assembly 8448509.*

(1) ITEM NO	(2) SMR CODE	(3) CAGEC	(4) PART NUMBER	(5) DESCRIPTION AND USABLE ON CODES (UOC)	(6) QTY
				GROUP 0101 FIG C-3 BOLT ASSEMBLY 8448509	
1	PAFZZ	19204	8448511	RING,BOLT	3
2	XAFZZ	19204	8448510	BOLT	1
3	PAOZZ	19204	8448513	PIN,EXTRACTOR	1
4	PAOZZ	96906	MS16562-98	PIN,SPRING	1
5	PAOZZ	19204	8448516	SPRING,HELICAL.	1
6	PAOZZ	19204	8448515	EJECTOR,CARTRIDGE	1
7	PAOZZ	19204	8448512	EXTRACTOR,CARTRIDGE	1
8	PAOZZ	19200	8448755	SPRING ASSEMBLY,EXT EXTRACTOR	1

END OF FIGURE

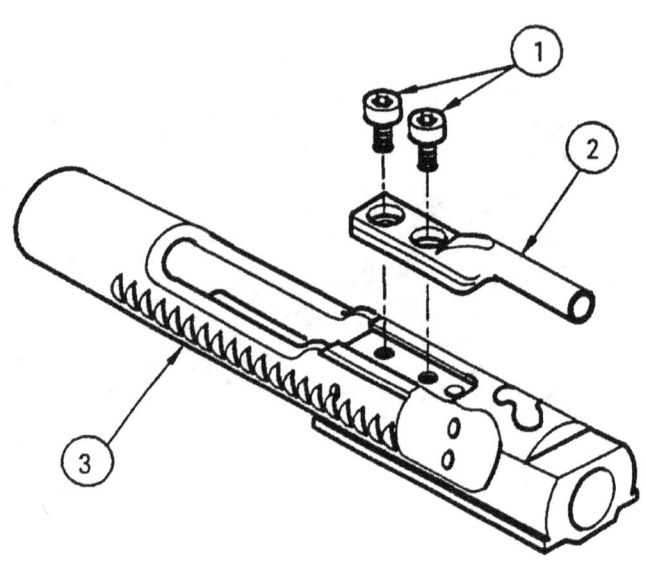

Figure C-4. Key and Bolt Carrier Assembly 8448505.

(1) ITEM NO	(2) SMR CODE	(3) CAGEC	(4) PART NUMBER	(5) DESCRIPTION AND USABLE ON CODES (UOC)	(6) QTY
				GROUP 0102 FIG C-4 KEY AND BOLT CARRIER ASSEMBLY 8448505	
1	PAFZZ	19204	8448508	SCREW,CARRIER AND KEY	2
2	PAFZZ	19200	8448506	KEY,BOLT CARRIER	1
3	PAFZZ	19200	8448507	CARRIER,BOLT	1

END OF FIGURE

C-4-1

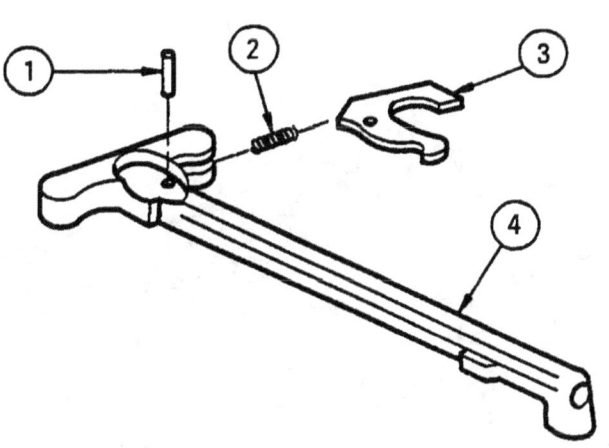

Figure C-5. Charging Handle Assembly 8448517.

(1) ITEM NO	(2) SMR CODE	(3) CAGEC	(4) PART NUMBER	(5) DESCRIPTION AND USABLE ON CODES (UOC)	(6) QTY
				GROUP 02 FIG C-5 CHARGING HANDLE ASSEMBLY 8448517	
1	PAOZZ	13629	8448521-2	PIN,SPRING	1
2	PAOZZ	19204	8448520	SPRING,HELICAL	1
3	PAOZZ	19200	8448519	LATCH,CHARGING HANDLE	1
4	XAOZZ	19204	8448518	HANDLE................................	1

END OF FIGURE

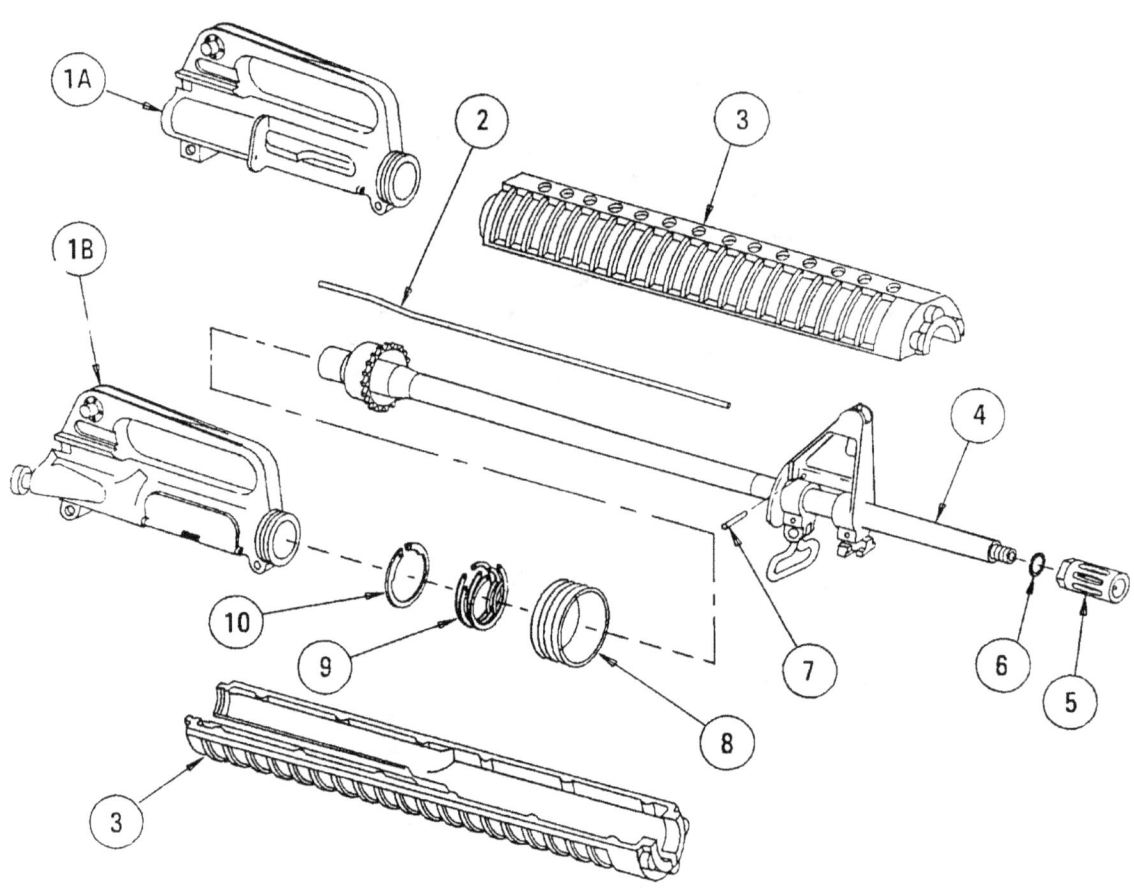

Figure C-6. Upper Receiver and Barrel Assembly M16, 8448601 and M16A1, 8448522.

(1) ITEM NO	(2) SMR CODE	(3) CAGEC	(4) PART NUMBER	(5) DESCRIPTION AND USABLE ON CODES (UOC)	(6) QTY
				GROUP 03 FIG C-6 UPPER RECEIVER AND BARREL ASSEMBLY M16 (8448601) AND M16A1 (8448522)	
1	AFFFF	19204	8448602	UPPER RECEIVER ASSY,M16 (SEE FIG.C-8 FOR BREAKDOWN) UOC:755	1
1	AFFFF	19204	8448523	UPPER RECEIVER ASSY,M16A1 (SEE FIG.C-8 FOR BREAKDOWN) UOC:194	1
2	PAFZZ	19200	8448567	TUBE,GAS	1
3	PAOZZ	19200	9349059	HANDGUARD ASSEMBLY	2
4	PAFFF	19204	8448663	BARREL ASSEMBLY, RIFLE (SEE FIG C-7 FOR BREADKDOWN)	1
5	PAFZZ	19204	8448576	SUPPRESSOR,FLASH	1
6	PAFZZ	19204	8448577	WASHER,LOCK,FLASH SUPPRESSOR	1
7	PAFZZ	96906	MS16562-106	PIN,SPRING	1
8	PAFZZ	19204	8448712	RING,SLIP,HAND GUAR GUARD	1
9	PAFZZ	19204	8448712	SPRING, SLIP RING, HANDGUARD	1
10	PAFZZ	96906	MS16626-1137	RING,RETAINING EXT, TAPERED SECTION	1

END OF FIGURE

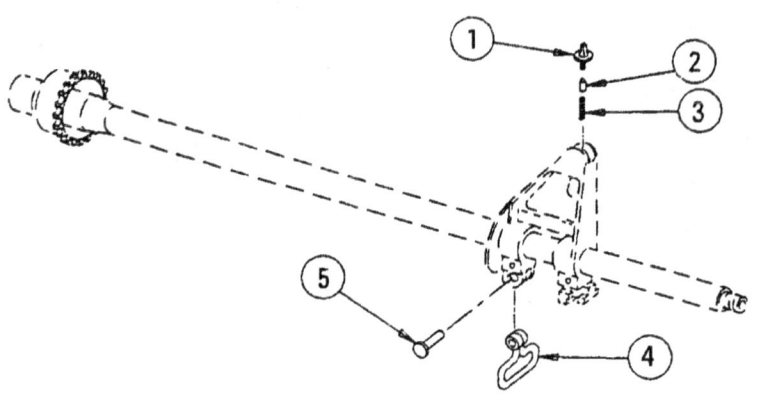

Figure C-7. Rifle Barrel Assembly 8448663.

(1) ITEM NO	(2) SMR CODE	(3) CAGEC	(4) PART NUMBER	(5) DESCRIPTION AND USABLE ON CODES (UOC)	(6) QTY
				GROUP 0301 FIG C-7 RIFLE BARREL ASSEMBLY 8448663	
1	PAOZZ	19200	9349056	POST,FRONT SIGHT	1
2	PAOZZ	19204	8448573	DETENT,FRONT SIGHT	1
3	PAOZZ	19204	8448574	SPRING,HELICAL	1
4	PAOZZ	19204	8448571	SWIVEL, SLING,SMALL	1
5	PAOZZ	19204	8448697	RIVET,TUBULAR	1

END OF FIGURE

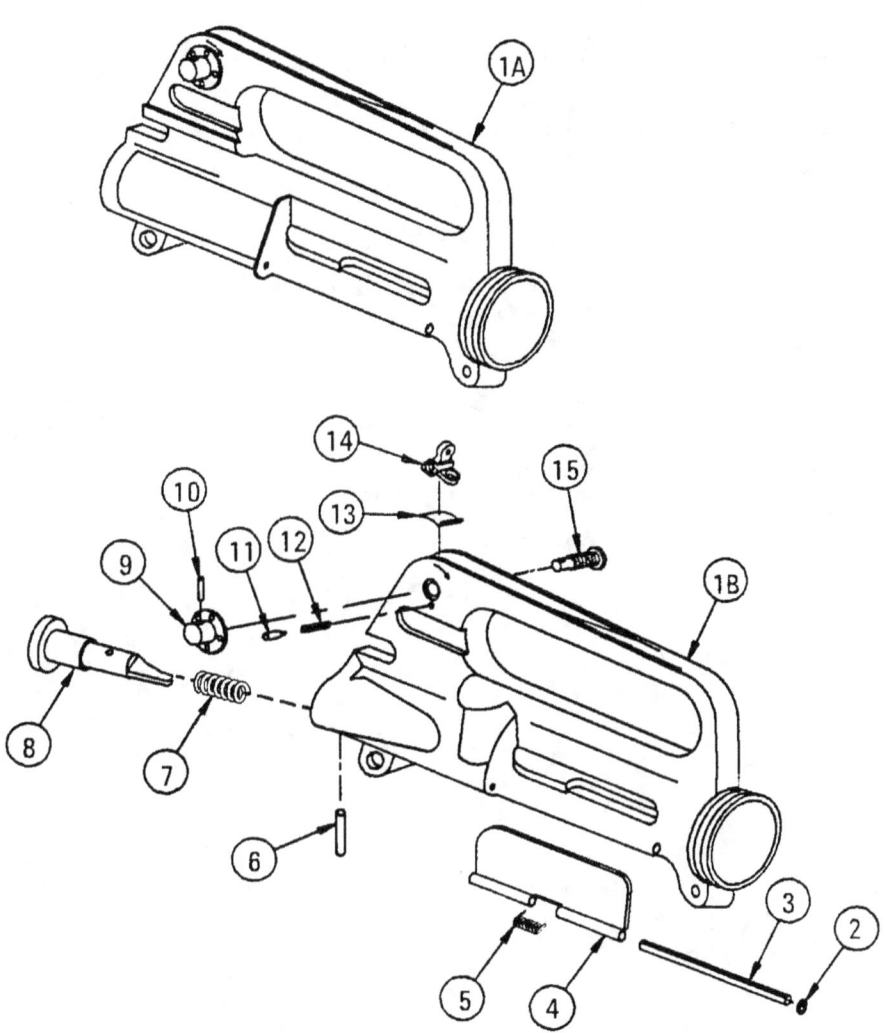

Figure C-8. Upper Receiver Assembly M16, 8448602 and M16A1, 8448523.

(1) ITEM NO	(2) SMR CODE	(3) CAGEC	(4) PART NUMBER	(5) DESCRIPTION AND USABLE ON CODES (UOC)	(6) QTY
				GROUP 0302 FIG C-8 UPPER RECEIVER ASSEMBLY M16 (8448602) AND M16A1 (8448523)	
1	PAFZZ	19204	8448603	RECEIVER,UPPER M16 UOC:755	1
1	PAFZZ	19200	12576280	RECEIVER,CARTRIDGE M16A1 UOC:194	1
2	PAOZZ	96906	MS16632-1012	RING,RETAINING	1
3	PAOZZ	19204	8448533	PIN,GROOVED,HEADLES COVER	1
4	PAOZZ	19204	8448525	COVER,EJECTION	1
5	PAOZZ	19204	8448532	SPRING,HELICAL	1
6	PAFZZ	96906	MS16562-121	PIN,SPRING (FORWARD ASSIST PIN) UOC:194	1
7	PAFZZ	19200	8448540	SPRING,HELICAL,COMP COMPRESSION UOC:194	1
8	AFFFF	19204	9349086	FORWARD ASSIST ASSY (SEE FIG.C-9 FOR BREAKDOWN) UOC:194	1
9	PAFZZ	19200	8448535	DIAL,CONTROL WINDAGE	1
10	PAFZZ	96906	MS16562-96	PIN,SPRING	1
11	PAFZZ	19200	8448537	DETENT,REAR SIGHT	1
12	PAFZZ	19200	8448538	SPRING,HELICAL,COMP COMPRESSION	1
13	PAFZZ	19200	8448536	SPRING,FLAT	1
14	PAFZZ	19204	8448539	APERTURE SIGHT	1
15	PAFZZ	19204	8448534	SCREW,REAR SIGHT WINDAGE	1

END OF FIGURE

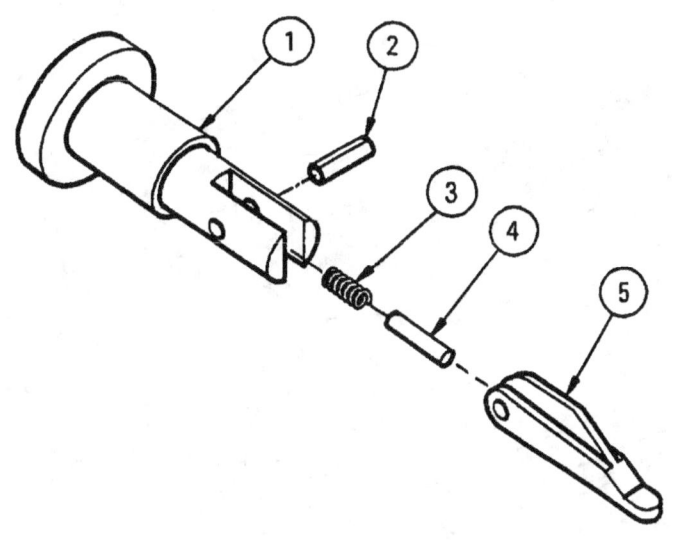

Figure C-9. Forward Assist Assembly M16A1, 9349086.

(1) ITEM NO	(2) SMR CODE	(3) CAGEC	(4) PART NUMBER	(5) DESCRIPTION AND USABLE ON CODES (UOC)	(6) QTY
				GROUP 030201 FIG C-9 FORWARD ASSIST ASSEMBLY M16A1 (9349086)	
1	PAFZZ	19200	9349085	PLUNGER ASSEMBLY UOC:194	1
2	PAFZZ	13629	95113	PIN,SPRING , FORWARD ASSIST PAWL... UOC:194	1
3	PAFZZ	19200	8448542	SPRING,HELICAL,COMP COMPRESSION UOC:194	1
4	PAFZZ	19204	8448544	DETENT,PAWL UOC:194	1
5	PAFZZ	19204	8448543	PAWL,FORWARD ASSIST UOC:194	1

END OF FIGURE

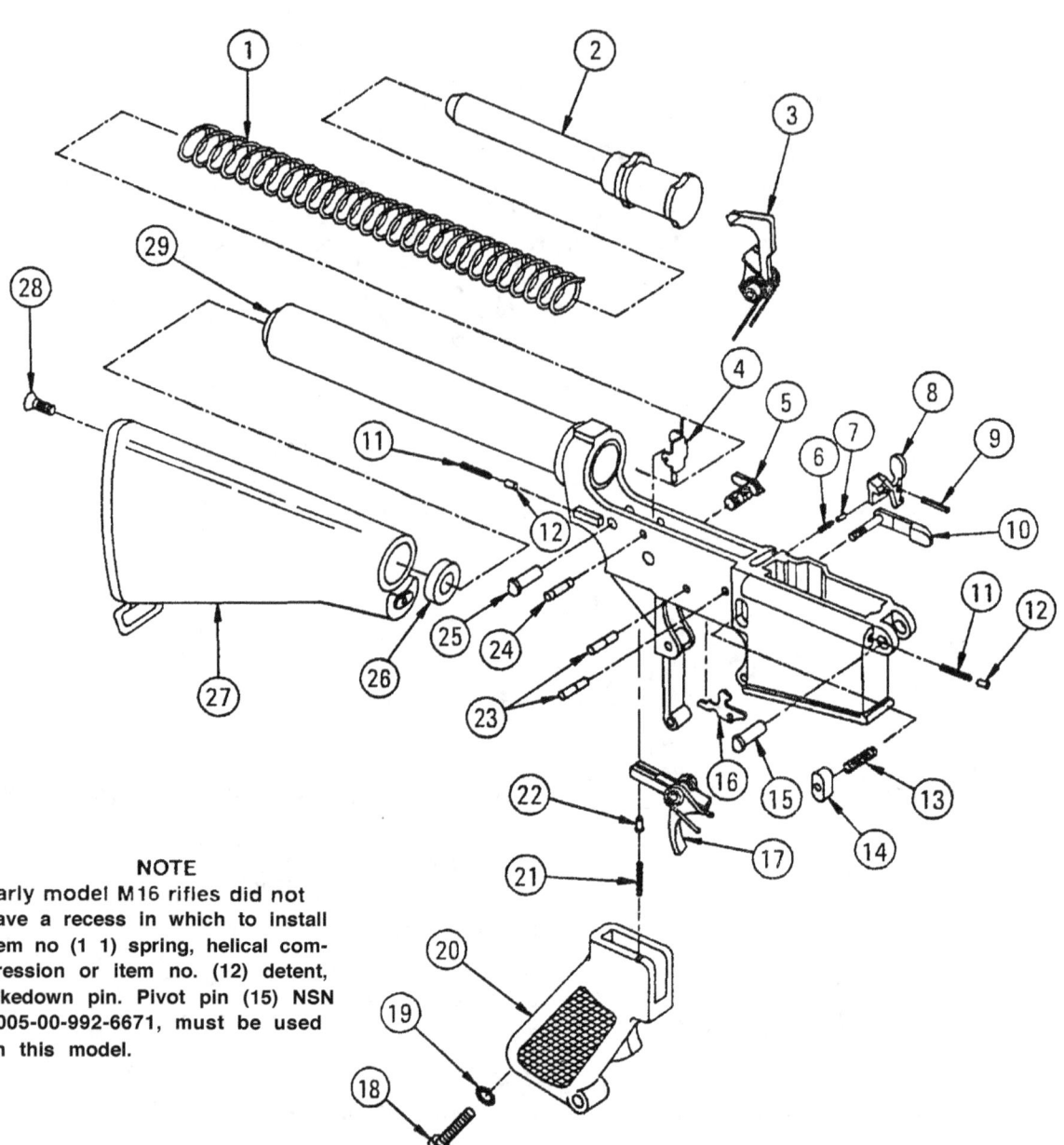

NOTE
Early model M16 rifles did not
have a recess in which to install
item no (1 1) spring, helical compression or item no. (12) detent,
takedown pin. Pivot pin (15) NSN
1005-00-992-6671, must be used
on this model.

Figure C-10. Lower Receiver and Extension Assembly M16, 8448604 and M16A1, 8448578.

(1) ITEM NO	(2) SMR CODE	(3) CAGEC	(4) PART NUMBER	(5) DESCRIPTION AND USABLE ON CODES (UOC)	(6) QTY
				GROUP 04 FIG C-10 LOWER RECEIVER AND EXTENSION ASSEMBLY M16 (8448604) AND M16A1 (8448578)	
1	PAOZZ	19204	8448629	SPRING,HELICAL, COMPRESSION	1
2	PAOZZ	19200	8448615	BUFFER ASSEMBLY	1
3	AFFFF	19204	8448610	HAMMER ASSY (SEE FIG.C-12 FOR BREAKDOWN)	1
4	PAFZZ	19200	8448595	SEAR AUTOMATIC ASSEMBLY	1
5	PAFZZ	19204	8448630	LEVER,SELECTOR	1
6	PAFZZ	19204	8448633	SPRING,HELICAL, COMPRESSION	1
7	PAFZZ	19204	8448634	PLUNGER,BOLT CATCH	1
8	PAFZZ	19200	8448628	CATCH,BOLT	1
9	PAFZZ	96906	MS16562-119	PIN,SPRING STEEL	1
10	PAFZZ	19204	8448638	CATCH,MAGAZINE	1
11	PAOZZ	19204	8448586	SPRING,HELICAL, COMPRESSION	2
12	PAOZZ	19204	8448585	PIN,STRAIGHT,HEADLE PIN	2
13	PAFZZ	19204	8448637	SPRING,HELICAL, COMPRESSION	1
14	PAFZZ	19204	8448636	BUTTON,MAGAZINE CAT CATCH	1
15	PAOZZ	19204	8448621	PIN,PIVOT	1
15	PAOZZ	13629	95601	PIN,PIVOT (SEE NOTE ON FIG C-10) UOC:755	1
16	PAFZZ	19200	8448635	DISCONNECTOR	1
17	AFFFF	19204	8448591	TRIGGER ASSY (SEE FIG.C-13 FOR BREAKDOWN)	1
18	PAOZZ	88044	AN501D416-18	SCREW,MACHINE,FILLI	1
19	PAOZZ	96906	MS35335-61	WASHER,LOCK	1
20	PAOZZ	19200	9349127	GRIP,RIFLE PLASTIC,BLACK	1
21	PAOZZ	19204	8448516	SPRING,HELICAL, COMPRESSION	1
22	PAOZZ	19204	8448631	DETENT,SAFETY	1
23	PAFZZ	19204	8448609	PIN,GROOVED,HEADLES TRIGGER	2
24	PAFZZ	19204	8448599	PIN,GROOVED,HEADLES	1
25	PAOZZ	19204	8448584	PIN,TAKEDOWN	1
26	PROZZ	19200	9349129	SPACER,STEPPED	1
27	PAOOO	19200	9349119	BUTTSTOCK ASSEMBLY	1
28	PAOZZ	19200	9349128	SCREW,SELF-LOCKING	1
29	XAFFA	19204	8448605	LOWER RECEIVER, AND EXTENSION SUBASSEMBLY, M16 (SEE FIG C-14 FOR BREAKDOWN) UOC:755	1
29	XAFFA	19204	8448579	LOWER RECEIVER AND EXTENSION SUBASSEMBLY, M16A1 (SEE FIG C-14 FOR BREAKDOWN) UOC:194	1

                          END OF FIGURE

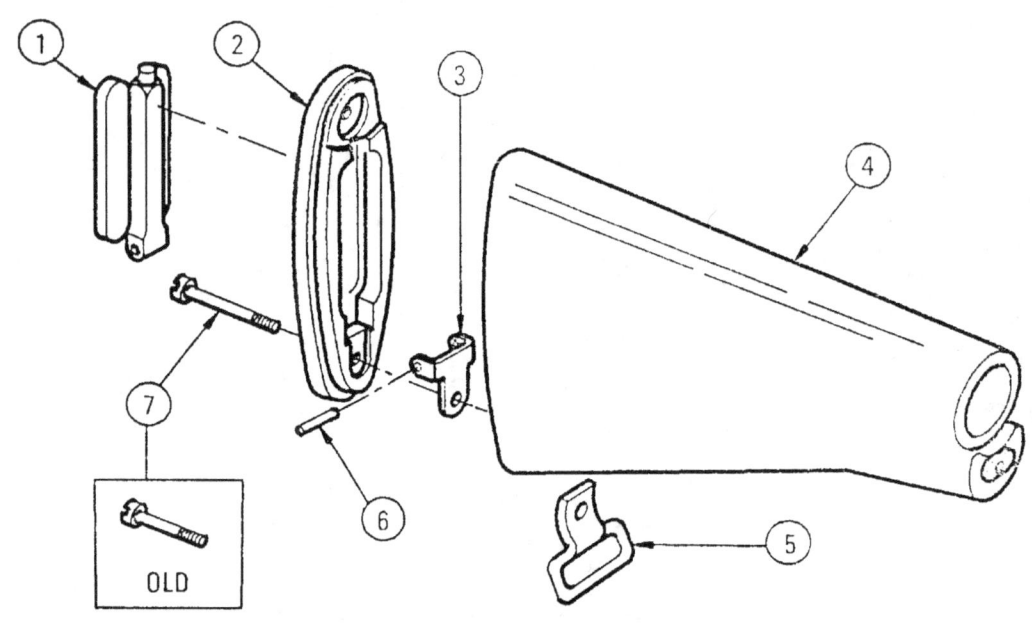

Figure C-11. Buttstock Assembly 9349119

(1) ITEM NO	(2) SMR CODE	(3) CAGEC	(4) PART NUMBER	(5) DESCRIPTION AND USABLE ON CODES (UOC)	(6) QTY
				GROUP 0401 FIG C-11	
				BUTTSTOCK ASSEMBLY 9349119	
1	PAOZZ	19200	9381380	DOOR ASSEMBLY,THUMB	1
2	PAOZZ	19200	9349130	PLATE,BUTT, SHOULDER	1
3	PAOZZ	19200	8448653	HINGE,ACCESS DOOR ACCESS DOOR BUTT PLATE.	1
4	XAOZZ	19200	9349121	BUTTSTOCK	1
5	PAOZZ	19204	8448652	SWIVEL, SLING, SMALL	1
6	PAOZZ	19204	8448655	PIN,STRAIGHT, HEADLESS	1
7	PAOZZ	19200	9349120	SCREW, SELF-LOCKING	1

END OF FIGURE

TM 9-1005-249-23&P
AIR FORCE TO 11W-3-5-5-24
COAST GUARD CMDTINST M8370.9

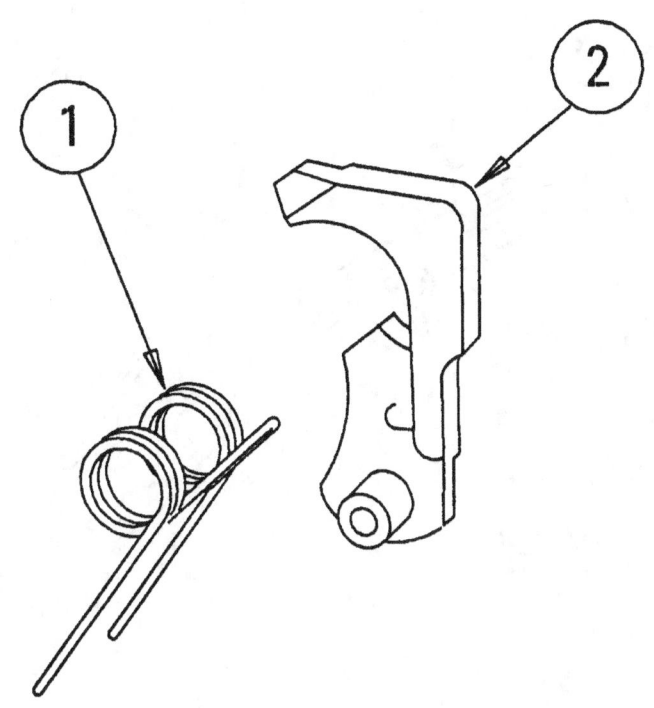

Figure C-12. Hammcr Assembly 8448610.

(1) ITEM NO	(2) SMR CODE	(3) CAGEC	(4) PART NUMBER	(5) DESCRIPTION AND USABLE ON CODES (UOC)	(6) QTY
				GROUP 0402 FIG C-12 HAMMER ASSEMBLY 8448610	
1	PAFZZ	19204	8448611	SPRING,HELICAL, TORSION	1
2	PAFZZ	19200	8448612	HAMMER,FIRING,SMALL	1
				END OF FIGURE	

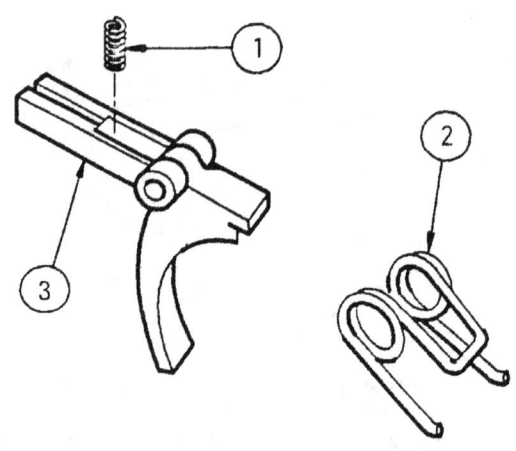

Figure C- 13. *Trigger Assembly 8448591.*

(1) ITEM NO	(2) SMR CODE	(3) CAGEC	(4) PART NUMBER	(5) DESCRIPTION AND USABLE ON CODES(UOC)	(6) QTY
				GROUP 0403 FIG C-13 TRIGGER ASSEMBLY 8448591	
1	PAFZZ	19200	8448594	SPRING,HELICAL,COMP COMPRESSION	1
2	PAFZZ	19204	8448593	SPRING,HELICAL , TORSION	1
3	PAFZZ	19204	8448592	TRIGGER	1

END OF FIGURE

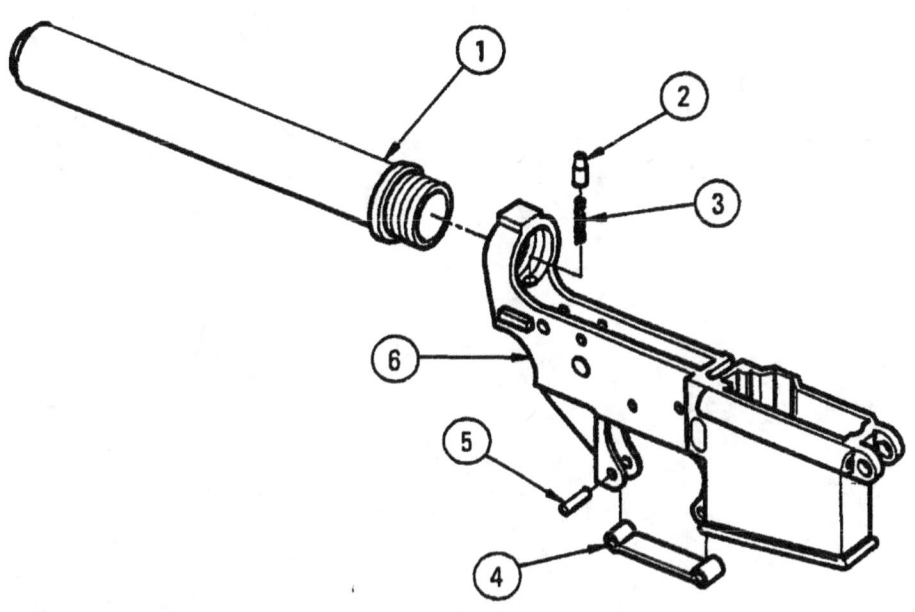

Figure C-14. Lower Receiver and Extension Subassembly M16, 8448605 and M16A1, 8448579.

(1) ITEM NO	(2) SMR CODE	(3) CAGEC	(4) PART NUMBER	(5) DESCRIPTION AND USABLE ON CODES (UOC)	(6) QTY
				GROUP 0404 FIG C-14 LOWER RECEIVER AND EXTENSION SUBASSEMBLY M16 (8448605) AND M16A1 (8448579)	
1	PAFZZ	19200	8448581	HOLDER,SPRING RECEIVER	1
2	PAFZZ	19204	8448582	PIN,SHOULDER,HEADLE	1
3	PAFZZ	19200	8448583	SPRING,HELICAL,COMP COMPRESSION	1
4	PAFZZ	19204	8448587	GUARD,TRIGGER	1
5	PAFZZ	96906	MS16562-35	PIN,SPRING	1
6	XAFDD	19204	8448606	RECEIVER, LOWER NOTE: SERIAL NUMBER CONTROL M16 . . . . UOC:755	1
6	XAFDD	19204	8448580	RECEIVER, LOWER NOTE: SERIAL NUMBER CONTROL M16A1 . . . . UOC:194	1

END OF FIGURE

TM 9-1005-249-23&P
AIR FORCE TO 11W-3-5-5-24
COAST GUARD CMDTINST M8370.9

Section III. SPECIAL TOOLS LIST

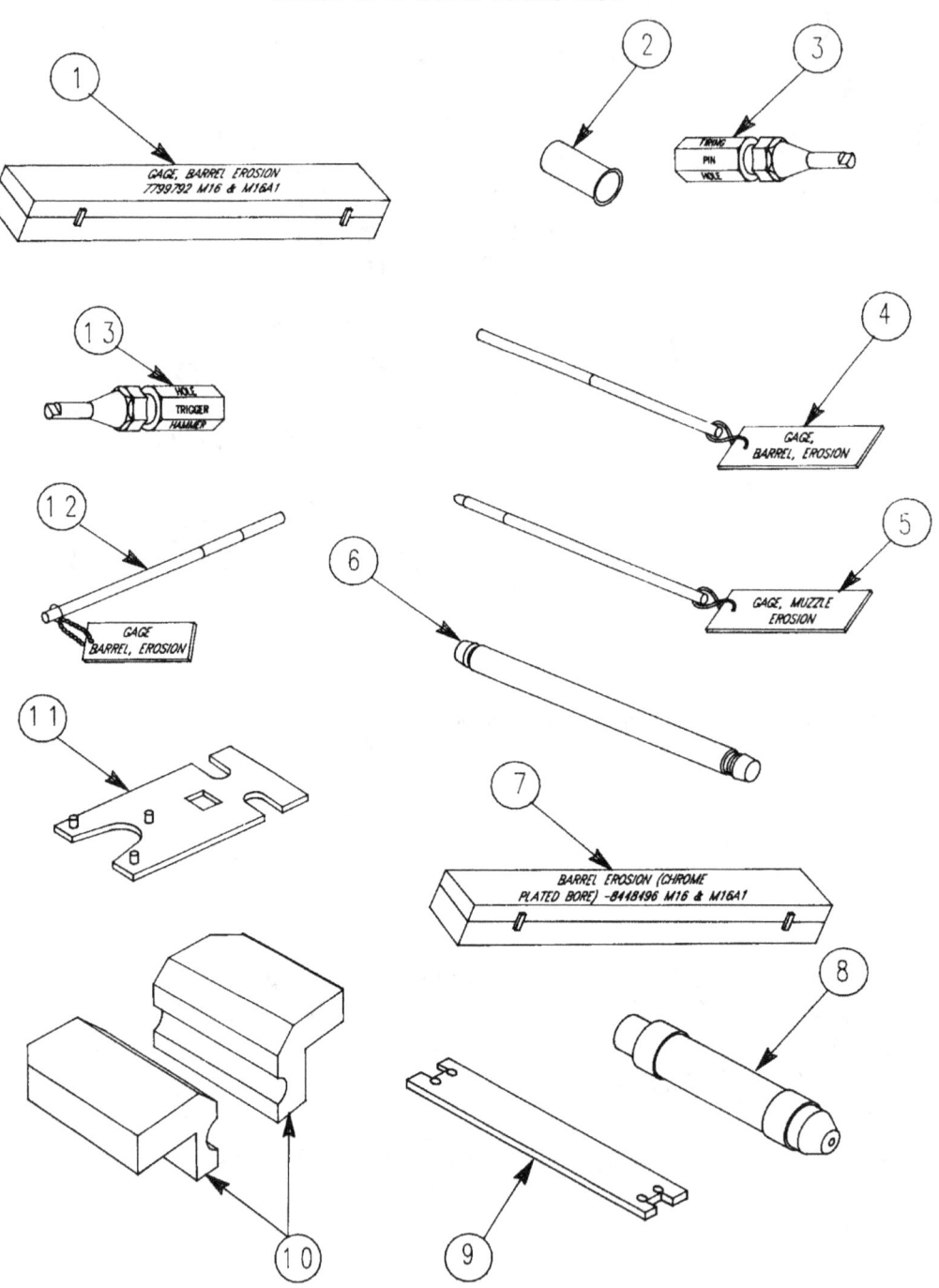

Figure C-15. Special tools.

SECTION III

(1) ITEM NO	(2) SMR CODE	(3) CAGEC	(4) PART NUMBER	(5) DESCRIPTION AND USABLE ON CODES (UOC)	(6) QTY
				GROUP 9500 FIG C-15 SPECIAL TOOLS	
1	ADFFA	19204	8426685	TOOL AND GAGE SET DS/GS SUPPORT MAINTENANCE FOR 5.56MM RIFLE M16 RIFLE SERIES BOI: 2 PER SUPPORTING DSU/GSU	
1	PAFZZ	19205	7799809	..CASE,CARRYING,GAGE PART OF KIT P/ N 8426685 (M16 ONLY)	
2	PAFZZ	19204	8448201	..REFLECTOR TOOL, CHAMBER,PART OF KIT P/N 8426685	
3	PAFZZ	19200	12620101	..GAGE,PLUG,PLAIN PART OF KIT P/N 8426685	
4	PAFZZ	19204	8448496	..GAGE,BARREL,EROSION PART OF KIT P/N 8426685 (CHROME BARREL)	
5	PAFZZ	19204	8448677	..GAGE,MUZZLE EROSION PART OF KIT P/N 8426685 (NON-CHROME BARREL)	
6	PAFZZ	19204	8448202	..GAGE,STRAIGHTNESS PART OF KIT P/ N 8426685	
7	PAFZZ	19204	12006359	..CASE,BORE GAGE PART OF KIT P/N 8426685	
8	PAFZZ	19204	7799734	..GAGE,HEADSPACE PART OF KIT P/N 8426685	
9	PAFZZ	19204	7799735	..GAGE,FIRING PIN PROTRUSION PART OF KIT P/N 8426685	
10	PAFZZ	19204	11010032	..FIXTURE,BARREL REMOVAL PART OF KIT P/N 8426685	
11	PAFZZ	19204	11010033	..WRENCH,COMBINATION PART OF KIT P/ N 8426685	
12	PAFZZ	19205	7799792	..GAGE,BARREL EROSION PART OF KIT P/N 8426685 (NON-CHROME BARREL)	
13	PAFZZ	19204	12006472	..GAGE,PLUG,TAPER CYLINDER PART O KIT P/N 8426685	

END OF FIGURE

CROSS-REFERENCE INDEXES

NATIONAL STOCK NUMBER INDEX

STOCK NUMBER	FIG.	ITEM	STOCK NUMBER	FIG.	ITEM
5315-00-017-9537	C-10	15	5360-00-979-3931	C-7	3
3040-00-017-9539	C-9	5	5360-00-992-6648	C-12	1
1005-00-017-9540	C-9	4	1005-00-992-6649	C-10	4
5360-00-017-9541	C-8	7	5315-00-992-6650	C-10	24
1005-00-017-9543	C-7	4	5315-00-992-6651	C-14	2
1005-00-017-9546	C-1	2	5360-00-992-6652	C-14	3
1005-00-017-9547	C-2	1	5315-00-992-6653	C-10	25
1005-00-017-9548	C-10	8	5315-00-992-6654	C-10	12
1005-00-017-9551	C-12	2	5360-00-992-6655	C-10	11
5315-00-017-9552	C-9	2	5360-00-992-6665	C-10	1
1005-00-056-2201	C-10	10	5340-00-992-6666	C-10	5
5360-00-056-2246	C-10	6	1005-00-992-6667	C-10	22
1005-00-056-2247	C-10	7	1005-00-992-6671	C-10	15
5315-00-058-6044	C-6	7	1005-00-992-7280	C-6	6
5365-00-064-2652	C-8	2	5315-00-992-7283	C-4	2
5220-00-070-7814	C-15	8	5305-00-992-7284	C-4	1
6695-00-070-7815	C-15	9	1005-00-992-7285	C-2	4
4933-00-070-9151	C-15	10	1005-00-992-7287	C-3	1
5120-00-070-9152	C-15	11	1005-00-992-7288	C-3	7
1005-00-087-8998	C-6	8	1005-00-992-7290	C-3	3
	C-6	9	1005-00-992-7291	C-3	6
1005-00-152-3441	C-6	4	5360-00-992-7292	C-3	5
5220-00-155-4925	C-15	5		C-10	21
5220-00-221-9391	C-15	6	5315-00-992-7294	C-2	3
5365-00-252-6853	C-6	10	5340-00-992-7297	C-14	1
5315-00-282-3642	C-8	10	1005-00-992-7299	C-14	4
1005-00-403-0964	C-11	5	5360-00-992-7301	C-10	13
5340-00-463-3892	C-11	3	1005-00-992-7302	C-10	14
5315-00-463-3894	C-11	6	1005-00-992-7307	C-13	3
5360-00-523-8084	C-9	3	5360-00-992-7308	C-13	2
5310-00-527-3634	C-10	19	5315-00-992-7309	C-10	23
5315-00-597-5086	C-3	4	5360-00-992-7311	C-13	1
1005-00-738-6213	C-4	3	5360-00-999-0404	C-5	2
1005-00-760-3768	C-3	8	5340-00-999-0405	C-5	3
4933-00-800-7508	C-15	2	1005-00-999-0406	C-10	16
5315-00-812-3312	C-10	9	1005-00-999-1509	C-2	2
5315-00-814-3530	C-14	5	5220-01-014-8183	C-15	4
1005-00-921-5004	C-1	4	5315-01-027-4759	C-8	6
1005-00-933-8089	C-6	5	4933-01-035-5607	C-15	7
1005-00-937-3078	C-10	2	5220-01-043-9473	C-15	13
1005-00-978-1022	C-8	4	5320-01-063-7635	C-7	5
5315-00-978-1023	C-8	3	5220-01-075-5004	C-15	3
5360-00-978-1025	C-8	5	1005-01-134-3625	C-7	1
1005-00-978-1026	C-8	14	1005-01-134-3629	C-6	3
5360-00-978-1027	C-8	13	1005-01-135-4973	C-10	27
5355-00-978-1029	C-8	9	1005-01-144-1468	C-9	1
1005-00-978-1030	C-8	11	5305-01-144-1494	C-11	7
5360-00-978-1032	C-8	12	1005-01-146-7685	C-11	2
4710-00-978-1038	C-6	2	5365-01-146-7692	C-10	26
5315-00-979-3930	C-7	2	5305-01-147-8585	C-10	28

CROSS-REFERENCE INDEXES

NATIONAL STOCK NUMBER INDEX

STOCK NUMBER	FIG.	ITEM	STOCK NUMBER	FIG.	ITEM
1005-01-148-4805	C-10	20			
1005-01-216-4510	C-1	5			
1005-01-228-8504	C-11	1			
1005-01-248-5858	C-8	1			
5305-01-268-1191	C-10	18			

SECTION IV

CROSS-REFERENCE INDEXES

PART NUMBER INDEX

CAGEC	PART NUMBER	STOCK NUMBER	FIG.	ITEM
88044	AN501D416-18	5305-01-268-1191	C-10	18
96906	MS16562-106	5315-00-058-6044	C-6	7
96906	MS16562-119	5315-00-812-3312	C-10	9
96906	MS16562-121	5315-01-027-4759	C-8	6
96906	MS16562-35	5315-00-814-3530	C-14	5
96906	MS16562-96	5315-00-282-3642	C-8	10
96906	MS16562-98	5315-00-597-5086	C-3	4
96906	MS16626-1137	5365-00-252-6853	C-6	10
96906	MS16632-1012	5365-00-064-2652	C-8	2
96906	MS35335-61	5310-00-527-3634	C-10	19
19204	11010032	4933-00-070-9151	C-15	10
19204	11010033	5120-00-070-9152	C-15	11
19204	12006359	4933-01-035-5607	C-15	7
19204	12006472	5220-01-043-9473	C-15	13
19200	12576280	1005-01-248-5858	C-8	1
19200	12620101	5220-01-075-5004	C-15	3
19204	12624561	1005-01-216-4510	C-1	5
19204	7799734	5220-00-070-7814	C-15	8
19204	7799735	6695-00-070-7815	C-15	9
19205	7799792		C-15	12
19205	7799809		C-15	1
19204	8426685		C-15	1
19204	8448201	4933-00-800-7508	C-15	2
19204	8448202	5220-00-221-9391	C-15	6
19204	8448496	5220-01-014-8183	C-15	4
19204	8448501		C-1	1
19204	8448502	5315-00-992-7294	C-2	3
19204	8448503	1005-00-017-9547	C-2	1
19204	8448504	1005-00-999-1509	C-2	2
19204	8448505		C-2	5
19200	8448506	5315-00-992-7283	C-4	2
19200	8448507	1005-00-738-6213	C-4	3
19204	8448508	5305-00-992-7284	C-4	1
19200	8448509	1005-00-992-7285	C-2	4
19204	8448510		C-3	2
19204	8448511	1005-00-992-7287	C-3	1
19204	8448512	1005-00-992-7288	C-3	7
19204	8448513	1005-00-992-7290	C-3	3
19204	8448515	1005-00-992-7291	C-3	6
19204	8448516	5360-00-992-7292	C-3	5
			C-10	21
19204	8448517	1005-00-017-9546	C-1	2
19204	8448518		C-5	4
19200	8448519	5340-00-999-0405	C-5	3
19204	8448520	5360-00-999-0404	C-5	2
13629	8448521-2		C-5	1
19204	8448522		C-1	3
19204	8448523		C-6	1
19204	8448525	1005-00-978-1022	C-8	4
19204	8448532	5360-00-978-1025	C-8	5
19204	8448533	5315-00-978-1023	C-8	3

SECTION IV

CROSS-REFERENCE INDEXES

PART NUMBER INDEX

CAGEC	PART NUMBER	STOCK NUMBER	FIG.	ITEM
19204	8448534		C-8	15
19200	8448535	5355-00-978-1029	C-8	9
19200	8448536	5360-00-978-1027	C-8	13
19200	8448537	1005-00-978-1030	C-8	11
19200	8448538	5360-00-978-1032	C-8	12
19204	8448539	1005-00-978-1026	C-8	14
19200	8448540	5360-00-017-9541	C-8	7
19200	8448542	5360-00-523-8084	C-9	3
19204	8448543	3040-00-017-9539	C-9	5
19204	8448544	1005-00-017-9540	C-9	4
19200	8448567	4710-00-978-1038	C-6	2
19204	8448571	1005-00-017-9543	C-7	4
19204	8448573	5315-00-979-3930	C-7	2
19204	8448574	5360-00-979-3931	C-7	3
19204	8448576	1005-00-933-8089	C-6	5
19204	8448577	1005-00-992-7280	C-6	6
19204	8448578		C-1	6
19204	8448579		C-10	29
19204	8448580		C-14	6
19200	8448581	5340-00-992-7297	C-14	1
19204	8448582	5315-00-992-6651	C-14	2
19200	8448583	5360-00-992-6652	C-14	3
19204	8448584	5315-00-992-6653	C-10	25
19204	8448585	5315-00-992-6654	C-10	12
19204	8448586	5360-00-992-6655	C-10	11
19204	8448587	1005-00-992-7299	C-14	4
19204	8448591		C-10	17
19204	8448592	1005-00-992-7307	C-13	3
19204	8448593	5360-00-992-7308	C-13	2
19200	8448594	5360-00-992-7311	C-13	1
19200	8448595	1005-00-992-6649	C-10	4
19204	8448599	5315-00-992-6650	C-10	24
19204	8448601		C-1	3
19204	8448602		C-6	1
19204	8448603		C-8	1
19204	8448604		C-1	6
19204	8448605		C-10	29
19204	8448606		C-14	6
19204	8448609	5315-00-992-7309	C-10	23
19204	8448610		C-10	3
19204	8448611	5360-00-992-6648	C-12	1
19200	8448612	1005-00-017-9551	C-12	2
19200	8448615	1005-00-937-3078	C-10	2
19204	8448621	5315-00-017-9537	C-10	15
19200	8448628	1005-00-017-9548	C-10	8
19204	8448629	5360-00-992-6665	C-10	1
19204	8448630	5340-00-992-6666	C-10	5
19204	8448631	1005-00-992-6667	C-10	22
19204	8448633	5360-00-056-2246	C-10	6
19204	8448634	1005-00-056-2247	C-10	7
19200	8448635	1005-00-999-0406	C-10	16

SECTION IV

CROSS-REFERENCE INDEXES

PART NUMBER INDEX

CAGEC	PART NUMBER	STOCK NUMBER	FIG.	ITEM
19204	8448636	1005-00-992-7302	C-10	14
19204	8448637	5360-00-992-7301	C-10	13
19204	8448638	1005-00-056-2201	C-10	10
19204	8448652	1005-00-403-0964	C-11	5
19200	8448653	5340-00-463-3892	C-11	3
19204	8448655	5315-00-463-3894	C-11	6
19204	8448663	1005-00-152-3441	C-6	4
19200	8448670	1005-00-921-5004	C-1	4
19204	8448677	5220-00-155-4925	C-15	5
19204	8448697	5320-01-063-7635	C-7	5
19204	8448712	1005-00-087-8998	C-6	8
			C-6	9
19200	8448755	1005-00-760-3768	C-3	8
19200	9349056	1005-01-134-3625	C-7	1
19200	9349059	1005-01-134-3629	C-6	3
19200	9349085	1005-01-144-1468	C-9	1
19204	9349086		C-8	8
19200	9349119	1005-01-135-4973	C-10	27
19200	9349120	5305-01-144-1494	C-11	7
19200	9349121		C-11	4
19200	9349127	1005-01-148-4805	C-10	20
19200	9349128	5305-01-147-8585	C-10	28
19200	9349129	5365-01-146-7692	C-10	26
19200	9349130	1005-01-146-7685	C-11	2
19200	9381380	1005-01-228-8504	C-11	1
13629	95113	5315-00-017-9552	C-9	2
13629	95601	1005-00-992-6671	C-10	15

CROSS-REFERENCE INDEXES
FIGURE AND ITEM NUMBER INDEX

FIG.	ITEM	STOCK NUMBER	CAGEC	PART NUMBER
C-1	1		19204	8448501
C-1	2	1005-00-017-9546	19204	8448517
C-1	3		19204	8448522
C-1	3		19204	8448601
C-1	4	1005-00-921-5004	19200	8448670
C-1	5	1005-01-216-4510	19204	12624561
C-1	6		19204	8448578
C-1	6		19204	8448604
C-2	1	1005-00-017-9547	19204	8448503
C-2	2	1005-00-999-1509	19204	8448504
C-2	3	5315-00-992-7294	19204	8448502
C-2	4	1005-00-992-7285	19200	8448509
C-2	5		19204	8448505
C-3	1	1005-00-992-7287	19204	8448511
C-3	2		19204	8448510
C-3	3	1005-00-992-7290	19204	8448513
C-3	4	5315-00-597-5086	96906	MS16562-98
C-3	5	5360-00-992-7292	19204	8448516
C-3	6	1005-00-992-7291	19204	8448515
C-3	7	1005-00-992-7288	19204	8448512
C-3	8	1005-00-760-3768	19200	8448755
C-4	1	5305-00-992-7284	19204	8448508
C-4	2	5315-00-992-7283	19200	8448506
C-4	3	1005-00-738-6213	19200	8448507
C-5	1		13629	8448521-2
C-5	2	5360-00-999-0404	19204	8448520
C-5	3	5340-00-999-0405	19200	8448519
C-5	4		19204	8448518
C-6	1		19204	8448523
C-6	1		19204	8448602
C-6	2	4710-00-978-1038	19200	8448567
C-6	3	1005-01-134-3629	19200	9349059
C-6	4	1005-00-152-3441	19204	8448663
C-6	5	1005-00-933-8089	19204	8448576
C-6	6	1005-00-992-7280	19204	8448577
C-6	7	5315-00-058-6044	96906	MS16562-106
C-6	8	1005-00-087-8998	19204	8448712
C-6	9	1005-00-087-8998	19204	8448712
C-6	10	5365-00-252-6853	96906	MS16626-1137
C-7	1	1005-01-134-3625	19200	9349056
C-7	2	5315-00-979-3930	19204	8448573
C-7	3	5360-00-979-3931	19204	8448574
C-7	4	1005-00-017-9543	19204	8448571
C-7	5	5320-01-063-7635	19204	8448697
C-8	1		19204	8448603
C-8	1	1005-01-248-5858	19200	12576280
C-8	2	5365-00-064-2652	96906	MS16632-1012
C-8	3	5315-00-978-1023	19204	8448533
C-8	4	1005-00-978-1022	19204	8448525
C-8	5	5360-00-978-1025	19204	8448532
C-8	6	5315-01-027-4759	96906	MS16562-121

SECTION IV

CROSS-REFERENCE INDEXES
FIGURE AND ITEM NUMBER INDEX

FIG.	ITEM	STOCK NUMBER	CAGEC	PART NUMBER
C-8	7	5360-00-017-9541	19200	8448540
C-8	8		19204	9349086
C-8	9	5355-00-978-1029	19200	8448535
C-8	10	5315-00-282-3642	96906	MS16562-96
C-8	11	1005-00-978-1030	19200	8448537
C-8	12	5360-00-978-1032	19200	8448538
C-8	13	5360-00-978-1027	19200	8448536
C-8	14	1005-00-978-1026	19204	8448539
C-8	15		19204	8448534
C-9	1	1005-01-144-1468	19200	9349085
C-9	2	5315-00-017-9552	13629	95113
C-9	3	5360-00-523-8084	19200	8448542
C-9	4	1005-00-017-9540	19204	8448544
C-9	5	3040-00-017-9539	19204	8448543
C-10	1	5360-00-992-6665	19204	8448629
C-10	2	1005-00-937-3078	19200	8448615
C-10	3		19204	8448610
C-10	4	1005-00-992-6649	19200	8448595
C-10	5	5340-00-992-6666	19204	8448630
C-10	6	5360-00-056-2246	19204	8448633
C-10	7	1005-00-056-2247	19204	8448634
C-10	8	1005-00-017-9548	19200	8448628
C-10	9	5315-00-812-3312	96906	MS16562-119
C-10	10	1005-00-056-2201	19204	8448638
C-10	11	5360-00-992-6655	19204	8448586
C-10	12	5315-00-992-6654	19204	8448585
C-10	13	5360-00-992-7301	19204	8448637
C-10	14	1005-00-992-7302	19204	8448636
C-10	15	1005-00-992-6671	13629	95601
C-10	15	5315-00-017-9537	19204	8448621
C-10	16	1005-00-999-0406	19200	8448635
C-10	17		19204	8448591
C-10	18	5305-01-268-1191	88044	AN501D416-18
C-10	19	5310-00-527-3634	96906	MS35335-61
C-10	20	1005-01-148-4805	19200	9349127
C-10	21	5360-00-992-7292	19204	8448516
C-10	22	1005-00-992-6667	19204	8448631
C-10	23	5315-00-992-7309	19204	8448609
C-10	24	5315-00-992-6650	19204	8448599
C-10	25	5315-00-992-6653	19204	8448584
C-10	26	5365-01-146-7692	19200	9349129
C-10	27	1005-01-135-4973	19200	9349119
C-10	28	5305-01-147-8585	19200	9349128
C-10	29		19204	8448579
C-10	29		19204	8448605
C-11	1	1005-01-228-8504	19200	9381380
C-11	2	1005-01-146-7685	19200	9349130
C-11	3	5340-00-463-3892	19200	8448653
C-11	4		19200	9349121
C-11	5	1005-00-403-0964	19204	8448652
C-11	6	5315-00-463-3894	19204	8448655

SECTION IV

CROSS-REFERENCE INDEXES
FIGURE AND ITEM NUMBER INDEX

FIG.	ITEM	STOCK NUMBER	CAGEC	PART NUMBER
C-11	7	5305-01-144-1494	19200	9349120
C-12	1	5360-00-992-6648	19204	8448611
C-12	2	1005-00-017-9551	19200	8448612
C-13	1	5360-00-992-7311	19200	8448594
C-13	2	5360-00-992-7308	19204	8448593
C-13	3	1005-00-992-7307	19204	8448592
C-14	1	5340-00-992-7297	19200	8448581
C-14	2	5315-00-992-6651	19204	8448582
C-14	3	5360-00-992-6652	19200	8448583
C-14	4	1005-00-992-7299	19204	8448587
C-14	5	5315-00-814-3530	96906	MS16562-35
C-14	6		19204	8448580
C-14	6		19204	8448606
C-15	1		19204	8426685
C-15	1		19205	7799809
C-15	2	4933-00-800-7508	19204	8448201
C-15	3	5220-01-075-5004	19200	12620101
C-15	4	5220-01-014-8183	19204	8448496
C-15	5	5220-00-155-4925	19204	8448677
C-15	6	5220-00-221-9391	19204	8448202
C-15	7	4933-01-035-5607	19204	12006359
C-15	8	5220-00-070-7814	19204	7799734
C-15	9	6695-00-070-7815	19204	7799735
C-15	10	4933-00-070-9151	19204	11010032
C-15	11	5120-00-070-9152	19204	11010033
C-15	12		19205	7799792
C-15	13	5220-01-043-9473	19204	12006472

APPENDIX D

EXPENDABLE/DURABLE SUPPLIES AND MATERIALS LIST

Section 1. INTRODUCTION

D-1. SCOPE. This appendix lists expendable/durable supplies and materials you will need to operate and maintain the 5.56mm Rifle M16 and M16A1. This listing is for informational purposes only and is not authority to requisition the listed items. These items are authorized to you by CTA 50-970, Expendable/Durable Items (Except Medical, Class V, Repair Parts, and Heraldic Items), or CTA 8-100, Army Medical Department Expendable/Durable Items.

D-2. EXPLANATION OF COLUMNS.

a. **Column (1)—Item Number.** This number is assigned to the entry in the listing and is referenced in the narrative instructions to identify the material (e.g., "Use cloth, abrasive, crocus, item 12, app D").

b. **Column (2)—Level.** This column identifies the lowest level of maintenance that requires the listed item.

C - Operator/Crew
O - Unit Maintenance
F - Direct Support Maintenance
H - General Support Maintenance

c. **Column (3)—National Stock Number.** This is the National stock number assigned to the item; use it to request or requisition the item.

d. **Column (4)—Description.** indicates the Federal item name and, if required, a description to identify the item. The last line for each item indicates the Federal Supply Code for Manufacturer (FSCM) in parentheses followed by the part number.

e. **Column (5)—Unit of Measure (U/M).** Indicates the measure used in performing the actual maintenance function. This measure is expressed by a two-character alphabetical abbreviation (e.g., ea, in., pr). If the unit of measure differs from the unit of issue, requisition the lowest unit of issue that will satisfy your requirements.

Section II. EXPENDABLE/DURABLE SUPPLIES AND MATERIALS LIST

(1) Item Number	(2) Level	(3) National Stock Number	(4) Description	(5) U/M
1	F	8040-00-944-7292	ADHESIVE KIT: (81 348) MMM-A-1754	KT
2	C	1005-00-242-5687	BOTTLE ASSEMBLY, CYLINDRICAL (19204) 8448444	EA
3	O	8020-00-244-0153	BRUSH, ARTIST'S: metal furrule, flat chisel edge 7/1 6 w, 1 1/8, exposed bristle (81 348) H-B-241	EA
4	C	1005-00-903-1296	BRUSH, CLEANING, SMALL ARMS; bore (1 9204) 11686340	EA
5	C	1005-00-999-1435	BRUSH, CLEANING, SMALL ARMS: chamber (1 9204) 8432358	EA
6	C	1005-00-494-6602	BRUSH, CLEANING, SMALL ARMS: tooth (1 9204) 8448462	EA

(1)	(2)	(3)	(4)	(5)
Item Number	Level	National Stock Number	Description	U/M
7	O	7920-00-205-2401	BRUSH, CLEANING, TOOLS AND PARTS: (96906) MS 16746-29	EA
8	F	6850-00-965-2332	CARBON REMOVING COMPOUND (81348) P-C-111	GL
9			CLEANER, LUBRICANT AND PRESERV-ATIVE: (27412)	
	C	9150-01-102-1473	CLP 1/2 OZ BOTTLE	EA
	O	9150-01-079-6124	CLP-4 4 OZ BOTTLE	EA
	O	9150-01-054-6453	CLP-5 PT BOTTLE	EA
	O	9150-01-053-6688	CLP-7 GAL BOTTLE	EA
10	C	9920-00-292-9946	CLEANER, TOBACCO PIPE: (92849) DILLS (32 PER PK)	EA
11			CLEANING COMPOUND,RIFLE BORE: SMALL ARMS BORE CLEANING SOLUTION (RBC) (81349) MIL-C-372	
	C	6850-00-224-6656	2-OZ (59.15-ML) BOTTLE	OZ
	O	6850-00-224-6657	8-OZ (236.59-ML) CAN	OZ
	O	6850-00-224-6663	1-GAL (3.79-L) CAN	GL
12	O	5350-00-221-0872	CLOTH, ABRASIVE (58536) A-A-1206	SH
13	O	8010-00-181-7859	COATING COMPOUND,FLUORESCENT: PAINT FOR BLANK FIRING ATTACHMENT (81349) MIL-P-21563 1 PT CAN	EA
14	F		DICHLOROMETHANE, TECHNICAL: (81349) MIL-D-6998	
		6810-00-244-0290	5 GAL PAIL	CN
		6810-00-616-9188	600 LB DRUM	DR
15	O	6850-00-281-1985	DRY CLEANING SOLVENT (58536) A-A-711 1 GAL CAN	GL
16	O	8415-00-823-7457 SIZE 11 8415-00-823-7456 SIZE 10 8415-00-823-7455 SIZE 9	GLOVES, CHEMICAL AND OIL PROTECTIVE (81348) ZZ-G-381	PR

(1) Item Number	(2) Level	(3) National Stock Number	(4) Description	(5) U/M
17	F	9150-00-754-2595	GREASE, MOLYBDENUM DISULFIDE (81349) MIL-G-21164	LB
18	C	1005-01-113-0321	HANDLE SECTION, CLEANING ROD, SMALL ARMS: (19204) 8436776	EA
19	O	9150-01-260-2534	LUBRICANT, SOLID FILM: (81349) MIL-L23398 16 OZ SPRAY CAN	OZ
20	C	9150-00-292-9689	LUBRICATING OIL, WEAPONS: (LAW) (81349) MIL-L-14107 1 QT (0.95-L) CAN	QT
21			LUBRICATING OIL, WEAPONS: (LSA), SEMIFLUID (81349) MIL-L-46000	
	C	9150-00-935-6597	2-OZ (59.15-ML) PLASTIC BTL	OZ
	C	9150-00-889-3522	4-OZ (118.30-ML) PLASTIC BTL	OZ
	O	9150-00-687-4241	1-QT (O.95-L) CAN	QT
	O	9150-00-753-4686	1-GAL (3.79-L) CAN	GL
22	O	4940-00-795-3595	PAN, WASH: (94453) 1211	EA
23	F	6850-00-826-0981	PENETRANT KIT: KT (81349) MIL-L-25135	KT
24	C	7920-00-205-1711	RAG, WIPING: (81348) DDD-R-30 50 LB BDL	LB
25	C	1005-00-050-6357	ROD SECTION, CLEANING, SMALL ARMS: (19204) 8436775 (3 REQUIRED)	EA
26	F	8030-00-670-8553	SEALING COMPOUND: (93648) DEVCONF	KT
27	C	1005-00-937-2250	SWAB HOLDER SECTION, CLEANING ROD, SMALL ARMS: (19204) 11686327	EA
28	C	1005-00-912-4248	SWAB, SMALL ARMS: (19204) 11686408	EA
29	F	8115-00-190-5002	BOX,SHIPPING, FIBERBOARD (81348) PPP-B-636	EA
30	F	8115-00-023-0301	BOX, SHIPPING, FLAPS (81348) PPP-B-601	EA

(1)	(2)	(3)	(4)	(5)
Item Number	Level	National Stock Number	Description	U/M
31	F	8135-00-855-6969	CUSHIONING MATERIAL (81348) PPP-C-843	EA
32	F	7510-00-297-6655	TAPE, PRESSURE SENSITIVE (81348) PPP-T-76	YD
33	F	8135-00-810-4075	BARRIER MATERIAL. GREASE-PROOFED, WATERPROOFED FLEXIBLE (81349) MIL-B-121	YD
34	F	8105-00-264-5523	ENVELOPE PACKAGING (81349) MIL-B-117	EA
35	F	8135-00-938-1565	FIBERBOARD, CORRUGATED (81348) PPP-F-320	EA
36	F	8115-00-616-9151	BOX, SHIPPING (81348) PPP-B-640	EA
37	F	8115-00-685-5171	BOX, SHIPPING (81348) PPP-B-621	EA
38	F	8135-01-019-1691	SHEET, POLYETHYLENE (84744) PE88-80-2	EA

APPENDIX E

ILLUSTRATED LIST OF MANUFACTURED ITEMS

INTRODUCTION.

a. This appendix includes complete instructions for making items authorized to be manufactured or fabricated at unit or direct support level.

b. A part number in alphanumeric order is provided for cross-referencing the part number of the item to be manufactured to the figure which covers fabrication criteria.

c. All bulk materials needed for manufacture of an item are listed in a tabular list on the illustration.

d. Figures E-1 and E-3 may be fabricated by Direct Support Maintenance.

e. Figure E-2 may be fabricated by Unit Maintenance.

INDEX

Item	Figure Number
Front sight post and low light level front sight post removing and installation tool	E-1
Pivot pin removing tool	E-2
Key tool	E-3
Front sight detent depressor	E-4
Pivot pin installation tool	E-5

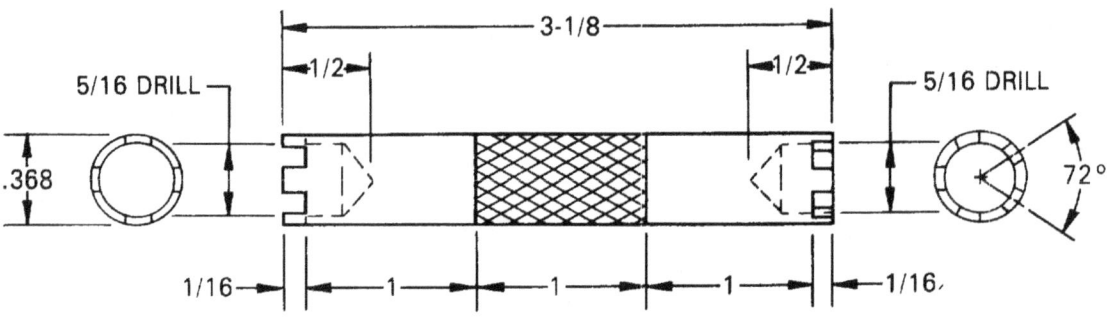

MATERIAL BLOCK
FSCM 81346 ASTM A686 METAL BAR
STEEL, GRADE C, GLASS W2-09
HOT ROLLED, ROUND, 0.375 INCH NOMINAL
DIAMETER, 3 FOOT NOMINAL LONG
NSN 9510-00-640-4407 OR EQUIVALENT

MATERIAL: MILD STEEL

NOTE

Teeth must be hand filed to fit front sight post.

NOTE: ALL DIMENSIONS SHOWN ARE IN INCHES AND KNURLING IS OPTIONAL IF DESIRED.

Figure E-1. Front sight post and low light level front sight post removing and installation tool.

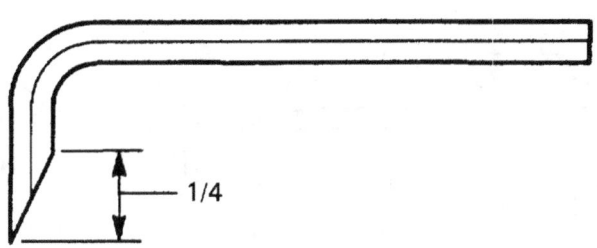

NOTE: 1. FABRICATE FROM 1/16 IN, SOCKET HEAD SCREW KEY NSN 5120-00-198-5398 OR EQUIVALENT

2. ALL DIMENSIONS ARE IN INCHES.

AR 922734

Figure E-2. Pivot pin removing tool.

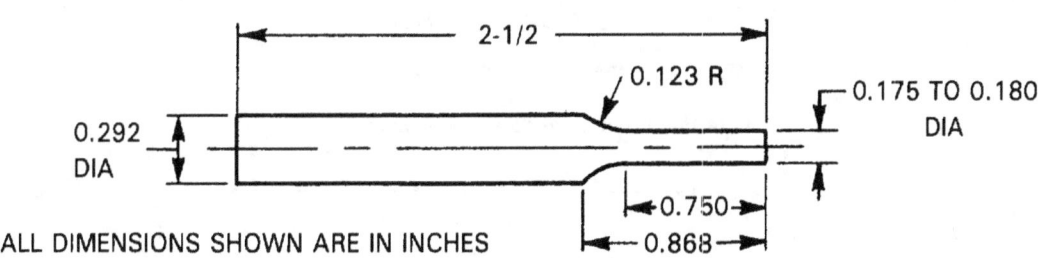

ALL DIMENSIONS SHOWN ARE IN INCHES

NOTE: ALL DIMENSIONS SHOWN ARE IN INCHES

MATERIAL BLOCK
FSCM 81346 ASTM A686 METAL BAR
STEEL, GRADE C, CLASS W209
HOT ROLLED, ROUND 0.375 INCH NOMINAL
DIAMETER, 3 FOOT NOMINAL LONG
NSN 9510-00-640-4407 OR EQUIVALENT

AR 922842

Figure E-3. Key tool.

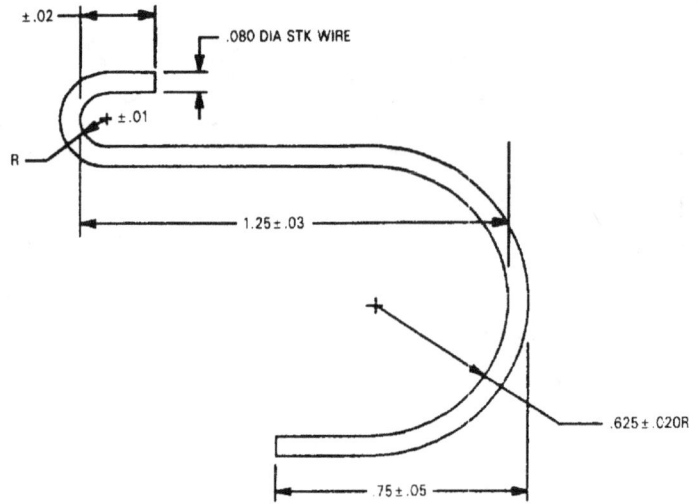

FABRICATE FROM .08 IN. MUSIC WIRE OR EQUIVALENT.

FINISH: NO. 5. 3.1.2 OR 5.3.2.2 OF MIL-STD-17

NOTE: ALL DIMENSIONS ARE IN INCHES.

Figure E-4. Front sight detent depressor.

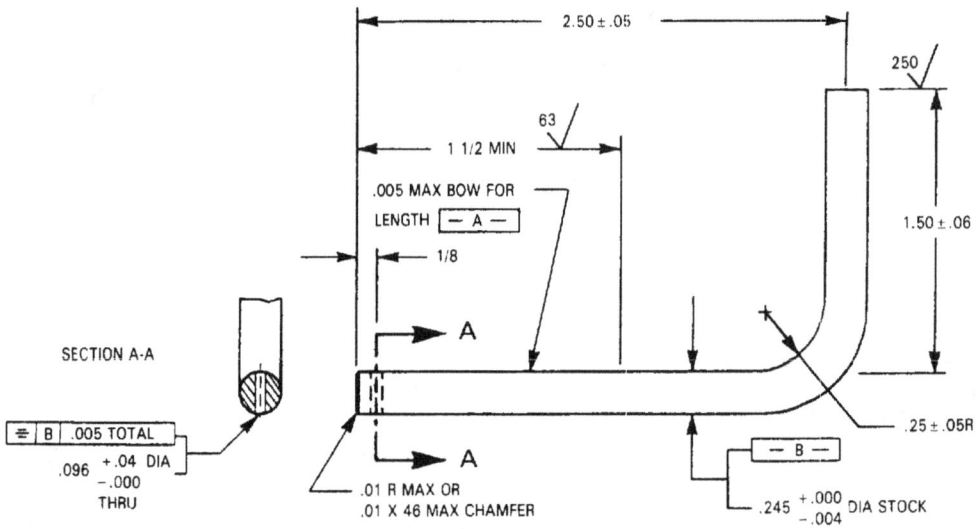

FABRICATE FROM .249 IN. STEEL A1S1 1095 OR EQUIVALENT.

HARDEN AND TEMPER TO RC-57-61 FOR LENGTH A-
FINISH 5.3.1.2 OR 5.3.2.2 OR MIL.-STD-171.

NOTE: ALL DIMENSIONS ARE IN INCHES.

Figure E-5. Pivot pin installation tool.

APPENDIX F

TORQUE LIMITS

INTRODUCTION.

a. This appendix includes a standard torque table of the most commonly torque screws, bolts, and nuts.

b. These torque values may be used when torque values are not specified.

c. The torque table values are given in inch-pounds. If a torque wrench is calibrated in foot-pounds, you need to divide the listed number by 12 to obtain the desired torque.

STANDARD TORQUE TABLE (INCH-POUNDS)

Torque Values In Inch-Pounds for Tightening Nuts				
Bolt, Stud, or Screw Size	On standard bolt, studs, and screws having a tensile strength of 125,000 to 140,000 psi.		On bolts, studs, and screws having a tensile strength of 140,000 to 160,000 psi.	On high-strength bolts, studs, and screws having a tensile strength of 160,000 psi and over.
	Sheer type nuts (AM320, AN364, or equivalent)	Tension type nuts and threaded machine parts (AN310, AN365, or equivalent)	Any nut, except shear type	Any nut, except shear type
8-32	7-9	12-15	14-17	15-18
8-36	7-9	12-15	14-17	15-18
10-24	12-15	20-25	23-30	25-35
1/4-20	25-30	40-50	45-49	50-68
1/4-28	30-40	50-70	60-80	70-90
5/16-18	48-55	90-90	85-117	90-114
5/16-24	60-85	100-140	120-172	140-203
3/8-16	95-110	160-186	173-217	185-248
3/8-24	95-110	160-190	175-271	190-351
7/16-14	140-155	235-255	245-342	255-428
7/16-20	270-300	450-500	475-628	500-756
1/2-13	240-290	400-480	440-636	480-792
1/2-20	290-410	480-690	585-840	690-990
9/16-12	300-420	500-700	600-845	700-990
9/16-18	480-600	800-1,000	900-1,220	1,000-1,440

ALPHABETICAL INDEX

Subject   Page

A

Annual Inspection and Gaging, M16 and M16A1 3-72
Assemblies
  Bolt Assembly 2-29, 3-15
  Bolt Carrier Assembly 2-24, 3-11
  Buttstock Assembly 2-52
  Charging Handle Assembly 2-33
  Forward Assist Assembly 3-47
  Hammer Assembly 3-60
  Key and Bolt Carrier Assembly 3-19
  Lower Receiver and Extension Assembly 2-45, 3-50
  Lower Receiver and Extension Subassembly 3-62
  Trigger Assembly 3-61
  Upper Receiver and Barrel Assembly 2-35, 3-23
  Upper Receiver Assembly 3-40
Auxiliary Equipment
  Bayonet-Knife M7 4-1
  Bayonet-Knife Scabbard M8A1 or M10 4-1
  Blank Firing Attachment M15A2 4-12
  Lock Plate 4-4
  Low Light Level Front Sight 4-2
  Rifle Bipod M3 4-10
  Top Sling Adapter 4-7

B

Bayonet-Knife M7 4-1
Bayonet-Knife Scabbard M8A1 or M10 4-1
Blank Firing Attachment M15A2 4-12
  Cleaning 4-13
  inspection 4-13
  installation 4-12
  Removal 4-12
  Repainting 4-13
  Replacement 4-13
Bolt Assembly 2-29, 3-15
  Cleaning 2-30, 3-18
  Disassembly 2-29, 3-15
  inspection/Repair 2-30, 3-15
  Lubrication 2-31, 3-18
  Reassembly 2-31, 3-18
Bolt Carrier Assembly 2-24, 3-11
  Cleaning 2-25
  Disassembly 2-24, 3-11
  Inspection 2-25, 3-12
  Reassembly 2-27, 3-14
  Repair 2-25, 3-14
  Test 3-13
Buttstock Assembly 2-52
  Disassembly 2-52
  inspection 2-53
  Reassembly 2-54
  Repair 2-54

Subject	Page

C

Characteristics, Capabilities, Features, and Equipment 1-2
Charging Handle Assembly 2-33
    Disassembly 2-33
    Inspection/Repair 2-34
    Lubrication 2-34
    Reassembly 2-34
Checks and Services, Preventive Maintenance 2-3
Cleaning
    Blank Firing Attachment M15A2 4-13
    Bolt Assembly 2-30, 3-18
    Bolt Carrier Assembly 2-25
Common Tools and Equipment 2-1, 3-1

D

Data Equipment 1-3
Decontamination of Rifles and Arms Rooms 2-21
Decontamination of Sights Activated with Tritium (H3) 2-21, 3-9
Destruction of Army Materiel to Prevent Enemy Use 1-1
Differences between Models 1-3
Disassembly
    Bolt Assembly 2-29, 3-15
    Bolt Carrier Assembly 2-24, 3-11
    Buttstock Assembly 2-52
    Forward Assist Assembly 3-48
    Hammer Assembly 3-60
    Key and Bolt Carrier Assembly 3-19
    Low Light Level Sight 4-2
    Lower Receiver and Extension Assembly 2-45, 3-50
    Lower Receiver and Extension Subassembly 3-62
    Trigger Assembly 3-61
    Upper Receiver and Barrel Assembly 2-35, 3-23
    Upper Receiver Assembly 3-40

E

Equipment Characteristics, Capabilities, and Features 1-2
Equipment Description and Data 1-2
Equipment Improvement Recommendations (EIR), Reporting 1-1
Expendable/Durable Supplies and Materials List D-1

F

Features, Equipment Characteristics, Capabilities and 1-2
Final Inspection, M16 and M16A1 Rifle 3-70
    Gaging 3-73
    Inspection 3-70
Firing Pin Protrusion Gaging 3-71
Forward Assist Assembly 3-47
    Disassembly 3-48
    Inspection 3-48
    Repair 3-49
    Reassembly 3-49

Subject   Page

G

Gaging (See applicable module)

H

Hammer Assembly 3-60
   Disassembly 3-60
   inspection/Repair 3-61
   Reassembly 3-61
How to Use This Manual III

I

Illustrated List of Manufactured items E-1
Inspection
   Blank Firing Attachment M15A2 4-13
   Bolt Carrier Assembly 2-25, 3-12
   Buttstock Assembly 2-53
   Forward Assist Assembly 3-48
   Hammer Assembly 3-61
   Low Light Level Sight 4-13
   Lower Receiver and Extension Assembly 2-47, 3-53
   Lower Receiver and Extension Subassembly 3-64
   Trigger Assembly 3-62
   Upper Receiver and Barrel Assembly 2-36, 3-26
Inspection/Repair
   Bolt Assembly 2-30, 3-15
   Key and Bolt Carrier Assembly 3-20
inspection, Final M16 and M16A1 3-70
Inspection, Preembarkation of Materiel in Units Alerted for Overseas Movement 3-73
Installation
   Blank Firing Attachment M15A2 4-12
   Lock Plate 4-4
   Low Light Level Front Sight 4-3
   Major Components of M16/M16A1 Rifle 3-10
   Rifle Biped M3 4-10
   Top Sling Adapter 4-7

K

Key and Bolt Carrier Assembly 3-19
   Disassembly 3-19
   Repair 3-20
   Reassembly 3-20

L

Location and Description of Major Components 1-2
Lock Plate
   installation 4-4
   Removal 4-5

Subject   Page

L (Cont)

Low Light Level Front Sight
    Disassembly 4-2
    Inspection 4-3
    Installation 4-3
    Reassembly 4-3
    Wrapping and Packaging 4-3
Lower Receiver and Extension Assembly
    Disassembly 2-45, 3-50
    inspection 2-47, 3-53
    Reassembly 2-49, 3-58
    Repair 2-48, 3-55
    Test 3-56
Low Receiver and Extension Subassembly
    Disassembly 3-63
    Inspection 3-64
    Reassembly 3-67
    Repair/Modify 3-65
    Test 3-66
Lubrication
    Bolt Assembly 2-31, 3-18
    Bolt Carrier Assembly 2-27
    Lubrication General 2-22

M

Maintenance Allocation Chart B-1
Maintenance Forms, Records and Reports 1-1
Major Components of M16 and M16A1 Rifle 2-23, 3-10
    Disassembly 2-23, 3-10
    Reassembly 2-55, 3-68
    Stowage 2-56
    Test 3-69
Manufactured Items, illustrated List of E-1
Materials List, Expendable/Durable Supplies and D-1
M7 Bayonet-Knife 4-1
M8A1 or M10,Bayonet-Knife Scabbard 4-1
M16 and M16A1 Rifle Annual inspection and Gaging 3-72
M16 and M16A1 Rifle Final inspection 3-70
Mechanical Zero Procedures 2-43, 3-46

O

Official Nomenclature, Names and Designations 1-1
Operation, Principles of 1-4

Subject	Page

P

Parts, Repair, Special Tools, TMDE, and Support Equipment 2-1
Preembarkation Inspection of Materiel in Units Alerted for Overseas Movement 3-73
Preparation for Storage or Shipment 1-1,4-13
Preventive Maintenance Checks and Services 2-3
Principles of Operation 1-4
Purpose of M16/M16A1 Rifle 1-1

R

Reassembly
    Bolt Assembly 2-31, 3-18
    Bolt Carrier Assembly 2-27, 3-14
    Buttstock Assembly 2-54
    Forward Assist Assembly 3-49
    Hammer Assembly 3-61
    Key and Bolt Carrier Assembly 3-20
    Low Light Level Front Sight 4-3
    Lower Receiver and Extension Assembly 2-49, 3-58
    Lower Receiver and Extension Subassembly 3-67
    Trigger Assembly 3-62
    Upper Receiver and Barrel Assembly 2-36, 3-30
    Upper Receiver Assembly 3-45
References . . . . A-1.
Removal
    Blank Firing Attachment 4-12
    Lock Plate 4-5
    Rifle Biped M3 4-11
    Top Sling Adapter 4-8
Repair
    Bolt Assembly 2-30, 3-15
    Buttstock Assembly 2-54
    Forward Assist Assembly 3-49
    Lower Receiver and Extension Assembly 2-48, 3-55
    Lower Receiver and Extension Subassembly 3-65
    Upper Receiver Assembly 3-42
Repair Parts and Special Tools List C-1
Repair Parts C-1-1
Special Tools C-15-1
Replacement
    Blank Firing Attachment M15A2 4-13
Reporting Equipment Improvement Recommendations (EIR) 1-1
Restamping Serial Numbers 3-66
Rifle Bipod M3
    Installation 4-10
    Removal 4-11
Rifles and Arms Rooms, Decontamination of 2-21

Subject   Page

S

Serial Numbers 3-66
Service Upon Receipt of Materiel 2-1, 3-1
Sights Activated with Tritium (H3), Decontamination of 2-21, 3-9
Stowage
    Major Components of M16 and M16A1 Rifle 2-56

T

Test
    Bolt Carrier Assembly 3-13
    Lower Receiver and Extension Assembly 3-56
    Lower Receiver and Extension Subassembly 3-66
    Major Components of M16 and M16A1 Rifle 2-56
    Upper Receiver and Barrel Assembly 3-35
Top Sling Adapter 4-7
    Installation 4-7
    Removal 4-8
Torque Limits F-1
Trigger Assembly 3-61
    Disassembly 3-61
    Inspection 3-62
    Reassembly 3-62
Troubleshooting 2-12, 3-2

U

Upper Receiver and Barrel Assembly 2-35, 3-22
    Disassembly 2-35, 3-23
    Inspection 2-36, 3-26
    Repair 2-36, 3-28
    Reassembly 2-36, 3-30
    Test 3-35
Upper Receiver Assembly
    Disassembly 3-40
    Inspection/Repair 3-42
    Reassembly 3-45

W

Wrapping and Packaging 4-3, 4-13

Z

Zero Procedures, Mechanical 2-43, 3-46

By Order of the Secretary of the Army:

GORDON R. SULLIVAN
General, United States Army
chief of Staff

Official:

PATRICIA P. HICKERSON
Brigadier General, United States Army
The Adjutant General

By Order of the Secretary of the Air Force:

MERRILL A. McPEAK, General USAF
Chief of Staff

Offical:

CHARLES C. McDONALD, General, USAF
Commander, Air Force Logistics Command

W.T. LELAND, Rear Admiral
Chief, Office Law
Enforcement and Defense Operations
U.S. Coast Guard

DISTRIBUTION :

To be distributed in accordance with DA Form 12-40E, (Block 0136), Unit, Direct and General Support Maintenance requirements for TM 9-1005-249-23&P.

RECOMMENDED CHANGES TO PUBLICATIONS AND BLANK FORMS For use of this form, see AR 310-1; the proponent agency is the US Army Adjutant General Center.	Use Part II (reverse) for Repair Parts and Special Tool Lists (RPSTL) and Supply Catalogs/Supply Manuals (SC/SM).	DATE

TO: (Forward to proponent of publication or form) (Include ZIP Code) Commander U. S. Army AMCCOM ATTN: AMSMC-MAS Rock Island, IL 61299-6000	FROM: (Activity and location) (Include ZIP Code)

PART I - ALL PUBLICATIONS (EXCEPT RPSTL AND SC/SM) AND BLANK FORMS

PUBLICATION/FORM NUMBER	DATE	TITLE
TM 9-1005-249-23&P	19 June 1991	Rifle, M16 and M16A1

ITEM NO.	PAGE NO.	PARA-GRAPH	LINE NO.*	FIGURE NO.	TABLE NO.	RECOMMENDED CHANGES AND REASON (Provide exact wording of recommended change, if possible).
1	1-1	1-6				Change zip code from 61201 to 61299. Reason: Change in zip code.
2	1-5	1-13				Change zip code from 61201 to 61299. Reason: change in zip code.

SAMPLE

*Reference to line numbers within the paragraph or subparagraph.

TYPED NAME, GRADE OR TITLE	TELEPHONE EXCHANGE/AUTOVON, PLUS EXTENSION	SIGNATURE
		Your name

DA FORM 2028, FEB 74   REPLACES DA FORM 2028, 1 DEC 68, WHICH WILL BE USED.

TO: *(Forward direct to addressee listed in publication)* Commander U. S. Army AMCCOM ATTN: AMSMC-MAS Rock Island, IL 61299-6000	FROM: *(Activity and location) (Include ZIP Code)*	DATE

PART II - REPAIR PARTS AND SPECIAL TOOL LISTS AND SUPPLY CATALOGS/SUPPLY MANUALS

PUBLICATION NUMBER				DATE				TITLE	
TM 9-1005-249-23&P				19 June 1991				Rifle, M16 and M16A1	

PAGE NO.	COLM NO.	LINE NO.	NATIONAL STOCK NUMBER	REFERENCE NO.	FIGURE NO.	ITEM NO.	TOTAL NO. OF MAJOR ITEMS SUPPORTED	RECOMMENDED ACTION

PART III - REMARKS *(Any general remarks or recommendations, or suggestions for improvement of publications and blank forms. Additional blank sheets may be used if more space is needed.)*

SAMPLE

TYPED NAME, GRADE OR TITLE	TELEPHONE EXCHANGE/AUTOVON, PLUS EXTENSION	SIGNATURE

<table>
<tr><td colspan="2">RECOMMENDED CHANGES TO PUBLICATIONS AND BLANK FORMS
For use of this form, see AR 310-1; the proponent agency is the US Army Adjutant General Center.</td><td>Use Part II (reverse) for Repair Parts and Special Tool Lists (RPSTL) and Supply Catalogs/Supply Manuals (SC/SM).</td><td>DATE</td></tr>
</table>

TO: *(Forward to proponent of publication or form) (Include ZIP Code)*

Commander
U.S. Army AMCCOM
ATTN: AMSMC-MAS
Rock Island, IL 61299-6000

FROM: *(Activity and location) (Include ZIP Code)*

PART I - ALL PUBLICATIONS (EXCEPT RPSTL AND SC/SM) AND BLANK FORMS

PUBLICATION FORM NUMBER	DATE	TITLE
TM 9-1005-249-23&P	19 June 1991	Rifle, M16 and M16A1

ITEM NO.	PAGE NO.	PARA-GRAPH	LINE NO.*	FIGURE NO.	TABLE NO.	RECOMMENDED CHANGES AND REASON *(Exact wording of recommended change must be given)*

*Reference to line numbers within the paragraph or subparagraph.

TYPED NAME, GRADE OR TITLE	TELEPHONE EXCHANGE/AUTOVON, PLUS EXTENSION	SIGNATURE

DA FORM **2028**, 1 FEB 74   REPLACES DA FORM 2028, 1 DEC 68, WHICH WILL BE USED.

TO: *(Forward direct to addressee listed in publication)*	FROM: *(Activity and location) (Include ZIP Code)*	DATE
Commander U.S. Army AMCCOM ATTN: AMSMC-MAS Rock Island, IL 61299-6000		

PART II - REPAIR PARTS AND SPECIAL TOOL LISTS AND SUPPLY CATALOGS/SUPPLY MANUALS

PUBLICATION NUMBER	DATE	TITLE
TM 9-1005-249-23&P	19 June 1991	Rifle, M16 and M16A1

PAGE NO.	COLM NO.	LINE NO.	FEDERAL STOCK NUMBER	REFERENCE NO.	FIGURE NO.	ITEM NO.	TOTAL NO. OF MAJOR ITEMS SUPPORTED	RECOMMENDED ACTION

PART III - REMARKS *(Any general remarks or recommendations, or suggestions for improvement of publications and blank forms. Additional blank sheets may be used if more space is needed.)*

TYPED NAME, GRADE OR TITLE	TELEPHONE EXCHANGE/AUTOVON, PLUS EXTENSION	SIGNATURE

<table>
<tr><td colspan="3">**RECOMMENDED CHANGES TO PUBLICATIONS AND BLANK FORMS**
For use of this form, see AR 310-1; the proponent agency is the US Army Adjutant General Center.</td><td colspan="2">Use Part II *(reverse)* for Repair Parts and Special Tool Lists (RPSTL) and Supply Catalogs/Supply Manuals (SC/SM).</td><td>DATE</td></tr>
</table>

RECOMMENDED CHANGES TO PUBLICATIONS AND BLANK FORMS	Use Part II *(reverse)* for Repair Parts and Special Tool Lists (RPSTL) and Supply Catalogs/Supply Manuals (SC/SM).	DATE
For use of this form, see AR 310-1; the proponent agency is the US Army Adjutant General Center.		

TO: *(Forward to proponent of publication or form) (Include ZIP Code)*	FROM: *(Activity and location) (Include ZIP Code)*
Commander U.S.Army AMCCOM ATTN: AMSMC-MAS Rock Island, IL 61299-6000	

PART I - ALL PUBLICATIONS (EXCEPT RPSTL AND SC/SM) AND BLANK FORMS

PUBLICATION FORM NUMBER	DATE	TITLE
TM 9-1005-249-23&P	19 June 1991	Rifle, M16 and M16A1

ITEM NO.	PAGE NO.	PARA-GRAPH	LINE NO.*	FIGURE NO.	TABLE NO.	RECOMMENDED CHANGES AND REASON *(Exact wording of recommended change must be given)*

Reference to line numbers within the paragraph or subparagraph.

TYPED NAME, GRADE OR TITLE	TELEPHONE EXCHANGE/AUTOVON, PLUS EXTENSION	SIGNATURE

DA FORM 2028
1 FEB 74

REPLACES DA FORM 2028, 1 DEC 68, WHICH WILL BE USED.

TO: *(Forward direct to addressee listed in publication)* Commander U.S. Army AMCCOM ATTN: AMSMC-MAS Rock Island, IL 61299-6000	FROM: *(Activity and location) (Include ZIP Code)*	DATE

PART II - REPAIR PARTS AND SPECIAL TOOL LISTS AND SUPPLY CATALOGS/SUPPLY MANUALS

PUBLICATION NUMBER	DATE	TITLE
TM 9-1005-249-23&P	19 June 1991	Rifle, M16 and M16A1

PAGE NO.	COLM NO.	LINE NO.	FEDERAL STOCK NUMBER	REFERENCE NO.	FIGURE NO.	ITEM NO.	TOTAL NO. OF MAJOR ITEMS SUPPORTED	RECOMMENDED ACTION

PART III - REMARKS *(Any general remarks or recommendations, or suggestions for improvement of publications and blank forms. Additional blank sheets may be used if more space is needed.)*

TYPED NAME, GRADE OR TITLE	TELEPHONE EXCHANGE/AUTOVON, PLUS EXTENSION	SIGNATURE